Praise for *Blindsight*

"*Blindsight* is a rigorous examination of how top brands sneak into our brains and grab the best real estate. Deftly mixing neuroscience, psychology, and fun stories, the book is a delight to read; it will grip you from the start, and leave you feeling smarter."

—Rich Karlgaard, publisher at *Forbes*

"Ghuman and Johnson's *Blindsight* is beautifully written and fascinating—a behind-the-scenes tour of the marketing schemes designed to cajole, sway, and hook us. Why do we spend decades of our lives playing games and scrolling through social media feeds? Why do we prefer predictability, but spend so much of our time seeking unpredictable rewards? Why do we ask for dozens of options, but ultimately regret our purchases more often when the choice set is large? *Blindsight* teaches us how to be smarter consumers who make wise decisions that will ultimately leave us happier, wealthier, and healthier."

—Adam Alter, *New York Times* bestselling author of *Drunk Tank Pink* and *Irresistible*

"Somewhere hidden between the bright colors, catchy jingles, and strategic placement of advertisements is the psychology behind their influence. This book uncovers this hidden layer of the consumer world and how it affects our thoughts, emotions, and spending habits. A must-read for consumers and marketers alike."

—Kendis Gibson, Emmy award-winning journalist and reporter for MSNBC

"*Blindsight* engrosses the reader from the very first page. With an entertaining blend of storytelling and science, *Blindsight* is a truly eye-opening look into the complex dynamics underlying how brands drive consumer behavior. A must-read book that will have you re-examining both information around you and your own purchase decisions at every turn."

—Abigail Sussman, associate professor of marketing at The University of Chicago Booth School of Business

"A fun, accessible dive into the ways marketing defines the modern human experience. Prince Ghuman and Matt Johnson bring to life the science behind how Facebook holds your attention, how Star Wars captured the hearts of generations of moviegoers, and selling billions in bottled water to consumers with taps in their homes. This is the perfect book for readers looking to understand what happens when the magic behind modern branding meets the machinery of the mind."

—Drew Jacoby-Senghor, assistant professor of management at Berkeley Haas School of Business

"*Blindsight* is a delightful book that opens your eyes to the hidden forces behind every decision and every choice in the consumer world. The book draws on scientific evidence from cognitive psychology, neuroscience, and decision science, and makes it fun and relatable to any audience. If you want to understand the driving forces behind your decisions, if you

want to be smarter about your purchases, if you want to know how to improve your spending habits, read this book!"
—Jiaying Zhao, associate professor of psychology at the University of British Columbia

"Johnson and Ghuman artfully combine science, business, and storytelling to help us understand the invisible forces which shape our decisions and experiences. Along the way, they reveal to us all how deeply interwoven consumerism is into the perception of reality itself. The result is a rare book which enriches our understanding of everyday life. A must-read for anyone curious to better understand the world around them and the psychological forces that shape it."
—Blake Sherwin, assistant professor of applied mathematics and theoretical physics at Cambridge University

"This is not your average 'marketer's how-to' book. Fast-paced, clever, and utterly fascinating, *Blindsight* sheds new light on the deeply rooted beliefs and mental gymnastics that brands tap with precision to create preference. Johnson and Ghuman weave meticulously chronicled science into great stories with thoroughly modern examples that will leave consumers, marketers, brands, or just neuro-curious readers with something to chew on and lots to discuss at your next dinner party."
—Carol Caruba, principal at Highwire PR

"Equal parts science and storytelling, *Blindsight* changes the way we see ourselves as consumers. Why does the same wine taste better to us if we think it's expensive? Why does a $10 fee seem less significant when tacked on to a larger purchase than a smaller one? Why do we judge original works of art to have greater value than replicas? This book is an engaging journey into the science of marketing's influence, and how it impacts how we see the world around us."
—Judy Fan, assistant professor of psychology at University of California at San Diego

"*Blindsight* is a refreshing, timely book that will make you examine the secret ways marketing influences you. You won't be able to think about your own consumer life the same way."
—Sheryle Bolton, serial entrepreneur

"In *Blindsight*, Ghuman and Johnson make the neuroscience of marketing accessible to all. Drawing creative and insightful connections between scientific studies and the effectiveness of today's marketing strategies, this book achieves a perfect balance of humor and rigor. *Blindsight* will make you understand yourself better—as a consumer, and as a person."
—Natalia Córdova, psychology lecturer at Yale University

"*Blindsight* is an ideal way to gain insight into the incredibly complex interactions between psychology and neuroscience that are underlying the seemingly simple concept of human intuition. Ghuman and Johnson are able to adroitly juggle entertaining, and often hilarious, stories with rigorous scientific ideas that provide marketers, as well as consumers, an important understanding of why we buy what we buy."
—James Newell, managing director at Voyager Capital

BLINDSIGHT

The (Mostly) Hidden Ways
Marketing Reshapes
Our Brains

**Matt A. Johnson, PhD,
and Prince Ghuman**

BenBella Books, Inc.
Dallas, TX

BenBella

BenBella Books, Inc.
10440 N. Central Expressway, Suite 800
Dallas, TX 75231
www.benbellabooks.com
Send feedback to feedback@benbellabooks.com

BenBella is a federally registered trademark.

Printed in the United States of America
10 9 8 7 6 5 4 3 2 1

Library of Congress Cataloging-in-Publication Data:
Names: Johnson, Matt A., 1985- author. | Ghuman, Prince, author.
Title: Blindsight : the (mostly) hidden ways marketing reshapes our brains
   / Matt A. Johnson, PhD, and Prince Ghuman.
Identifiers: LCCN 2019054236 (print) | LCCN 2019054237 (ebook) | ISBN
   9781950665068 (hardback) | ISBN 9781950665235 (ebook)
Subjects: LCSH: Consumer behavior. | Marketing—Psychological aspects. |
   Neuromarketing.
Classification: LCC HF5415.32 .J645 2020 (print) | LCC HF5415.32 (ebook)
   | DDC 658.8/342—dc23
LC record available at https://lccn.loc.gov/2019054236
LC ebook record available at https://lccn.loc.gov/2019054237

Editing by Leah Wilson
Copyediting by James Fraleigh
Proofreading by Lisa Story and Sarah Vostok
Indexing by WordCo Indexing Services
Text design and composition by Katie Hollister
Cover design by Sarah Avinger
Cover illustration by Ralph Voltz
Author photos by Prince Ghuman (Johnson) and Tamer Abu-Dayyeh (Ghuman)
Printed by Lake Book Manufacturing

Distributed to the trade by Two Rivers Distribution, an Ingram brand
www.tworiversdistribution.com

To Marlene and Santiago, for their endless support and inspiration. And to my parents, for always encouraging my writing.
—Matt

To my mother, Ruby Ghuman. Thank you for your boundless source of love, support, and positivity.
—Prince

CONTENTS

THE POWER OF BLINDSIGHT

I n 2010, a series of experiments floored the scientific community. A subject named T.N. navigated a twenty-yard hallway littered with boxes, cabinets, and chairs without touching a single object.[1] Pretty easy, right? The thing is, T.N. is legally blind. He is one of a rare group of people who have what neuroscientists call *blindsight*.

People with blindsight cannot see, but they do still process visual information. If you sit someone with blindsight down in front of a computer and flash a set of dots on the screen—as researchers have—they'll insist they can't see the screen or the dots. Yet if you convince them, with enough patience and prodding, to humor you with a guess, that "guess" will be staggeringly accurate.

How is this possible?

Turns out, the processing of visual information in the brain is complicated, involving multiple steps in multiple regions. While most blindness results from damage or impairment to the eyes—meaning visual information never enters the brain in the first place—sometimes, as with T.N., blindness is caused by damage somewhere in the brain. Residual information from the eyes is still processed in other brain regions, allowing the person to react to these stimuli (e.g., walking around obstacles) despite never consciously processing them.

In other words, the brain receives information that the person isn't aware of having received.

This doesn't just happen to the blind. *All* of our brains are receiving information all the time that we aren't consciously aware of. Blindsight is more than a fascinating window into how the brain produces visual awareness; it's also a window into our relationship with the consumer world.

When someone with blindsight walks down an obstacle-filled room hallway, they don't know *why*, at each encounter with an object, they suddenly feel they should go right or left. The reaction comes intuitively, outside the reaches of their conscious mind. This is also how we navigate the consumer world.

Our decisions as consumers to buy or not to buy are influenced by the ads we see all around us, by the way website "buy" buttons are placed, by the design of packages—often in ways outside our consciousness. We don't necessarily understand *why* we want to buy one brand of toothpaste or another; we just know that we do.

That's where this book comes in. It reveals the blueprint behind the consumer world, the code behind its design. The brand logos you see, the ads you scroll past on your newsfeed, the commercials you absorb on TV, the apps you use daily—these are only the outermost, visible layer of the consumer world. There is another, deeper layer, carefully designed to exploit our brains' peculiar architecture, that influences us without our knowledge or consent.

Blindsight like T.N.'s is a neuropsychological condition. What we want to give you, with this book, is a different kind of blindsight—the ability to see the unseeable in our consumer world. We want to help you look beyond *what* is printed on a billboard to see *how* the image influences your brain and *why* it may ultimately make you want to buy what it's selling.

PREPARE FOR TAKEOFF

Think of navigating the world of consumer neuroscience like flying an airplane. The airplane represents your brain, a complex machine that functions via a particular set of rules and limits. The wind all around the plane is the consumer world, where exposure to brands and marketing constantly tugs on the mechanisms of the brain, pulling our thoughts and desires this way and that.

Then there's the person aboard the plane—you, or rather, your conscious mind. The question is, are you a pilot or a passenger?

Which role you inhabit depends on your knowledge of the plane and the wind. A pilot possesses this knowledge and can safely navigate the plane where they want it to go. A passenger, by contrast, is clueless about the plane and the wind—how the brain and the consumer world interact—and goes wherever they're flown.

In that sense, this is a book about taking control of your flight. It's about understanding the airplane and the wind, about understanding the brain and how marketing impacts it, so *you* can better navigate the choppy winds of today's consumer world.

CLOSING THE KNOWLEDGE GAP

We believe it is not just beneficial, but necessary for you to understand your consumer behavior. Why the urgency? Well . . .

Today more than ever, *brands know you better than you know yourself!*

You're not the only one with a vested interest in understanding this relationship between your brain and the consumer world. With every click, swipe, and heartbeat recorded on a smart device, brands learn *even more* about how best to separate you from your cash. The knowledge gap between consumers and brands gets wider by the day.

With that context firmly at heart, this book is written for you, the consumer—and for anyone determined to close the disturbingly large knowledge gap between psychology and marketing.

In the next twelve chapters, we reveal the deep interaction between our brains and the consumer world. Within the context of marketing, we illuminate the neuroscience of memories and experiences, pleasure and pain, emotion and logic, perception and reality, attention, decision making, addiction, novelty, likeability, empathy, communication, storytelling, and subliminal messaging.

On the surface, you will learn how the brain works and see how brands design for it. But peel back a layer and you'll find a sharper image of yourself: a better understanding of your psychology as reflected in the mirror of your consumer behavior.

To be a pilot, one needs to be an expert in both the wind and the airplane. To gain our new kind of blindsight in the consumer world, one needs to be an expert in both marketing and the brain. That's why this book has two authors. It combines Matt Johnson's experience as a neuroscientist with Prince Ghuman's experience as a marketer to provide a rare window into the unseen world of consumer science.

Are you ready, like Neo in *The Matrix*, to see how deep the rabbit hole goes? Follow us.

Welcome to *Blindsight*.

This logo throughout the book marks optional supplementary material—logos, video and print ads, and other visuals we refer to in text—available online. To access it, please head over to www.popneuro.com/blindsight-material.

Chapter 1

EATING THE MENU

How Marketing Tricks Our Tongues

Imagine you're a judge on a cooking show. You're served five fancy plates of pâté-style meat, each carefully garnished and accompanied by imported crackers. All of them look equally amazing, and you sample each one. Then the host gives you the following task: "Identify which of the five pâtés is the dog food."

This wasn't a cooking show. This was the exact experience of participants in a 2009 research study,[1] bluntly titled "Can People Distinguish Pâté from Dog Food?" Four of the dishes contained human food, including expensive luxury pâtés. One was canned dog food that was blended through a food processor to give it the same look and consistency of pâté. The shade of the meat was slightly different in each pâté, but aside from that, their appearances were identical. The results? No one could tell which one was the dog food.

If your mother were to hand you a can of dog food and say, "Eat this, it tastes about the same as duck pâté at a fraction of the cost," you'd look at her as if she were crazy. Yet, when dog food is dressed up the same way as a pâté, your tongue can't tell them apart. And it's worth emphasizing that the participants in the study were *trying* to distinguish which dish was dog food, and they still couldn't. Just imagine what you could get away with in a restaurant full of unsuspecting eaters!

A skeptic might rightly argue that you might be able to fool a layperson into thinking dog food is pâté, but not a real foodie. Challenge accepted. This hasn't been tested with dog food and pâté, but something similar has been done with wine.

If anyone should be able to taste something for what it is, it's a sommelier. These wine experts go through years of reading, drinking, eating, and testing, better known as formal wine education, to be formally certified. Soms' sense of taste is amazing. One sip and they are able to tell the wine they are drinking, the species of grapes involved, what country it is from, and the vintage year of the bottle.

In a deliciously devious experiment,[2] Frederic Brochet at the University of Bordeaux showed that taste is fallible even for these supertasters. He provided sommeliers with two different glasses of wine, one red and one white, and had them review each wine. Unknown to the sommeliers, the red wine was the exact same wine as the white, just with red food coloring added. Not only were the wines perceived as tasting completely different, but the "red" wine was described as if it had red ingredients. Tasters of the white wine described it with flavors like "honey" and "citrus," while the red wine was described as tasting like "raspberry" and "mahogany." This is despite identical information reaching the tongue. The dog-food eaters shouldn't feel too bad; the pros get fooled, too.

Beyond suggesting a new approach for cost-cutting in high-end restaurants (kidding!), these findings illustrate a fundamental insight about how we experience the world: what we taste is much more than meets the tongue.

We don't experience the food we eat directly. There's a massive gap between the objective sensation of the food hitting our tongues and what our brains ultimately experience. As the late great philosopher Alan Watts describes, "We eat the menu, not the food." In other words, we're always one step removed—experiencing our own internal description of the world, rather than the world itself.

In neuroscience, this gap is humbling evidence of perceptual fallibility: we don't, perhaps *can't*, experience the world as it is. In marketing, this gap represents something else altogether: opportunity. The opportunity to tweak, influence, and fundamentally alter consumers' innermost experience of reality. What more could a marketer want, in their pursuit of persuasion, than the ability to alter reality itself in their favor?

At the most basic level, marketing tweaks the consumer's experience of one sense through use of others—restaurants curating not only our meal, but the music, the decor, and more. At a deeper level, it alters the consumer's beliefs about what's being consumed—dog food only tastes palatable when you *believe* it may be pâté. And finally, in the most extreme cases, it ingrains these perception-altering beliefs so deeply that a brand literally etches itself into the architecture of our brains.

The opportunity to do all of this exists because of the strange ways our brain copes with this gap between external, objective reality and internal, subjective perception. And over the years, brands have converged on clever ways of inserting themselves into this gap—fundamentally altering our experience of reality in the process. The gap between *objective* reality and *subjective* perception is the marketer's playground. To better understand this gap, and how it's filled, we first need to take a deeper dive into how our brain constructs our experience of day-to-day life.

THE GUESSING GAME: MENTAL MODELS

Our brains don't experience reality directly. Instead, they construct a model of it, which neuroscientists call a *mental model*. Our brains are constantly modeling. Each time you take a bite of food, you aren't experiencing the food per se, but your brain's best guess at what the experience of eating that food *should* be like. The sensation at the tongue contributes to this model, but many other things can, too. And while the brain does its best to accurately replicate reality, as we saw with the dog food and wine, these models are far from perfect.

Mental models are incredibly impressionable, and can be influenced by numerous factors. They're also hard, if not impossible, to "correct," because we can never compare them to reality and see where they've gone wrong; all we can ever experience is the mental model itself. So when a brand or business influences our mental models, they are directly influencing our experience of reality.

Restaurants, for example, rely heavily on the fact that mental models are highly prone to suggestion. When we sit down for a meal, we unconsciously take in everything around us: the restaurant environment, the music playing in the background, the cutlery, the location—everything. And all of these things fundamentally affect the mental model our brain creates. The same meal tastes very different eaten in an abandoned warehouse than in a decadent banquet hall.

Since mental modeling is always going on, we never notice it happening or how it works. But understanding how the brain creates these mental models—particularly for what we taste—is key to understanding how they are tweaked and altered in the consumer world.

The first thing to know is that when it comes to creating models, the brain does not treat all senses equally. Rather, it prioritizes the stronger senses over the weaker. Taste is incredibly weak (and therefore highly impressionable) in comparison to the others. Vision is by far our strongest. How do we know this? Vision dominates the brain's cortex volume; roughly one-third of the brain is dedicated just to processing and interpreting visual information. And when put in competition with other senses, vision dominates.

You can see this directly when vision is pitted directly against our second-strongest sense, hearing. The brain is like a biased traffic cop: if visual data approaches an intersection at the same time as, say, auditory data, the brain will give vision the right of way every time!

Here's how that tie-break plays out in the real world. Imagine watching a video of a man repeating the word *bah*. The sound is coming in clearly: *bah, bah, bah, bah*. Now, imagine another audio clip, with the same man repeating the word *fah*. Again, the sound is clear: *fah, fah, fah, fah*. Finally, imagine if the audio from the first clip were laid over the second clip—so that you are seeing a person's mouth articulating *fah*, but hearing the word *bah*. Which "sound" wins, *bah* or *fah*? Which piece of data, audio or visual, gets right of way in our mental model of the video? It's the visual one, every time. Even though, objectively, the sound we hear is *bah*, our mental model takes its cue from the visual domain, and we ultimately hear *fah* instead.

This phenomenon has been replicated dozens of times, and is known as the McGurk effect.[3,4] 🔊

It's no surprise, then, that vision has such a strong impact on our brain's model for taste, our weakest, least-developed sense. Recently, more studies[5,6] have replicated the results of the wine test with one key difference:

rather than food coloring, augmented reality (AR) was used to change the wine's color from white to red. And even though the change in appearance was digital, with participants viewing the wine only through AR lenses, the results were the same: "red" wine "tasted" like red things such as berries and dark spices, despite the actual substance remaining unchanged. It's like something straight out of *Black Mirror*: changing the color of food in the virtual world shifts our perception of food in the real world.

Other colors can make us not want to eat at all. In one experiment, researchers at the University of Hyogo investigated the influence color can have on soup consumption.[7] They fed several groups of subjects soup with the same ingredients, bowl, temperature, and so forth, with just one slight change: the color. Tasteless dyes were used to test the response to each color.

A striking pattern emerged. Blue dye decreased participants' willingness to eat, their reports of the soup's palatability, and their feeling of comfort associated with having soup more than any other color. Moreover, the blue soup elicited the most anxiety and the least satisfaction. In other words, subjects were unsatisfied simply because their soup was blue.

In the previous experiments we've discussed here, participants were duped while consuming a known item. Both pâté and red wine were familiar to the subjects; they knew what these items should taste like. Not so much with blue soup. And yet their perception of the blue food was still affected. This is because their mental model of blue soup was informed by what they thought blue food *means*.

Whether ingrained through evolution or based on our experiences in this lifetime, the brain implicitly understands that blue food may not be safe, since it doesn't occur naturally in healthy foods. When we do see blue in the food world (e.g., on spoiled meat), it is usually a bad sign.

As the late, great George Carlin explained:

Red is raspberry, cherry, and strawberry. Orange is orange. Yellow is lemon. Green is lime. Brown is meat . . . THERE'S NO BLUE FOOD! Don't say blueberries, we know they're purple. Blue cheese? No. Blue cheese is just white cheese with a bunch of mold in it.[8]

The soup eaters may not have had an explicit understanding that the color blue is suspicious when it comes to food. But, outside of their awareness, their brains used this latent meaning to, well, *color* their mental models of how they experienced the soup.

BELIEVING IS SEEING

The ability of a strong sense to influence our perception of a weaker one is a good illustration of how our mental models are imperfect and impressionable. But that's only the beginning. Mental models are even more heavily influenced by our beliefs—what we understand to be true about what we're consuming.

Imagine enjoying a meat dish with a glass of merlot at a Michelin three-star restaurant. It's savory, well cooked, and tastes amazing—at least until the waiter comes by and asks you how you're liking your "horse face" sausage. With this piece of knowledge penetrating your mental model, your next bite might taste very differently. In other words, your beliefs about eating horse meat influence your mental model of the dish, which in turn affect your perception of the dish's taste—even when you're in between bites! It was horse meat before you knew, and it is horse meat now. Yet somehow, one bite later, it just doesn't taste the same.[9]

While eating horse is common in many European and Asian countries, in America, it is somewhat taboo. There's nothing inherently unpalatable about horse meat. But your enjoyment of it depends on the beliefs you bring to the table. Your beliefs about what you're eating affect your mental model, and therefore the experience of eating itself.

In a famous sequence from *Pulp Fiction*, Jules (played by Samuel L. Jackson) philosophizes about this very point, refusing to even try pork because it comes from pig, based solely on his belief that the pig is a filthy animal: "Sewer rat may taste like pumpkin pie but I'd never know 'cause I wouldn't eat the filthy motherfucker." Just imagine Jules happily munching down on what he thinks is beef brisket, only to be told halfway through that he's actually eating pulled pork. He might just "strike down with great vengeance and fuuuurrrious anger."

Beliefs supercharge mental models, and the implications for the consumer world are far-reaching. An "organic" label biases how you taste the food it labels.[10] People find turkey tastes better when packaged with a national brand logo compared to the same piece of meat in a generic package.[11] Beliefs are part and parcel of the mental models we create, and they heavily influence our consumer experiences.

Now, a cynic might argue that the effect of belief is only superficial—that we just *tell* ourselves that coffee tastes better in a fancy cup, or that turkey tastes better when it comes from a reliable brand. That the experience of biting into an apple that is only labeled organic is not the same as eating an apple that is actually organic.

It's not an unreasonable position to take. But it doesn't hold up. Wine, again, provides a delicious testing ground. Countless studies have shown that if people *believe* they're drinking expensive wine, they report experiencing it as being more enjoyable. But one seminal piece of research went beyond self-reporting and looked directly at its participants' brains. Baba Shiv's research team at Stanford used functional MRI (fMRI) machines to observe subjects' pleasure centers, a region deep inside the brain called the nucleus accumbens,[12] as they tasted two different glasses of wine. One was described as very expensive, and the second as cheap. The research team found that neurons in the pleasure center fired actively when participants were told they were drinking an expensive wine. When they were told they were drinking cheap wine? No fireworks. Of course, both glasses of wine came from the same bottle.

This research shows how deeply mental models are influenced by beliefs, and how deeply those mental models influence our perceptions. This isn't trickery. We aren't actively fooling ourselves. Expensive wine actually tastes better at the measurable, neuroscientific level of the brain. The core of the brain experiences one identical thing in two entirely different ways because of its self-imposed beliefs. It's not that you're *saying* you like the more expensive wine better; you actually *feel* it tastes better. The belief behind expensive wine informs your mental model in such a way that it actually affects the taste of the wine. Mental models are not an addition to an experience, but rather, the experience itself.

HOW BELIEFS SCULPT MENTAL MODELS

As we've seen, beliefs weigh much more heavily in mental models than simple sensory information. But brands don't stop with the simple beliefs like *This is organic* or *This meat comes from a cow*. They are also in the business of creating complex, enduring beliefs about themselves and their products that create a lasting impact on the brain's basic architecture. Creating a belief like this requires serious integration in the brain. And to understand how that's done, we first need to step back for a second to understand how the brain organizes information.

The brain generally organizes stored data in a vast, interconnected web of what neuroscientists call "semantic networks." Knowledge and concepts are not stored in isolation but rather in association—in networks of related items. Whenever you bring one thing to mind, you also bring to mind all of the other concepts associated with it. For example, when you think of the word *tree*, you may naturally think of *apple*; when you think of *door*, you may automatically think of *key*. And so on.[13]

These webs of knowledge are housed in the brain's temporal lobe. People with damage to this region have a troubling disorder called *agnosia*, in which they are able to see and hear just fine but unable to connect what they see and hear with what the object is called.[14] If presented with a miniature fire truck, an agnostic patient can accurately describe all of its features—how it looks, what it feels like to hold, and what noises it makes. But they cannot *name* what the object is. In other words, they can't connect the sensory information with meaning.

Consistent with the idea that the brain stores knowledge in an organized network, distinct categories of knowledge can be selectively impaired. For example, you can lose your ability to remember or name *living* things, while still being able to name *nonliving* things, if a specific part of the temporal lobe is damaged.[15]

The associations that structure the neural networks in our temporal lobe are not inborn but are learned over time. *Tree* automatically makes us think *leaf* because they are often spoken about in the same breath. In the same way, emotions and other abstract concepts can also be associated with sensory input, or different abstract concepts, through experience. We automatically associate the sound of a siren with a police car or fire engine, but also with the emotion of fear and with alertness. And these emotional associations also hang out in the temporal lobe.

Our brains are able to learn these associations because they are inherently pattern-seeking machines. Neuroscientists call this *statistical learning*. Brains detect patterns in our environment effortlessly and automatically. Over time, these repeated patterns turn to associations. Unlike the associations themselves, the process that creates them seems to be innate. Infants as young as eight months can pick out sound patterns within natural speech, an ability that provides one of the key foundations of language acquisition.[16] Humans have an amazing ability to note patterns. We're pros at turning the statistics in our environment into knowledge without really noticing it. And because associations are paramount to establishing knowledge, their influence on mental models is especially vigorous.

BRANDS AS BELIEF-BASED MENTAL MODELS

Let's pause for a question. What is a brand exactly? Ask a neuroscientist and they'll define a brand as a set of associations. Brand*ing* is an exercise in association design.

Take Coca-Cola, for example. It's the number-one food and beverage brand in the world, and the number-five brand in the world overall, behind Apple, Google, Amazon, and Microsoft.[17] And it feels a little shocking to see it round out the top-five brands list, considering how dependent consumers are on the other four's products. Consider these scenarios:

Scenario 1: Life without Coke.
Scenario 2: Life without Google's search engine.

Which scenario hurts more to imagine? The latter, of course. Google search makes our lives infinitely easier. For better or worse, we'd have a hard time living in the modern world without it. A bottle of Coke? Not so much. If Coca-Cola were a resource-poor start-up today, it would fail based on the frivolous nature of its product. A bottle of Coke has minimal utility—perhaps negative utility, considering its health effects.

"Coke" the substance is brown, carbonated sugar water. That's all it is without the brand, anyway. But "Coke" the brand is something else entirely.

Coca-Cola spends billions on advertising and branding each year. Why? There is hardly a soul alive on the planet who has not heard of Coca-Cola. They do it because the advertising buys them much more than name recognition—it buys them psychological association, a large patch of real estate within the semantic network.

Or put another way, Coca-Cola spends billions on association design. And not just on any association. Coca-Cola spends billions to associate Coke with *happiness*. How do you sell soda to the masses? Associate said product with what the masses want: happiness. The successful association of sugar water with happiness has created $200 billion in value.

In the everyday consumer world, the effect on consumption of the company's brand—their association with an abstract concept such as happiness—is difficult to isolate. When you enjoy a sip of Coke, for example, you do not consciously attribute 25 percent of your perception to the sensory experience of the beverage itself, and 75 percent to the abstract associations you have with the brand. Instead, you have one congruent mental model—the kind of seamless experience that Coca-Cola is arguably the best at creating. This makes their brand all the more impressive.

How does Coca-Cola do it? By carefully crafting their place in our temporal lobes through association design. Coca-Cola spends $4 billion a year on association design, through advertisements and other digital and offline marketing campaigns. All of the above have one singular goal: to hammer into your brain that Coke = Happiness, so that this association will inform your choice of beverage the next time you want something to drink. Coca-Cola's most lasting slogan (ten years as of this writing!) is telling: "Open Happiness." No wonder Pepsi keeps coming up short. It's hard to compete with happiness.

It's clear that Coca-Cola's branding has a deep impact on how we perceive the taste of the beverage. But when a brand becomes deeply embedded like this, is it possible to quantify how effective the brand is at influencing our perception? In the real world, no—it's all one seamless integration. But in a controlled environment, certain experiments can help tease out the specific contribution of the brand to our mental model of the product compared to that of the substance itself. The most famous example of this is the Pepsi Challenge.

The Pepsi Challenge was a long-running marketing campaign that Pepsi launched in 1975. The inspiration came from its marketing team's anecdotal observation that when people didn't know what they were drinking was Pepsi, they actually preferred it over Coke. While the Pepsi Challenge is remembered now as an advertising ploy, its results were obtained using the highest experimental standards. Painstaking detail was applied to ensure that all relevant variables were controlled. Both drinks had to be poured at the same time and served at the same temperature. All trials were randomized, run double blind, and orchestrated by an independent judge not affiliated with the Pepsi brand. The experimental precision rivaled that of clinical drug testing.

S. I. Lee, Pepsi's marketing director for the Asia-Pacific region during the 1990s, described Pepsi's thinking: "We know our product actually tastes better, so let's create a campaign around this."[18] With Pepsi's sales trailing Coca-Cola's by a significant margin at the time, they had little to lose by putting their product's taste to a formal, well-publicized test.

The results were shockingly consistent. When tasters knew which brand they were drinking, 80 percent preferred Coke, while only 20 percent preferred Pepsi. However, when brand information was withheld, blind taste-testers preferred Pepsi to Coke 53 to 47! The results were touted by the marketing team and quickly replicated in every region in which both colas were sold. Based on taste alone, Pepsi was consistently superior.

However, the main marketing victory for Pepsi came from an unexpected source: die-hard Coke fans. Coke loyalists were confident that their soft drink was better and were sure they knew the difference between it and other sodas. These loyal Coke fans ended up being a major focus of the campaign. They were asked ahead of time what they liked most about Coke, and nearly all of them said the taste. However, based on the experiment, they didn't *really* like the taste of Coke as much as they thought. They only liked it when they thought they were drinking Coke. The branding did the majority of the tasting work by influencing Coke fans' mental model of the cola.

Coca-Cola has a major advantage in the soda market because its name has been etched into the brain's semantic network. The mere *idea* of Coke activates the brain in a profound way.

In a set of fMRI experiments inspired by the original Pepsi Challenge marketing campaigns, scientists eavesdropped on the brain as participants drank Coke.[19] One group of participants were told in advance they were drinking Coke, while the other, "control" group were told only that they were drinking a "cola." Compared to the control group, the Coke group showed increased activation in a variety of brain regions, most prominently in the temporal lobe—the region of the brain where your semantic and emotional associations live. This means—just like with expensive wine—people aren't just telling themselves Coke tastes better. Coke actually does taste better to them, because of association design. We can see exactly in the brain where the Coke association is being activated!

This brings us back to the neuroscientists' definition of branding: association design, or the process of repeatedly exposing an audience to a consistent message that a company wants their product to elicit. When this branding is both consistent and repetitive enough, it teaches us an association and alters the underlying architecture of our brains' semantic network. Just as you learned over time during childhood that *leaf* and *tree* go together based on proximity of use, so, too, through countless, consistent advertisements, have you learned that *Coke* and *Happiness* are associated. Our semantic network informs our mental model of the product, which is synonymous with our perception of it. The association has been physically etched—dare we say, *branded*—into your temporal lobes. Coca-Cola is literally renting real estate in your brain, but you are the one paying for it, every time you buy a Coke. Concerned? Don't worry, just "Have a Coke and a Smile."

FROM BLINDSIGHT TO BLIND SPOTS

We've discussed mental models primarily with respect to taste, because of all our senses, it is easiest with taste to see the flexibility of mental models, and how they can be shaped by brands. Because taste is our weakest sense, our brain takes many more liberties. That is, the mental model for what we eat and drink is much more prone to the influence of beliefs—like those elicited by the fanciness of the restaurant we're eating at, the brand of the cola we're drinking, or the organic sticker on the apple we're about to bite into.

But even vision—our most dominant, reliable sense—is subject to the influence of belief. Our brains are constantly creating mental models for what we see, making the world up as we go along. The greatest example of this is the existence of the perceptual blind spot.

The brain sees by processing visual information received by the retina—the millions of cells in the back of each eye that register light from the outside world. The retina sends these visual signals via the optic nerve to the rest of the brain for processing. However, at the point in each eye where the optic nerve meets the retina, there aren't actually any retinal cells—meaning each eye has a blind spot, where we receive no information from the outside world. This blind spot is about the size of a thumbnail and is located 15 degrees from the center of our field of vision.

You can actually "see" your blind spot for yourself, with the demonstration on the next page.

Chances are you have never noticed the existence of this blind spot. One reason, of course, is that we have two eyes—what one eye misses, the other can pick up. But when we close one eye, we don't see a blob of empty, black space. The reason is mental modeling: our brain is constantly making things up as it goes, "filling in" what we expect to be there.

To fill in our blind spot, our brain guesses at reality, based either on other sensory data or on internal belief. And its guesses are pretty remarkable. Think about it: we go our entire lives unaware this blind spot even exists.

Our blind spot also illustrates just how prevalent mental modeling is. It's not something our brain does every once in a while, when in an ambiguous situation with conflicting signals like eating fancy-looking dog food or hearing the sound *fah* when a person's mouth is saying *bah*. The brain is in modeling mode *all the time.*

And of course, this modeling goes well beyond taste or vision or any other specific sense. Our brain is constantly modeling the full experience of reality itself, in all of its complexity and detail. And just like models for taste, our model of reality, too, is incredibly impressionable.

This is why Coca-Cola is far from alone in working hard to deeply integrate themselves into our brains. Brands strive to become synonymous in your mind with abstract, inspirational ideals. BMW has associated its products with perfection; Ford Motors with toughness and reliability; Apple with sleek minimalism; Corona with relaxing on the beach; and on and on. Branding—the systematic altering of our beliefs about a company—fundamentally changes how we experience a company's products. This, again, is why established companies with almost universal name recognition continue to spend billions of dollars a year on advertising. Branding is much more than just getting your name out there; it's about becoming engrained with exactly the right attributes and associations in the customer's brain.

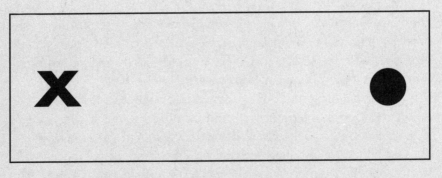

1. Hold the above image at eye level, about an arm's length away, in your right hand.
2. Cover your **left** eye with your **left** hand.
3. With your **right** eye, look at the **X**. Focus on the **X**, but be aware of the dot.
4. SLOWLY bring the image closer to your face, maintaining the focus on the **X**.

As you move the page toward your face, the dot disappears, and then reappears. (If it doesn't work, try it again, this time moving the image toward your face even slower, at half your previous speed or less.) It may take a bit of practice, but once you find the right distance, the dot completely disappears! Congratulations—you've found your blind spot!

Blindsight
The (Mostly) Hidden Ways Marketing Reshapes Our Brains
www.popneuro.com/book

Nike is a great example. The brand has associated itself with the demigods of sports and striving to become the personification of the brand's namesake, the Greek goddess of victory. As a result, it *feels* different wearing a pair of Nikes than it does a generic brand—emotionally and psychologically, above and beyond the physical feel of the shoes themselves. Our mental model for the experience of wearing Nike shoes brings in not only the sensory data involved, but the latent brand knowledge that we have come to associate with Nike over time.

Red Bull has pulled off a similar feat, but with "extreme energy," illustrating that brands don't just influence how we *taste*, but how we *feel*. Controlled studies—think Pepsi Challenge, but for energy drinks—have found that consumers have taken Red Bull's branding quite seriously. In a 2017 experiment,[20] 154 Parisian men were randomly placed into three groups. Each participant was given the same cocktail made with vodka, fruit juice, and Red Bull, but the three groups were each told they were drinking something different. For one group it was a "vodka cocktail," for the second it was a "fruit juice cocktail," and for the last it was "vodka Red Bull." Compared to the other two groups, the group who knew they were drinking Red Bull reported feeling more intoxicated, showed riskier behavior, and were more confident when it came to approaching women. It's your associations with the brand, and not the drink itself, that really "give you wings."

Branding like this works on the same principle as a phenomenon the medical community has known about for decades: the placebo effect. As long as the person taking it *believes* it's medicine, a sugar pill labeled as medicine will often work just as well as the medicine itself. This is exactly what brands are doing: labeling sugar pills as medicine. Except the sugar pill is their product, and the medicinal effects are the abstract emotions and concepts they have calculated.

Recent work using fMRI has found a consistent pattern of brain activation in placebo responders that suggests the effects of a placebo are just as real as that of any biological agent.[21,22] "For years, we thought of the placebo effect as the work of imagination," Kathryn Hall, a molecular biologist studying the biology of placebo effects, told the *New York Times* in 2018.[23] "Now through imaging you can literally see the brain lighting up when you give someone a sugar pill." Just like in Shiv's wine studies, belief informs our mental model of what we experience, right down to our brains' visceral, biological reactions.

If you are led to deeply believe that your chosen shoe brand makes you a better basketball player, who's to say that it doesn't? Call it the placebo effect, confidence, or self-fulfilling prophecy—your beliefs can manifest. Athlete hopefuls who want to "be like Mike" may actually perform just a little bit better with a pair of Jordans on, purely due to the beliefs the brand has produced by associating itself with athletic excellence. And in fact, controlled experiments have found that if you're led to believe you're using a Nike golf driver, you'll drive the ball harder and more accurately than if you were using one that is generically branded—despite the fact that the equipment itself is identical.[24]

The same goes for nearly every product with a strong brand. Expensive makeup brands spend millions to associate their brand with beauty and confidence because, if the buyer believes it to be true, their actual experience of wearing the product reflects that. Expensive luxury clothes with brands synonymous with style, coolness, and confidence create these feelings in the people who wear them. Ultimately, brands matter because beliefs matter.

Brands use the term "mind share" in a figurative sense to describe where one brand stands in comparison to its competitors in the minds of consumers. But the biggest brands know that mind share is quite literal. A brand can dominate competitors right down to the anatomy of the brain, as Coke does Pepsi.

When brands create associations, they are actually creating an enduring change in your brain's semantic network. Let's take a moment to truly let the weight of that set in. Brand associations are not ephemeral, untouchable concepts. They literally take up biological space inside your brain, living as connections between neurons in your temporal lobe. And they have the power to heavily influence, if not actually construct, our experience of reality.

We experience life through our senses. When we see, hear, smell, touch, or taste, the brain takes in this objective raw data as input. Then, combining that data with our existing beliefs about the world, it creates an internal subjective model. This model isn't superficial, a framework in which you perceive new data; it stands in for perception itself. Perception really *is* reality.

We are never consciously aware of the mental modeling process—what happens in our brains between taking in objective data and producing subjective experience. And for marketers, that lack of awareness, as much as that gap between experience and perception itself, represents opportunity. Through tweaking other senses, instilling beliefs, and etching themselves deep into the brain, brands can commandeer this modeling process—and in turn, fundamentally alter our perception of reality.

All of this is unique to *Homo sapiens*. Do you think your dog experiences the taste of their food differently depending on whether it's labeled as Alpo or a generic brand? Not a chance. But humans are strange creatures. Our experience of the world is complex and impressionable. For better or worse, we eat the menu, not the food. Brands probably aren't putting dog food on the menu, but we also probably wouldn't be able to tell if they did.

Chapter 2

DROPPING ANCHORS

The Neuroscience of Relativity

W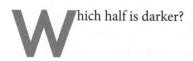hich half is darker?

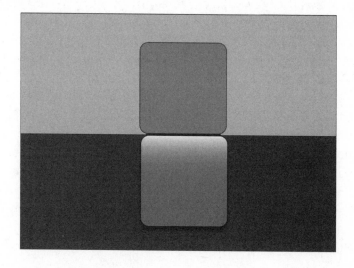

Clearly the top one, right?

Guess again. The shades of gray are exactly the same. When you cover up the seam in the middle with your finger, it reveals that the two halves are exactly the same.

The reason they look different initially is because of something called *mental anchoring*. The brain automatically processes input relative to a reference point. Here, the image's background is acting as that reference point, an anchor directing your brain to process the shade of the squares in relation to it: darker against the lighter background, and lighter against the darker one. Despite the same exact wavelengths of color meeting your eyes, they appear fundamentally different because of that background anchor. Anchors change our perception. They can also affect our attention and our sense of value.

The world is a complex stream of never-ending data, and the brain cannot pay attention to it all. To deal with this sheer volume of information, the brain uses shortcuts. The biggest shortcut of all is anchoring. Anchors help direct our attention to what's most likely to be important, and away from what's likely to be unimportant.

Anchors are everywhere, from the images we see to the sounds we hear. A plain white spot is most visible against the anchor of a black surface. When you grow up in a city, you're used to street noises at night: cars driving, people walking, even the occasional alarm going off. This constant, reliable level of city noise is your aural anchor. When you then go camping out in the countryside for the first time, the silence at night is deafening. You notice it because it's different. The opposite is true for people growing up in the country. Silent nights are their anchor, making obvious the nighttime noise in the city that you've learned to ignore.

Anchors serve as the mental background against which foregrounds stand out. A foreground can be anything from a gray-colored square to a new car. Even foregrounds as abstract as success are processed in relation to an anchor. Being a vice president of a company feels amazing if you're being promoted—say, from being a general manager. You'd likely be reaching for the champagne. But what if you became vice president after being demoted from the position of president? You're not popping any corks for that one. It's a much different life event now.

The brain's perception of the foreground depends on its anchors. The tricky part is, we're hardly ever aware of the anchors themselves, let alone their impact on our behavior.

Brands use this to their benefit. When we're processing the consumer world—for example, assessing if a product is worth its sticker price—we feel as if we're doing so in absolute terms. But really, we're processing it relative to an anchor—which was likely placed by a brand. Brands create anchors for two fundamental reasons: to capture our attention and to alter our perception of value.

The brain is always looking for a place to anchor. And brands, being the sailing experts that they are, plan accordingly. Let's start our look at how they do this by examining attention.

ANCHORING OUR ATTENTION

The impetus for paying attention to something generally comes from one of two places: inside of us, or outside of us. The fancy words for these sources are *endogenous* and *exogenous*, respectively. Endogenous attention is what you use when you shop with a grocery list in hand. Your guiding goal is to find the items on the list; what you are paying attention to is directed *internally* (the *endo* in *endogenous* means "coming from within"). But imagine you're going to the mall to kill time and browse around. In this case, you don't have an internal goal. Instead, the things you pay attention to are generally directed *externally*, by whatever catches your eye. This is exogenous attention.

Brands love to hack our exogenous attention by using the anchors in our environment. TV ads play at a higher volume than the televised content. Billboards come in bright colors that stand out against the mundane hues of the landscape. Driving exogenous attention comes down to tapping into what you naturally pay attention to: change.

At a simple visual level, the brain is biased to pay higher attention to high-contrast objects—white against black, yellow against red, and so forth. Lines and contours can create high contrast as well. In fact, there are distinct systems in the brain that prioritize high-contrast information.[1] Studies with children as young as just a few days have demonstrated a consistent preference for high-contrast stimuli.[2,3] And adult-eye-tracking work has found that high-contrast areas can predict where people will look with 85 percent accuracy.[4]

User-experience designers know the brain's attraction to contrast very well and incorporate it intelligently. Take, for example, logout screens. It's in Facebook's best interest to keep you signed in. How else would they collect all their delicious data? To nudge the user's behavior away from logging out, they use contrast to draw attention to the cancel button.

Here's an example from Amazon's business meeting platform, Chime, that uses contrast to draw your attention to the option they want you to select. The dull background is the anchor; the blue button set against it draws more of your attention compared to the white buttons.

When it comes to making urgent purchase decisions, research has shown that the mere saliency of a product's appearance—its noticeability, arising from the combination of high-contrast visual features such as contours, edges, and color contrast—dramatically increases the likelihood of it being selected.[5] In other words, creating the starkest possible contrast between a product's appearance and its surroundings will increase the likelihood of it being selected.

Imagine being extremely thirsty and truly indifferent to price, brand, or size. Which bottle of water will you choose from a wall of refrigerated bottles? If VOSS is in the fridge, it is sure to *peak* past the rows of similar-looking competitors. This is exactly what VOSS water intended when designing their bottles, which look like something designed by Apple—made of glass, slender, with sharp contrasting lines and a clean, svelte silhouette. In a sea of bulgy plastic bottles (your visual anchor), VOSS grabs your attention.

The stakes only get higher when you're selling Russian water, a.k.a. vodka. After you graduate from Popov, vodka is mostly tasteless. Unlike with whiskey or mezcal, taste isn't such a strong deciding factor for which brand we choose. In a very thorough neuromarketing study,[6] market-ers examined which vodka bottle design received the highest degree of exogenous attention. Turns out, when it comes to attracting the highest amount of attention on the shelf, Absolut, Pinnacle, and Svedka came out on top. Sorry, hipsters: Tito's was dead last. More contrast needed! The use of contrast to catch consumers' attention goes beyond the visual. In the field of journalism, where grabbing attention has become increas-ingly important, getting someone to click an article requires contrast at a conceptual level. According to Katie Calautti, an NYC-based journalist who has written for *Vanity Fair*, *Kinfolk*, and *Huffington Post*, among oth-ers, grabbing attention is increasingly important. As she told the authors in a phone conversation, "There is a lot of noise, and chatter, so you have to do something different to stand out. The reader's time and attention are more constrained now than ever. You want to convey the basic gist of the article, but in a succinct and *distinct* manner."[7] Media companies are vying for attention in a clickbait arms race: all else being equal, the more a head-line contrasts with the other headlines the reader sees, the more likely the reader will be to click it.

PATTERN SEEKING

Recall from chapter one that our brains are pattern-seeking machines. Outside of our awareness, we're constantly learning the patterns in our environment. Over a lifetime, our brains have internalized many such pat-terns, and these patterns provide the background, the anchors, that drive attention to potentially important violations.

This type of anchoring makes evolutionary sense. Survival doesn't depend on taking in and experiencing 100 percent of our environment. In fact, paying attention to every detail all the time would actually hurt our survival odds. Survival depends on quick action, and our brains have evolved to process just enough perceptual information in order to act. Is this berry a fruit I've eaten before, or something new and potentially poi-sonous? It's not necessary to see every pigment in the berry, only to notice whether it continues or interrupts my established pattern of safe-to-eat berries. Learning patterns helps save time and energy.

In fact, the brain likes patterns so much that it leads us to *dis*like true statistical randomness. When iTunes first released its shuffle feature, it received a slew of angry emails. The complaints came from customers who claimed the feature was broken because, when they clicked the "shuffle" button on their *NSYNC album, the tracks sometimes played in order. People felt cheated. How could a random algorithm produce three songs in the same order as they appear on the actual album? Random should mean 7, 11, 3, not 1, 2, 3, right? Except that when song selection is truly random, each song has the same probability of playing each time the current song ends. Sometimes that means 7, 11, 13, but sometimes that means 1, 2, 3 instead.

In response, iTunes changed their randomness algorithm to avoid such sequential ordering. The new algorithm *feels* more random to us humans despite it being objectively *less* random. Spotify went through a similar experience with their feature[18] when determining the optimal approach to shuffling songs in playlists. Mattias Peter Johansson, Spotify's algorithm developer, put it best: "The problem is that, to humans, truly random does not feel random. We updated [the shuffle feature] with a new algorithm that is intended to feel more random to a human."[19] We humans are strange creatures.

The Zig and the Zag

"Zig when everyone else zags" is a saying often applied to branding. It also perfectly captures the simplicity of the brain's attention system. The psychological anchor is the *zag*, the direction in which everyone is headed—the pattern. To capture the attention of the brain, you have to *zig* by going in a different direction.

Brands are great at zigging in order to get your attention. One of the ways they do so is by tapping existing associations, which act as a pre-made anchor. All a brand has to do is break from the anchoring association and voilà—our pattern-seeking brains detect the sudden change, and we respond by giving the brand our attention.

If you were asked to think of an exotic sports car, what color car comes to mind? Chances are, red or bright yellow. If you are a car brand releasing a new sports car, how do you stand out among a sea of red sports cars? For Nissan's 350Z, the answer was to use orange. Specifically, burnt orange. In a sea of red sports cars (the zag), the "350Z Orange" (the zig) grabs attention. For many years, brands selling products to women have used pink to signal femininity, and the more brands that have done this over time, the more of an associative anchor pink has become. How do you stand out, then, against the anchor of brands that associate femininity with pink? The easy answer here is to pick a different color—which is exactly what the jewelry brand Tiffany & Co. did. Then, Tiffany went further. By breaking through the existing associations enough times and doing so in a consistent manner, they ended up creating a new association. This is the reason why Tiffany blue is so powerful: it broke through a sea of pink and, over time, became an association in itself.

If you zig hard enough, you can achieve the ultimate outcome in pattern breaking: surprise. In late 2006, UK-based Cadbury Chocolates was in the middle of a public relations storm. A salmonella outbreak had sickened more than forty people, greatly damaging the brand image. After the PR team performed some initial damage control, they were desperate for something to rejuvenate the once-classic brand. Cadbury's PR savior was a four-hundred-pound gorilla, in an ad campaign that went viral before *viral* was a household term. The commercial opens with a close-up of a gorilla's face. No background is visible. The only audio is the beginning of Phil Collins's "In the Air Tonight": a slow vocal buildup to a musical crescendo punctuated by perhaps the most famous drum break in pop music history. As the song builds up to the break, the camera slowly zooms out to reveal the gorilla is actually a drummer patiently waiting to jam out the crescendo. Imagine being in the meeting to hear this pitch! "Bob, I've got a way out of our salmonella nightmare. All I need is Phil Collins and a gorilla suit."[8]

The zig worked. The video quickly received over half a million views on YouTube.[9] And more than attention, Cadbury reported an overwhelmingly positive consumer impression from the campaign,[10] along with a significant uptick in sales.

Patterns create expectations, which act as anchors. See enough doors with a pull handle, you'll expect doors to pull to open. See enough high fives, and when someone raises their right hand in the air with their palm facing you, you'll know to slap their hand in like fashion. Breaking this expectation results in a very specific sensation: surprise. In fact, "violation of expectation" is exactly how neuroscientists define surprise. What

Cadbury did here was use the silly but existing association of drummers as human as an anchor to surprise the audience. We don't live in a world where gorillas are drummers (as epic as that would be). So our surprise at seeing one—the ad's violation of our expectation—attracted our attention.

The most interesting aspect of this ad, though, was its one-and-done nature. A few iterations later, the allure of the gorilla evaporated. The sequels exhibited sharp diminishing returns. Why? Because the attention value of the initial surprise is fleeting. You can only be surprised by a four-hundred-pound gorilla once, before you start to learn the new pattern and perceive things relative to this new anchor. Fool me once, shame on the gorilla. Fool me twice . . .

Violation of Expectation

Neuroscientists have studied violation of expectation deeply. Using an EEG machine, neuroscientists can measure the fluctuation of brain activity linked to surprise. This measurement is called N400, so named because it is roughly 400 milliseconds after hearing a surprising verbal punch line that your brain registers the surprise on the EEG.

The N400 response is primarily associated with linguistic surprise.[11] As a general rule, every word elicits an N400 response, but the more uncommon a word is, the greater in amplitude its N400 response. For example, an uncommon word like *superfluous* creates a much greater N400 response than a common word like *chapter*.

However, the interesting thing about the N400 response is that the contextual anchor is hugely important. While each word has its own inherent N400 amplitude, this amplitude changes dramatically based on how likely the word's use is in the context in which it's presented. For example, take the sentence: "I long to marry my one and only true _____." You wouldn't be surprised if this sentence ended with *love*. However, if the last word in the sentence were *elephant*, you'd be extremely surprised. It would score high on the N400 scale. While *elephant* itself isn't a rare word, it's surprising in the context of the sentence.

Dozens of EEG studies[12] have documented this phenomenon. The greater the mismatch between the word and the contextual anchor, the greater the amplitude of the N400 response—the greater the surprise. The context itself acts as an anchor, creating an expectation that can then be either fulfilled or violated. And when it's violated, you can't help but pay attention to it.

Comedians know this intuitively, and perhaps no one utilizes this tool better than Anthony Jeselnik. Jeselnik is an N400 professional, a comedian who's made a career out of "violation of expectation" jokes. His formula is simple and yet irresistible. He paints a verbal picture that takes the listener in one direction, but ultimately leads to a surprising punch line. The truest sign of his mastery of surprise? Even though the audience quickly figures out the formula, they never see the punch line coming. Jeselnik is able to surprise his audiences repeatedly for over an hour despite those audiences' keen awareness of his use of surprise and misdirection.

Here are a few examples, minus Jeselnik's comedic timing. See if you can predict the punch lines.

My dad was amazing. He raised five boys. All by himself. Without the rest of us knowing.

We just found out my little brother has a peanut allergy, which is very serious, I know. But still I feel like my parents are totally overreacting—they caught me eating a tiny little bag of airline peanuts and they kicked me out of his funeral.

I've got a kid in Africa that I feed, that I clothe, that I school, that I inoculate for 75 cents a day. Which is practically nothing compared to what it cost to send him there.

The power of a deliberate violation of expectation isn't lost on big brands. Consider IHOP's publicity stunt in 2018. The American breakfast chain committed blasphemy by announcing they were changing their name from IHOP, International House of Pancakes, to IHOB, International House of Burgers. The change garnered massive attention, quantified via digital metrics: they saw a 6,477 percent increase in social media mentions in just one day, boosting brand awareness significantly. Moreover, the hashtags #IHOP and #IHOB received more than 297 million impressions in the weeklong lead-up to its big reveal: that they were kidding all along.[13]

They'd pulled the stunt to grab consumer attention for the rollout of their new product, burgers.

Burgers are not themselves surprising stimuli. In its normal context, the word *burger* would generate no N400 at all. But in context of *IHO*, with *pancakes* as the anchor? Massive N400 and a massive grab of our attention.

ENDOGENOUS ATTENTION: VIGILANCE AGAINST SHINY THINGS

From billboards to flashy packaging to zig advertising, anchors are used to drive consumer attention. But our exogenous attention is finite. You as the consumer can only be pulled in so many directions. How do companies protect against the competition constantly attempting to grab their customers' attention? Enter the brand.

Powerful brands—ones that have garnered your loyalty—have the ability to drive *endogenous* attention. Recall that endogenous attention comes from within; it's going to the market with a shopping list instead of just browsing. Brands drive endogenous attention by being the name on the list:

> Buy (Kraft) macaroni and cheese
> Buy (Doritos) chips

Say you have a strong preference for a brand of water, like Dasani. At the moment of purchase, you will search for bottled water in endogenous mode; you'll search for Dasani. Companies don't have to grab your attention externally if they are already in your head.

What's interesting about endogenous attention is that it also serves as protection against exogenous attention grabs from competitors. The more we favor Dasani, the less likely we are to see the alternatives. We are *literally blind* to Dasani's competition—a massive win for Dasani.

Being in an endogenous mode for a brand dulls the visual, attention-grabbing effects of sharp angles, colors, and contrasts. Remember the previously quoted study where visual attention could be predicted with 85 percent accuracy based on visually salient features? That was in browsing (exogenous) mode. The moment you give test subjects a goal, the prediction accuracy plummets to 40 percent. Which is to say that, when in endogenous mode, visual-attention-grabbing tricks are not very effective.

This may seem like a moment to celebrate. After all, endogenous mode seems to undo the effects of the previous attention hack. But pause the high fives and let's take a moment to reflect. When the brain shifts from browsing attention (exogenous) to goal-oriented attention (endogenous), the brain literally sees less. The brain goes selectively blind.

In a study by Harvard researcher Daniel Simons,[14] blindness is exactly how you would describe it. The experiment design is brilliant: A person playing a tourist holding a map walks up to a stranger to ask for directions. While the stranger is looking at the map, a pair of movers walk past holding a painting, and the tourist changes places with one of the movers. The new tourist continues to speak to the stranger—and the stranger has no idea the tourist is a whole new person![15] 🔄

Another classic study by Simons validated our tendency to be blinded by attention.[16] If you're not familiar with this already, you should try it yourself[17] before reading on. 🔄

In the study, subjects watched a video of a group of people bouncing a ball back and forth and were asked to count the number of bounces. With their endogenous attention directing their gaze onto the ball, the subjects completely miss a man in a gorilla suit walking through the middle of the group. When our attention is anchored endogenously on things like reading a map or counting bounces, we are mentally blind. A strong enough anchor has the power to blind us to everything else—even gorillas. Don't gloss over the importance of this. One of the top wishes a genie could grant a company is to physically blind customers to its competition. But companies don't need a genie for this. Our loyalty to the brand flips our brain into goal-oriented endogenous mode. Recall from chapter one how a brand can fundamentally alter our perception; it can also fundamentally alter our attention in its favor.

FROM ATTENTION TO VALUE

Back to the original point: brains are like boats, always looking for places to anchor, because our brains use anchors to process and contextualize the world. The brain's reliance on anchors is key to the psychology of surprise, perception, and attention. But anchors can do more than distort our attention. They also have the power to distort our sense of value.

To understand this, first we need to understand the strange effect that numbers have on us. Throw some numbers at the brain and anchoring kicks into overdrive. Whenever numbers are present, the brain uses these numerical references as anchors of value. Anchoring makes us fall for numerical as well as visual illusions.

In a study by the famous behavioral scientist Daniel Kahneman, participants spun a gameshow-style wheel on which each placard contained a random number between 1 and 100. After each spin, the subjects were asked impossible numerical questions designed to make them guess. For example, "What percentage of Zimbabwe's population has traveled outside the country?" or "What is the average temperature in Bozeman, Montana?" Fascinatingly, their answers correlated to the numbers they received when spinning the wheel. If they'd spun a high number, they were more likely to respond with a high estimate, and vice versa for low numbers. Despite the fact that participants were fully aware that the number they'd landed on was random and had nothing to do with their question, the number nonetheless anchored and biased their response.

And here's where the stakes are raised. When these anchors are amounts of money, they have a major effect on what we're willing to spend. In a real-world experiment outside the Exploratorium Museum in San Francisco, passersby were asked if they'd be willing to donate money to help wildlife affected by a recent oil spill. Being good West Coast Samaritans, most people were willing to donate some amount of money—a generous $64 on average. But when participants were given a subtle numerical anchor, via being asked if they would donate a specific number of dollars, it warped their responses significantly. When this number was $5, it shrunk the donation average to $20. When the anchor was $400, their response ballooned to $143!

Similarly, when Williams-Sonoma placed a $429 bread maker on the shelf near a $279 model, the $429 unit, predictably, did not sell. However, sales of the cheaper $279 model doubled. Knowing nothing of bread makers, and facing the option of only one model at $279, your brain is lost. Is $279 a fair price? Is it a steal? Is it overpriced? We can't figure this out. But put the same $279 bread maker next to one for $429, and the brain is no longer lost. The $429 serves as an anchor that puts $279 in perspective.

Next to this anchor,[18] $279 seems like a good deal. Similar effects have been found on menus. If you put an expensive entrée first, no one may actually buy it, but everything else looks much cheaper, and therefore much more appealing, by contrast.

The brain is so receptive to numerical anchors that companies don't even need an expensive alternative to make us think their price is a steal. Fast-food restaurant ads are filled with proud declarations of "the best dollar menu." This makes sense: a dollar for a burger feels like a really good deal. What doesn't make sense is trying to charge $4 for a burger while the competition is shouting about their $1 burger. Yet Carl's Jr. did exactly that—and succeeded. While the rest of the industry engaged in a race to the bottom, Carl's Jr. introduced "The Six Dollar Burger," which you could have for the tasty price of $4. The name itself provided an anchor for value; it told you how much you *should*, or rather *would*, pay elsewhere. Priced at $4, you think you're getting a great deal. Carl's Jr. changed its customers' anchor.

This brings us to MSRPs. What in the world is an MSRP? It stands for *manufacturer's suggested retail price*. You may know that already. What you may not know is the psychological impact of an MSRP. MSRPs act as anchors for our sense of value. Amazon consistently uses them to anchor value; their product listings proudly display the original (much higher) price. Seeing the $300 MSRP for a set of Bose noise-canceling headphones next to the Amazon price of $150 makes the purchase feel like a hot buy—never mind the fact most internet retailers are selling at or near Amazon's price.

Numerical limits also drive up purchasing by serving as an anchor in your mind. If a grocery store puts up a big sign in the produce section stating that "the maximum number of apples you can buy is fifteen," your brain picks up that number as the all-important anchor for deciding. Researchers tested this directly with soup and found that people are much more likely to buy four cans of soup than two when they are told there is a four-can limit.[19]

We saw earlier how brands, to capture our attention, create or tap into a consistent pattern in our minds, only to violate that pattern. They do the same thing with price. Macy's, for example, is famous—or rather, infamous—for exactly this type of strategy. The company plans periods of no sales paired with shorter yet consistent periods of sales. You walk into a Macy's and see a Ralph Lauren men's suit priced at $700. That is the reference point your brain uses to anchor the suit's value. You walk in a month later on Presidents' Day weekend, and the same suit is on sale for $400. Since the value is already anchored at $700, $400 sounds like a great deal—despite the fact that every major holiday brings a Macy's sale with a similar discount.

Old Navy takes this to another level by always having items on sale. Think about it: When was the last time you walked past an Old Navy and *didn't* see a window advertisement for a sale? The original price is always knocked off at Old Navy—and yet consumers keep buying into the anchor.

Some criticize Macy's and Old Navy for exercising what is essentially fake pricing. JCPenney originally functioned the same way, with less than 1 percent of their revenues coming from items bought at full price. Then the company heard the critics and decided to take a stance against fake pricing by abandoning the never-ending sales and the fake MSRPs, instead offering everyday low prices.

The result? Calamity. Nearly $1 billion worth! JCP's revenue plunged $985 million in the fiscal year following their move to "fair and square" pricing. It turns out that customers *liked* the marked-down prices; their brains wanted the reference of the inflated, untrue price to help justify their purchases. JCP's CEO, Ron Johnson, the famous retail architect behind Target's "affordable chic" design and Apple's Genius Bars, stepped down, and marked-down sale prices returned. The result? Revenue recovered.

A moment of silence here is appropriate. A Historic American Business did something truly noble by saying their MSRPs were fake. For every item, they moved to one price, which was lower than the previous sale price. In theory, this made total sense—less noise and more savings to the customer. The fact that it failed shows how deeply ingrained the anchor mechanism is inside the brain. It is such a powerful influencer that a noble effort on JCP's part, one that was objectively good for the customer, was spurned by customers because, well, we wanted fake prices. Nonetheless, a hat tip to you, Mr. Johnson.

THE GOLDILOCKS BIAS

What if, in looking for numerical anchors, the brain sees three pricing options, rather than two? What then? Well, then the brain engages in something called the Goldilocks bias: given three options, we lean toward the middle one.

Marketers often deliberately set up the option they want us to choose as the middle one. Do you want a 12-ounce steak for $18, a 14-ounce steak for $22, or a 16-ounce steak for $26? Most people opt for 14 ounces. How do we know people don't just naturally prefer the 14-ounce steak on its own merit? Because when it becomes the lowest option—when the choices change to 14, 16, and 18 ounces—16 ounces becomes the more popular choice. It's the "middleness" of the option that is the persuasive factor.

BuyAutoParts.com, one of the earliest companies to sell auto parts online, used the middle option successfully during coauthor Prince's tenure there as the head of marketing. The auto parts sold came in three options, in order of price: remanufactured, unbranded new, and branded new. Over 80 percent of the time, customers chose the middle option—unbranded new. The middle was doubly appealing in this situation because the average shopper is not a car-parts expert. They know they need a radiator, but don't how to tell a good radiator from a bad one. Behavioral economists describe this as *operating under high uncertainty*: without other information to guide our sense of value, the Goldilocks bias is an even more effective anchor.

DIMINISHING RETURNS

The impact of anchors also gives rise to the phenomenon of diminishing returns, especially when it comes to money. Money seems less valuable the more of it there is. Your perception of the amount of value you receive from a $100 bill goes down depending on how much money you already have. If you're broke, $100 means the world. If you're Jeff Bezos, $100 is hardly worth the effort to bend over to pick it up. The amount of money you already have in the bank serves as a psychological anchor, which brings down the weighted psychological value of new gains. Each additional dollar means less and less.

This also works with anchors other than your existing wealth. Brands can create an anchor within a buying experience to distort how you value the money you're forking over. A prime example of this is add-on pricing. Buying a digital pen for $100 might sound like a lot of money. But if you've just committed to spending $2,000 on a Microsoft Surface Pro laptop, an additional $100 doesn't feel as heavy.

German luxury-car manufacturers are especially adept at this. Take BMW for example. Say you want to treat yourself for your promotion and buy a $68,000 BMW M3. Not a bad choice. If you aren't afraid of speeding tickets and want to go for broke with the color red (notorious for its magnetic attraction of police cruisers), you have to pay for it. That's right—BMW has the nerve to charge you for the color of the car! For $550 more, you can have your red M3. This is sadly humorous, considering "colorless" isn't the default option.

BMW does it because they know you will pay for it. Plus $500 for wireless charging and Bluetooth. And another $300 just to connect your Apple device (really!), $200 for the heated steering wheel, $1,100 for the mirror caps, and $430 to paint the grill black. It goes on and on. Why? Because what's a few hundred dollars when you're already paying nearly $70K for the car? Any time you make a big purchase like a car or a house, you're vulnerable to how that large anchor warps your perception of value. Everything else seems small by comparison.

When it comes to the mathematics of value, the calculation does not take place in a vacuum. Instead, our perception of value is fixed to a reference point—an anchor. Sometimes that reference point is the price of a recent purchase; sometimes it is a set of options; and other times, it's another random number in the vicinity. The lesson here is our brains are hardwired not to look for the objective value of an item, but rather to look to numbers, no matter how irrelevant, on which to hang our sense of the item's value.

From numbers to surprises, anchors like this exist because we need them. Life has evolved to contain more data points than ever. What was once a dirt path with an occasional signpost is now a street with cars, pedestrians, bike lanes, skateboarders, traffic lights, crosswalks, street signs, parked cars, parking meters, fire hydrants, curbs, and buildings with doors, windows, graffiti, and signs. If it weren't for shortcuts like anchoring that let our brain prioritize all of this information, we might never leave the house.

The consumer world is especially busy, with billboards, TV and radio commercials, social media ads, clickbait articles, influencer sponsorships, and much more. No wonder our attention span is shortening. With all the noise, brands have more incentive to design for our brain's tendency to look for anchors. How else would they capture our attention? And in the chaos of the modern environment, our overstimulated, overtaxed brains are even happier for an excuse to shut out alternative options or rely on convenient value-anchoring numbers.

The French philosopher Simone Weil was right when she said, "Attention is the rarest and purest form of generosity." Knowing how anchors work provides us with a newfound appreciation for our own most valuable resource. And instead of passively allowing it to be taken, we can at least make brands *earn* it.

Chapter 3

MAKING THE MOMENT

The Marketing Opportunity Between
Experience and Memory

On the east coast of the United Kingdom, on the banks of Welland River, rests a small town called Spalding. Dating back to the Roman period, the land served as an ancient salt factory. Today, you can take a water taxi down the river en route to the famous Spalding Flower Parade, which celebrates the town's production of tulips.

Spalding is also home to Michelle Philpots, who lives a life unique as the town itself. In 1994, she experienced a rite of passage many employees do: getting let go. Specifically, she was fired from her office job because she was found photocopying the same piece of paper over and over again. When asked, Michelle explained she knew she had to photocopy the page, but did not remember having already done so. She was stuck in a never-ending loop.

Michelle had been in two major car accidents four years apart, both resulting in head injuries. After her firing, local doctors diagnosed Michelle with a form of epilepsy caused by the injuries, and her memory continued to deteriorate until finally hitting a plateau years later. Today, she has all of her memories leading up to 1994. She wakes up every morning as a twenty-something-year-old woman (she is fifty-four at the time of writing) and thinks *Pulp Fiction* is a new movie by up-and-coming director Quentin Tarantino. Michelle remembers her husband Ian, because they met before 1994, but she does not remember marrying him, as they married in 1997.

Every single day, Michelle's memory is deleted. If this sounds like the plot for the movie *50 First Dates*, well, it is. Michelle has the same condition as Drew Barrymore's character, Lucy. Lucy re-meets her boyfriend Henry, played by Adam Sandler, for the first time every day, and uses her diary as a tool to remind herself of Henry. At one point, Lucy breaks up with him, and effectively erases any memory of him by erasing every mention of him in her diary.

This is where things get spooky. Lucy checks herself into an adult care clinic, where she spends her days painting. Weeks pass as she focuses on painting her masterpiece. The masterpiece turns out to be a portrait of Henry, a man she does not consciously remember and yet clearly has not truly forgotten. The subconscious memory of him has found a way to drive her behavior.

Patients like Michelle and her fictional counterpart Lucy suffer from what neuroscientists call anterograde amnesia, caused by a specific type of brain damage to the hippocampus and nearby regions of the medial temporal lobe. Studying this variety of amnesia patient has provided an amazing window into the mysteries of human memory.

WHAT IS MEMORY?

Intuitively, memory feels like a single thing. But what we think of as memory is actually a group of distinct neuroscientific phenomena. When you go to a museum, the region of the brain involved in gaining knowledge from the experience (semantic memory) is different from the region involved in the memory of the museum trip itself (episodic memory). Studying the facts of a city on Wikipedia (explicit memory) is very different from slowly gaining a sense of familiarity after moving to a new city (implicit memory). And learning a physical skill is considered yet another, separate form of memory (procedural memory). Say that you're practicing cursive, or writing notes with your off hand. Your ability to do this will get better with time, even if you forget the actual circumstances in which you practiced.

If we were to come up with a definition of memory that encapsulates all of these different strands, it would go something like this: *memory is our brain's attempt at connecting us to the past.*

All marketers, whether they realize it or not, are in the memory business. The most amazing, emotionally gripping thirty-second commercial in the world means absolutely nothing if viewers instantly forget it the second it's over. An incredibly designed in-store experience means zilch if it isn't remembered. In fact, when we talk about a brand, what we're really referring to is the cluster of memories of all our past experiences and previously acquired knowledge related to a particular company or product.

For brands, the transformation of experiences into memories, and the effective retrieval of those memories, is crucial. For them to connect with us, they need to become part of our memory—a part of our past. And as we'll see, the ways in which the brain attempts to connect us to the past through memory are systematically biased—and often, if not always and inherently, inaccurately so.

There's a lot to unpack here. As such, memory is the only topic in the book spread across two chapters. This chapter focuses on memory encoding, or how we transform experiences into memories; chapter four focuses on our recall of those encoded memories.

ENCODING MEMORIES

For an event to become a memory, it must first be encoded. *Encoding* is what neuroscientists call the process by which the brain turns an event into an impression. *Encoding* is the verb; an *impression* is the resulting noun. Impressions are physical things. They are consolidated in the brain's hippocampus, near the very center of the brain, and later integrated broadly into the cortex, the large, outermost region of the brain. For an experience to lead to a memory, it must literally and physically change our brains.

Not every event we experience results in an impression. If you have an amazing experience but can't remember any of it—say, because you drank too much—did it really happen? Of course it did. But thanks to the alcohol interrupting the consolidation process, it left no impression on the brain.

No impression means no memory. Michelle Philpots can't remember anything after 1994 because her brain hasn't encoded anything since 1994. Events in her life haven't been encoded because the region of her brain responsible for encoding was damaged.

For brands, the success of a campaign is defined by how strong an impression it leaves on the brain. As mentioned, if it does not leave an impression, it doesn't really matter; it can't affect your future behavior in any way. So brands are in the business of creating impressions—or, as a neuroscientist would put it, in the business of encoding. It's a tricky business, though, because the transition from event to impression is far from straightforward.

Clever brands are adept at creating experiences that optimize not only for the event itself, but for the resulting memory. There are certain characteristics of events that can "boost" encoding, resulting in stronger impressions on the brain. Using one or more of these impression boosters can mean a stronger memory that is better optimized to achieve a brand's goals.

BOOSTER #1: ATTENTION

One's state of mind during an event is incredibly important to whether it gets encoded. If we're not paying attention, it's unlikely the memory will stick. Thus, the first encoding booster is attention itself. We saw in chapter two the ways in which attention is captured and maintained—how our attention system only really cares for sudden changes relative to an anchor. But attention isn't just moment-to-moment experience; it's also the crucial first step in forming an explicit memory.

Attention isn't all or nothing, where we either pay close attention to a thing or barely notice it. Attention exists on a spectrum, and it is often split. Think about events like concerts and performances. You can count on a good chunk of the audience to be recording the event on their smartphones. Experiencing the event through a camera app means we are paying attention not just to the event in front of us, but also to the phone, the positioning of the lens, and the recording on the screen. We're multitasking.

Professor Diana Tamir at Princeton University[1] and colleagues reported in 2018 that when we record an event like a concert, our memory of that event is actually much worse than if we'd simply watched it. A similar study[2,3] that analyzed memory when taking still pictures found that memories of photographed events were reduced as well. Why? Because when we experience the world through a camera, still or recording, it subtracts from the attention we would otherwise be dedicating to the event unfolding in front of us, which decreases encoding. How ironic that the tools we use to save digital copies of our experiences end up impairing our ability to remember the experience itself.

In this context, mobile technology actually poses a mixed bag for marketers. On one hand, it allows for shareable content to proliferate on social media. But on the other, when the consumer is the one creating the shareable content, it seems to degrade the consumer's memory of the actual experience and attenuate the impression it leaves on them.

The influence of attention on encoding is why product placements are much more successful in video games than in movies. When watching a movie, viewers are passive, observing events that unfold in front of characters. But video game players are active, paying close attention to control an avatar of themselves. This increased focus results in stronger, more successful encoding—including of the products companies pay to place there.

BOOSTER #2: FRICTION

Attention is a broad phenomenon. As we saw in chapter two, our attention is naturally drawn to stimuli that have high visual contrast, and that violate expectation. Taking this a step further, certain types of stimuli not only draw our attention, but also force our attention into a deeper state. These friction-inducing stimuli make us think closely about what we're seeing. When what we're looking at is just a little bit difficult to process, it drives us to strain our attention to figure it out. And when we think deeply about something, we encode it more thoroughly, and remember it better.

This idea has been cleverly illustrated with fonts. Carnegie Mellon University professor Daniel Oppenheimer provided two groups of people with an identical story written in two different fonts. One version's font consisted of clean, easy-to-read block letters, whereas the other version's font consisted of irregular letters that were slightly difficult to read. Later, he quizzed the subjects on the story. Turns out, the students given the difficult-to-read font—the one with more friction—had much higher recall than those given the easy font.[4]

The more we strain our attention during an experience, the stronger the memory that's encoded. In other words, memories don't just happen; they have to be earned. Our brains have to work for them.

It's worth noting that you can't turn up the difficulty all the way and expect the memory to be maximized. If it's too difficult, the brain gives up, and remembers little if anything. Successful encoding is all about creating a balance between ease and difficulty. The font must have just the right amount of mental friction: enough to require the brain to exert attention, without making reading so difficult that the brain gives up trying. Interestingly, a team at RIMT has created a font that nails the balance. They call it Sans Forgetica. Evidence from their lab suggests that reading information written in Sans Forgetica provides a memory advantage above other fonts.[5,6] Sans Forgetica boosts memory because it strikes the perfect balance in our attention, what Oppenheimer describes as "desired difficulty."

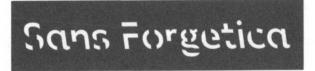

Source: https://sansforgetica.rmit/

In 2018, Burger King launched a campaign intended to draw attention to their mobile app. BK sold customers the Whopper cheeseburger for a penny, but only if the customer first drove or walked within 600 feet of the fast-food chain's competitor, McDonald's, snapped a picture, and uploaded it to the BK app. The publicity stunt not only succeeded at grabbing attention, it also helped encode the memory of BK's brand more deeply, by creating friction in the form of the required photograph. If BK gave away one-cent burgers to just anyone who downloaded the app, there would be minimal friction. By adding an exercise, the company created a layer of not-too-difficult friction that helped boost memory via encoding.

BOOSTER #3: EMOTIONAL AROUSAL

Emotion acts like superglue by sticking attention and memory together. Emotional experiences are readily prioritized by the brain.[7] Whether good or bad, if something is important enough to arouse our emotions, our brain assumes it is important and therefore should be remembered. This prioritization of emotional memories likely bears evolutionary importance. Highly emotional memories, such as being chased by an animal or eating berries that made us sick, are lessons worth remembering to increase survival. Emotions tell the brain what events to tag with a label reading "Important!" to boost encoding and strengthen the impression.

We see this memory prioritization effect with experiences—emotionally charged experiences, like being in a car crash, are more memorable than boring, mundane ones, like getting where you're driving successfully—but also with simple stimuli like text. Emotionally charged words like *love*, *hate*, and *happiness* are encoded and recalled with greater accuracy than neutral words like *desk*, *money*, and *highway*.[8] So it's no surprise that emotional words are used extensively to drive attention (and ultimately memory) in a wide array of marketing contexts, such as billboards, banner ads, and search results.[9]

The emotion we experience affects more than how much attention we pay to an experience; it also affects what we focus on, and therefore what we remember. In other words, emotion colors *how* we pay attention. Experiments have shown that when we're in a negative mood, we focus more on details, and when we're in a positive mood, our focus is much more on the big picture.[10] Imagine just getting out of a job interview that did not go well. You're likely to be ruminating on the details and what you should (or shouldn't) have said. In contrast, if it had gone well, you're more likely to be thinking about the experience as a whole.

BOOSTER #4: MUSIC

The next booster is something we are all very familiar with: music. Music has a profound effect on the brain, and musical memory is one of the longest-lasting, most durable forms of memory. Musical memories have an uncanny ability to burrow deep into our memories, almost hibernating. Even when you haven't heard a song in years, the melody and lyrics tend to come right back to you the next time you hear it.

The most striking examples of the persistence of musical memory come from observation of patients suffering from dementia. Late-stage Alzheimer's patients who have difficulty recognizing family members and familiar objects can still recognize familiar songs. In some instances, these patients are able to sing despite having lost the ability to speak.[11]

The unique strength of musical memory has puzzled researchers for years, but one possible reason for the robustness of musically encoded memory is that music is encoded by several different regions of the brain. While auditory regions are primarily involved, so are parts responsible for imagery and emotion.[12] Because musical memories are laid down in multiple brain regions, stimulating any one of these regions may spark their retrieval. It also may be the reason musical memory persists so long in dementia patients. If one brain region becomes damaged, the other, healthy regions can pick up the slack, theoretically providing "backups."

Anyone who has ever had their innocent shower interrupted by the question "Call me, maybe?" knows the experience of getting a song stuck in their head. As catchy as American music is, this phenomenon cuts across cultures. It's described by the French as *musique entêtante* ("stubborn music") and by Italians as *canzone tormentone* ("catchphrase song"). In English, they are colloquially known as ~~songs by Drake~~ earworms. Earworms are unlike other forms of auditory memory in that they are recalled and played continuously without our consent, persisting in our minds despite our wishes[13,14] (though in systematic studies, people reported these occurrences to be largely pleasant[15]).

All memory benefits from repetition; you unfortunately have to study your chemistry flashcards more than once to commit them to memory. Earworms provide natural, though often annoying, experiences of repetition. With each mental replay, the musical memory becomes even stronger—whether that memory is of a favorite song, or a brand's latest jingle.

Emotional, attention-grabbing, and interactive brand experiences, such as advertisements and commercials, are designed to be encoded in your brain, but what these experiences can't do is get stuck in your head. Imagine if a brand could freely pop its logo up in your brain repeatedly, even if you actively tried to block it. Branded jingles make that possible.

After all, what is a jingle if not an audio logo? Nike's *Just Do It* is great, but it doesn't get stuck in your head like McDonald's *I'm lovin' it* does. Why? Because musical memory.

IMPLICIT MEMORY

So far our discussion of memory encoding has addressed impressions of events we consciously experience. Turns out, though, that the brain also encodes memories of events beyond our conscious awareness. Memory is always "turned on," even when we don't think it is. Events leave impressions, even when we aren't aware of those impressions being made.

Intuitively, we feel that we have to try to "put down" memories, but that's not the case at all. The brain, being a pattern-seeking machine, is always taking in information. Much of this information forms memory traces—changes in the brain—that accumulate completely outside our awareness, whether we like it or not. Neuroscientists call this *implicit memory*, and this is the facet of memory preserved in amnesia patients.

Recall how Lucy from *50 First Dates* is able to paint a portrait of Henry without conscious, or explicit, memory of him—or of learning to paint. This is implicit memory. Implicit memory doesn't rely on the hippocampus, where explicit memories are stored, and so persists in patients whose hippocampi are damaged.

If you've played basketball before, you know that the only way to get better is through practice. Sure, instructions can be helpful, but you won't really improve unless you do it. Just by dribbling around the court for an hour a day, over time your skill levels will slowly but steadily increase. Now, if someone asks you what you learned, and how exactly you dribble a basketball, you'd be at pains to describe it explicitly. Learning has taken place—a significant impression has been left in your brain that changes your behavior—despite your not being aware of the details of the learning process.

As we learned earlier, the brain is constantly picking up on statistics in the environment. This process, statistical learning, is all implicit, and it has an immense impact on memory and, ultimately, your behavior. How many times have you seen the words *Coke* and *happiness* together in an advertisement? No idea, we're guessing. But somehow, through implicit statistical learning, you have made the connection. What about Corona and a beach? You may not be able to recall how often you've coupled the two, but the brain remembers and connects the concepts. And your brain does more than just connect them. Remembering that Corona is connected to the beach also affects behavior: if you're on the beach, you'll be more likely to consume a Corona. Did you try to commit these associations to memory? Of course not. Yet your brain picked up on these statistical regularities completely outside your awareness and without effort, and will use these remembered connections to influence future behavior.

IMPLICIT LEARNING AND THE YOUNG BRAIN

Nobody does implicit learning better than children. All of us are able to learn *at least* one language—a vast, complex, highly detailed system—and we're able to do this at a very young age, without even trying. None of us got a Duolingo or a Rosetta Stone subscription when we were six months old, nor did (most of us) use flashcards to study basic vocabulary. Yet by the age of four, most children know over five thousand words. And decades of research reveals that our parents don't teach us language explicitly, through any deliberate instruction. Instead, we soak up linguistic knowledge implicitly, from ambient language in our early environments. The idiom *kids are sponges* is a massive understatement.

This early implicit learning ability is not limited to language, either. Most forms of implicit learning are done much better as children than as adults: playing instruments, dance, sports. We learn all of these things much better early in life than later in life. Those of us who have tried to learn a second language in adulthood know this all too well. While we struggle with the notecards, it's hard not to be envious of native bilingual individuals who grew up with both languages.

The fact that the young brain is in a constant state of absorption should give us pause. Regulations are in place to prevent certain types of companies from marketing directly to children. These are good measures, but they also provide a false sense of security. Why? Just like with language learning, young children don't need ads explicitly directed at them to learn about a product, or the consumer world in general. Think about ads on websites, TV, mobile, and social media, and in video games. Children are showered with repeated exposure to thousands of ads for hundreds of brands, and their spongy, malleable brains are constantly taking this information in. In a Nickelodeon study, researchers discovered that kids are exposed to so many ads that they will have memorized three hundred to four hundred brands before their tenth birthday. Creepily, children grow up forming relationships with a select number of these brands that last well into the future, like friends you didn't know they had.

Imagine the implicit car-brand associations you have if your childhood memories of soccer practice and family road trips to Disneyland all involved riding around in a Toyota. Parents' brand choices bleed into their children's memories, which in turn influence children's choices as they grow up. Associations play a key part in the formation of memories, and when an adult's memories of a brand are associated with positive emotions like nostalgia, their preference is impacted. Memories can be insidious this way. Hard to believe? Just try to say no to a Capri Sun . . .

With this context, now plug in Ronald McDonald. Before kids even have the ability to pay for food, many have memories of one specific fast-food brand, McDonald's. The Ronald McDonald House Charities is legally a separate nonprofit foundation from McDonald's, and their official mission is to improve the well-being of children. But they are openly and heavily supported by McDonald's,[16] and one of their common initiatives[17] involves employees visiting elementary and middle schools dressed up as a basket of fries, a hamburger, and of course, Ronald McDonald the clown, to spread the (ironic) message of healthy eating. In the process, Mickey D's is implanting positive brand-associated memories in children's minds using the Trojan horse of the Ronald McDonald nonprofit organization. With the memories in place, when the kids grow up, their choice in fast food will nudge toward the golden arches.

Companies are only getting smarter—and more technologically sophisticated—at creating memories that lead to positive brand associations. Ever heard of Apple Jacks? If you guessed cereal, well, not entirely. Kellogg's has turned Apple Jacks into a video game where kids race cars and collect "points"—which, unsurprisingly, are just little Apple Jacks. In one way, this is a digital version of the Ronald McDonald strategy: create a positive associative memory early on so that kids develop a preference for your brand. Think about the encoding boosters discussed earlier. Interaction, because it heightens our attention, is a highly effective way to encourage memory encoding. Kids playing the Apple Jacks game aren't simply becoming aware of Apple Jacks cereal; their brains are absorbing the brand deeply, due to the interactive nature of the experience. What brand of cereal do you think this kid will reach for in the supermarket aisle?

Explicit and implicit memory are distinct systems, but they interact to produce our overall impression of the past experiences. Kids are explicitly encoding the episodic experience of playing the game. At the same time, implicit learning via brand associations is also happening as the kids' brains connect *Apple Jacks* with *fun*. The implicit learning happens completely outside of kids' awareness, yet can shape their preferences for years to come.

EMOTIONAL MEMORY AND THE PEAK-END EFFECT

Recall from earlier in this chapter how memory and emotion have a special relationship. There's more to this story. Emotion not only can distort *what* we remember, but *how* we remember it, shaping the nature of the memory itself. This affects the consumer's memory in unexpected ways, and many companies have converged on these quirks of the emotion–memory relationship to optimize the impressions they want to leave.

Not all parts of an event are encoded into memory equally. Think back on a recent trip you took. Do you remember all aspects of the experience equally? Of course not. Instead, certain aspects of the trip always leave stronger impressions than others. There is a pattern behind this, and it was uncovered using the unlikeliest of sources: colonoscopies.[18]

As if the procedure wasn't uncomfortable enough, in a study by Daniel Kahneman, colonoscopy patients were given the task of reporting how much discomfort they were currently experiencing using a handheld dial. Once the procedure was over, they also filled out a brief questionnaire about their memory of the experience. What they remembered (via the questionnaire) versus what they reported (via the dial) revealed a pattern behind how experiences are remembered.

Turns out, the study subjects' memory of the overall painfulness of the procedure had little to do with how much absolute pain they themselves reported. Rather, their memory was tied to two elements. The first was the *peak* of the pain they experienced. If there was a moment in the procedure in which pain suddenly spiked—the doctor's hand slipping, for example—patients would remember the entire experience as being much more painful overall, regardless of what they reported the rest of the time via the dial.

The peak of an event affects our memory of the event. It is not (just) that the peak stimulus during an event is encoded most deeply. Rather, the peak stimulus dictates our ultimate impression and colors our memory of the entire experience. In other words, if the average pain on the dial is a 5 on a scale of 1 to 10 but the peak pain was 8, our brains remember the whole experience as closer to an 8 than a 5.

The second element that impacted patients' memory of the experience was its *end*. Procedures that ended in pain were remembered as more painful than was actually reported via the dial, and those that ended "not so bad" were remembered as such despite what was reported during. If the pain at end of the procedure was a 7 and the average pain on the dial was a 4, the participants remembered the whole experience as closer to 7 than 4.

This second element prompted a follow-up experiment in which the procedure was actually extended! The additional minutes were relatively innocuous; the colonoscopy tube was merely left in longer than it needed to be, which is naturally uncomfortable but much less painful than the rest of the process. Remarkably, patients who received the extended version of the test actually remembered the procedure as being much *less* painful overall. Even though they experienced more objective pain, since they underwent a longer procedure, their memories of the event were far more favorable.

The duo of insights—that the memory of an event is heavily weighted by its peak and its end—is appropriately called *the peak-end effect*. While its discovery came through exploring pain and discomfort, it's a stable property of human memory that applies equally to positive experiences.

Imagine you're at a music festival. All of the acts from beginning to end are pretty mediocre, but somewhere in there, one of the bands' drummers delivers an earth-shattering fifteen-minute solo. When you think back on the festival months later, the amazing solo is likely the only thing you'll remember, and as a result, you'll recall the whole experience fondly.

The peak effect is further amplified by surprise. Say that, instead of a drummer, the band brought out a pro xylophone player for a fifteen-minute solo. The peak effect would be stronger still. With either the xylophone or drum solo, you forget the festival's poor start and instead remember the solo as a positive memory of the whole show.

The end part of the peak-end effect single-handedly explains our obsession with cliffhangers: we love them because they are designed to be memorable. What is less talked about, however, is our love of a finale with a reveal—a finale where the end is also the peak. When a story, be it a book or movie, ends in a surprising reveal, the whole experience is solidified in its audience's heads.

We will never forget that Bruce Willis was dead all along in *The Sixth Sense*. Or that Brad Pitt and Ed Norton were the same character in *Fight Club*. Or that the whole story told in *The Usual Suspects* was fake and Kevin Spacey was Keyser Söze. Perhaps the best example of combining a cliff-hanger and a reveal to maximize the peak-end effect is in *Inception*, when Leonardo DiCaprio finally returns home to his kids, yet the movie leaves the door open to the possibility that he may still be dreaming. As Shake-speare said, "All's well that ends well." This couldn't be truer for how we form memories of experiences.

The peak-end effect also explains why so many Hollywood endings tend to play it safe. Viewers can deeply enjoy ninety minutes of a hundred-minute movie, but if the ending, the last ten minutes, isn't to their liking, they are likely to discount the whole movie as horrible. A disproportionate amount of importance and weight is attached to the end of films, at least if you aren't aware of the peak-end effect. A disappointing ending can mean the difference between a $200 million blockbuster and a $200 million loss. Conversely, a below-average movie can be rescued by an above-average ending—or in the case of *Ant Man and the Wasp*, an excellent post-credits scene.

For many, the pinnacle of peak-end storytelling in television is *Game of Thrones*. The HBO show wove detailed tales of many characters intertwined within a meta-story. The tales all have both memorable peaks and memorable ends. Peaks come frequently and unpredictably in the form of the main characters' deaths—most of them gruesome.

Similarly, the end of each season left the audience in suspense because of the number of unanswered questions in the many characters' stories. Despite the series' controversial end, *Game of Thrones* holds the record for the most Emmys won by a series (59), the most pirated TV show, the most torrents sharing a single file (258,000), and the most-watched episode in the history of Nielsen ratings (16.5 million viewers).

The hospitality industry is especially keen on creating memories, and hotels are masters of designing mini-peaks designed for customers' enjoyment. Hand-stamped toilet paper, towels folded into swans, elaborate lobbies, "surprise" chocolates on pillows, and welcome glasses of champagne are all minor peaks designed to create a fond memory of the hotel stay.

Retail stores also pay a lot of attention to both the peak and peak-end effect—though, admittedly, not all of them. If you have FOMO (fear of missing out) because you've never experienced the rush of a Black Friday sale, fear not. You can get the same rush going to your nearest Fry's electronics store on any given weekend. The peak experience occurs somewhere in the disorganized checkout lines, the aisles that look like Roman ruins, and the employees who seem to be helping everyone but you. And of course, there's the very last touchpoint at Fry's: an employee who checks your receipt to make sure you aren't a looting thief. At Fry's, both the peak and the end are optimized to be remembered as pain.

But compare that to the Apple Store. Every employee is a checkout register. You are greeted upon walking in. You can have as much or as little interaction with the employees and the products as you like. And before you walk out, what do you get? A goodbye and a thank-you—an acknowledgment of your existence. The Apple Store ending is some friendly eye contact with one of the employees whose home base is a few feet from the exit. The last touchpoint at the Apple store is miles ahead of Fry's.

But even Apple can't hold a candle to the finest example of the peak-end effect in retail: the Amazon Go retail stores. Amazon has lately come full circle, from e-commerce to brick-and-mortar, by testing retail stores. Amazon Go, the first Amazon retail store concept, opened in Seattle in 2018. The concept is beautiful in its simplicity. There are no lines, no checkouts, no registers, no cash. In Amazon's own words, "Use the Amazon Go App to enter, then put away your phone and start shopping. Take whatever you like. Anything you pick up is automatically added to your virtual cart. If you change your mind, just put it back." In Amazon Go's case, the peak of the shopping experience is also its end. Consumers are able to check out and exit the store in a truly novel way, by walking right out, making the whole shopping experience, in comparison to those of other stores, more memorable and more pleasurable.

BRANDED EXPERIENCES AS ENCODERS

Another, newer form of marketing that adeptly ties together multiple boosters to ensure a memory is well associated with a specific brand and their products is experiential marketing. In experiential marketing, companies create experiences, or actual physical ways for consumers to interact with brands. Interaction augments both attention and friction in an experience, and, depending on the interaction, emotion as well. Interactive experiences make sense for making memories; they also make cents for brands. Event Track's research revealed three out of four consumers say a branded experience makes them more likely to buy.[19]

What does a branded experience look like? Imagine a piano manufacturer buys ad space on a set of subway stairs and paints piano keys onto them. They add their logo nearby, and voilà! A branded experience. Bonus points if walking on the keys makes a sound.

Making customers put up with a little pain is an effective way to create a branded experience, if a little lazy. Lean Cuisine was anything but lazy when they created their 2015 branded experience in New York's Grand Central subway terminal. First, instead of simply putting up advertising posters to promote their meals, Lean Cuisine put together an interactive mini-booth. This zig immediately grabbed the attention of subway passengers; a booth captures more attention than a poster. Next, they designed the booth itself to invite interaction, a form of friction. Instead of a simple billboard, the branded experience consisted of a scale that passersby could use to "weigh in"—except the scale was not for people. In a statement against unhealthy obsession with body weight, participants decided how they wanted to be weighed as a person and placed things representing this on the scale.

One student placed a letter from her university congratulating her for making the dean's list. When asked how much it weighed, she replied, "It is immeasurable." Another woman placed her divorce papers on the scale, to symbolize overcoming hardship. One participant placed her daughter on the scale, exclaiming that motherhood is what she wanted to be weighed by. The list goes on. In this campaign, Lean Cuisine was able to create an experience optimized for encoding using attention, friction, and emotion. If you were in Grand Central during the campaign or saw the video after, it encoded a much deeper memory of Lean Cuisine than even the catchiest poster could create. And ironically, it happened without using a single photo of the food Lean Cuisine is selling.

In 2015, Google created a branded experience with a twist.[20] The company decided to donate $5.5 million to select nonprofits based in the San Francisco Bay Area. The finalists were selected based on their innovative solutions to local issues, but then Google put the amount of their contributions to each of the final recipients to a public vote. Instead of taking the simple, predictable route and using an online registration-based voting system, Google created an experience out of the vote. The company placed booths all around the Bay Area—in coffee shops, bookstores, concert venues, and food truck parks. Each booth housed ten giant buttons that explained the goal of each nonprofit. Pressing a button recorded a vote. The number of votes collected? Over 400,000, which is more than half of San Francisco's population.

Google was already ubiquitous, but the company found a new way to touch their customers through deep interaction. Reading the socially conscious goals of almost a dozen nonprofits, choosing a favorite, and taking part in a physical vote involves a whole lot of mental and physical engagement on the part of the participant. And investing in innovative new ways to encode memories helps Google stay both on top of the market and in the front of consumers' minds.

EXPERIENCES AS THE FUTURE OF CONTENT

Branded experiences fall under the slightly larger umbrella of *experiential marketing*, which is business lingo for marketing a company's product and/or brand via an experience. For some content industries (radio, video, print, etc.), experiential marketing is not just about marketing the product; it *is* the product itself. This is especially the case for once-physical products that have become increasingly digitized.[21]

Remember VHS tapes and DVDs? Now there's Netflix. Binders full of CDs? Spotify. Instead of having your news delivered on newsprint every morning, endless streams of up-to-the minute stories are at your fingertips. Pirating has further driven the commodification of digital content by making it accessible to more people, at low or no cost. Accordingly, consumers have become much more entitled to get content for free. Nobody wants to pay for music beyond, at most, that $10 for a monthly Spotify or Apple Music subscription. Pay for news? Not a chance.

This is great for the consumer, but makes it difficult for content creators to make a living. Comedians such as Kevin Hart are now famous for strictly prohibiting cellphones at shows, to prevent audience members from undercutting sales by recording performances and giving away the real-life experience in a digital space.[22] You can get so much for free that it's increasingly difficult to put a price tag on anything digital and create a solvent business from it. As a result, many publishers and content creators have turned their focus away from physical products, like CDs and newspapers, and toward the one realm that can't (at least not yet) be put online and digitized: experiences.

What do you do when you're a news agency too highbrow for clickbait advertising, but you exist in a world where no one wants to pay for news? Make like the music industry and create a "news festival"—and charge admission. This is exactly what the esteemed *New Yorker* magazine has done. What started as an anniversary celebration in 2000 has turned into a proper cultural festival. Instead of listening to your favorite podcast (for free), or reading articles (mostly for free), you can see the people who write and produce this content up close and personal, along with thought leaders, politicians, comedians, filmmakers, musicians, artists, and more. It's like Coachella for *New Yorker* fans.

Journalist Katie Calautti says this investment in experience—"Journalism off the page," as she calls it—is on the rise. "We see it more and more now—editors and journalists giving talks, or serving on live panels at events. These have almost become celebrity events. It's a unique way of connecting with your readership in a way that can't easily be done through journalism and digital media itself."[23]

Digitization has been especially hard on musicians. While outlets such as Pandora and Spotify have helped soften the blow after the impact of Napster and its ilk and of newer peer-to-peer sharing sites like BitTorrent, it still takes an average of 220 streams for a musician to accrue a single dollar. Unsurprisingly, a 2017 report by the Music Industry Research Association found that the lion's share of musicians' income comes from live shows and concerts.[24] This has moved the bar for live performances. Fans can listen to your music for virtually free online; they come to the show for the experience. Hence the proliferation of music festivals.

In some ways, the focus on experience is good for the consumer. At the very least, it is much more entertaining; event production values are increasing. Experiencing Kendrick Lamar at Coachella is an unparalleled experience that listening to a Kendrick Lamar album at home can't touch. And for the music industry, at least, it appears to be working. In 2016, album downloads in the US netted the music industry $623 million[25] in revenue. A year later, this revenue rose to a shade under $1.6 billion (with a *b*!).[26]

Thanks to the rise in experiential marketing, the production cost of branding has never been higher—but neither has its potency to persuade. Remember, expensive branding experiences are not just looking for a piece of your wallet; they're looking for a piece of your mind.

When it's successful, a branding experience encodes a memory to be recalled at a later time. This encoding is immensely valuable because a memory is more than a pleasant replay of a past event. Memory has the power to drive behavior. This is precisely why companies spend millions on designing brand experiences. They know these experiences boost encoding, which provides a foundation for driving your future behavior around their products.

Which brings us to the second half of the equation: *how* the brain replays these encoded memories, and how brands use them to drive future behavior.

Chapter 4

MEMORY REMIXED

How the Trace of the Past Drives Us Forward

The experience of being stuck in bumper-to-bumper traffic doesn't rank highly on anyone's list of desirable activities. It's nothing but our own thoughts and our growing outrage at the stream of cars ahead of us. But Los Angeles native Bob Petrella, who finds himself in this situation often, considers it the perfect opportunity to entertain himself—with his own memories. He'll recall, in vivid, lifelike detail, memories of a date from years and decades past, mentally catalog the best Saturdays in June he's ever had, or go through 2002 day by day, recalling the events of each.[1]

These memory games are possible for Bob because he has one of the most advanced memories ever documented. If you ask Bob about any day in his past, he's able to replay it for you in incredible detail. Ask, "February 18th, 1966. Which day was that?" and he'll answer, "That was a Friday, and [high school football team] Beaver Falls beat Sharen." His memories include not only what happened, but exactly how he felt in that moment. As he describes, "It's almost like a time machine, where I can go back to a certain period, or a certain day, and almost feel like I'm back there." And how could you get bored in traffic when you have a time machine?

Bob has what neuropsychologists have called *highly superior autobiographical memory*,[2] of which there have only been sixty or so documented cases. James McGaugh, professor of neurobiology at UC Irvine, has studied Bob and other cases like his: "They can describe most of the days of their life the way you or I can describe yesterday."[3]

For those of us without this time machine in our heads, memory recall is a very different experience. Just like with perception, memory recall is limited. Most of us can hardly remember what we had for dinner last night, much less what we had for dinner fifteen years ago. We don't have a precise carbon copy of the past we can review in the present moment. Just like with perception, we only have a mental model—our brain's creative representation of the past.

Recall from the previous chapter our broad definition for memory: *Memory is our brain's attempt at connecting us to the past. Attempt* is the key word here. First, events we experience get encoded to become impressions. Then these impressions get recalled later as hazy movies we conjure up in our heads. But the relationship between events encoded and events recalled is far from direct. We conjure up images, sounds, and stories and feel as though they happened the way we recall them. We assume our recollections are accurate. We assume encoding is like hitting record and recall is like hitting play. But we are wrong.

In reality, our recall of the events we've encoded is murky. Whenever we hit play on an event, what comes out is closer to a remix than the original. Just like perception, memory is a best guess, heavily prone to bias and influence. Two people who experience the same event may remember it in very different ways. Moreover, our recall of an event can change depending on who we're with, our mood, and a number of other variables. We may even recall something from an event that didn't actually happen. What we think of as memory recall is really just a reconstruction of the encoded original.

Of course, just because memory recall is flawed doesn't mean it isn't powerful. As McGaugh emphasizes, "Memory is the most important ability . . . if human beings didn't have memory, there wouldn't be human beings." As such, memory is the jumping-off point for nearly all of our behavior.

Enter nostalgia marketing. If the Capri Sun reference from the previous chapter sent you back to your childhood, you are no stranger to nostalgia: your own personalized remix of the past, typically with a positive spin. Whether accurate or not, that internal, subjective remix is what forms the basis for our future. And so when it comes to marketing to your memories, nostalgia is hard to beat. Brands will often pick a throwback song, bring back an older version of their product, or even cast a previously used character in their ads to connect with our personalized sense of yesteryear in a deep and emotional way. Such a connection can profoundly guide our future behavior. One could even argue that Adidas's resurgence to sneaker relevance is due to their repurposing of '80s and '90s shoe models like Superstars and Stan Smiths.

A subtler way brands (and sometimes politicians) tap into nostalgia's effects is by portraying their products as throwbacks to "the way things used to be." Probably the greatest example of this is a classic Coca-Cola commercial from 1971[4] depicting a large, diverse crowd of young adults on a hillside singing in unity, "I'd like to teach the world to sing . . . I'd like to buy the world a Coke."[5] 🔗 At a time when the country was heavily mired in the Vietnam War and civil rights protests, the song attempted (successfully, most would argue) to capture the country's collective nostalgia for a simpler, more harmonious time, and to associate Coke with that nostalgic longing.

Now that millennials are becoming one of the highest-spending-power generations, dropping $1.4 trillion in the US annually,[6] we're seeing more and more products drawn directly from their '90s childhoods. Whether it's the sequel to *Top Gun*, the reintroduction of a Nintendo hand-held console,[7] the *Oregon Trail* mobile game, or the reboot of Tamagotchi toys (yes, those little gadgets you have to "keep alive"), there's an increasingly strong flow of items and media that can only be categorized as "millennial nostalgia." As millennial spending power continues to rise, don't be surprised if you see jorts and Pogs make a roaring comeback!

While nostalgia marketing is effective, upon further examination, much of its effectiveness is not based on our past experiences—at least not directly. Instead, marketing tends to game the strange mechanics of our brain's attempts to connect us to the past. Let's take a deeper look into the fallibility of memory and how clever marketing can play into the creative nature of our own memories.

THE FALLIBILITY OF MEMORY

What did you have for lunch last Tuesday? How about Tuesday the week before last? Tuesday three weeks ago? A month ago? These questions may sound trivial—who cares what you had for lunch last month?—but they are anything but to the family of Hae Min Lee, whose death journalist Sarah Koenig investigated in 2014 for the first season of her podcast *Serial*.

Lee was a Baltimore high school student who went missing in mid-January 1999. Her body was found in early February, and her boyfriend, Adnan Syed, was arrested on February 28 and charged with murder. Twenty years later, the case remains in limbo. Why? The fallibility of memory.

Syed did not have a clear and concise memory of the events that occurred on January 13, 1999, the day Lee went missing. It is hard enough remembering what you ate for lunch last week; how well would you remember exactly what you did six weeks ago between 2:15 PM and 2:36 PM? But what if your ambiguity is up against someone else's crystal-clear account of your whereabouts during those same twenty-one minutes?

Adnan's vague memory of that time was in competition with the account of another high school student, Jay Wilds. There are many layers to the story, but one thing quickly becomes clear in the podcast, and remains consistent: memory is not objective. The accounts of several high school students interviewed about January 13, 1999—both by police in 1999 and podcasters in 2014—vary wildly. Their recollections also show a whole range of confidence levels, from Adnan's weak ambiguity of the events to Jay's confident and clear recall. The case, reopened shortly after *Serial*'s airing, remains unresolved.

All of this ambiguity and the conflicting stories comes down to the fact that our memories are notoriously fallible.

One common example of this is how we're easily tricked by our existing semantic network. Imagine I give you a list of the following items and have you memorize them:

Donut
Cake
Scone
Pastry

Candy bar
Ice cream sandwich

If I were to ask you a week later, "Hey, remember that list of items I gave you? Was *pie* on it?" you'd be likely to misremember that it was—much more likely than if I had asked you about an unrelated word, like *bicycle* or *chair*. Recall from chapter one that your brain stores knowledge in categories. So, in addition to making you hungry, reading this list of items activated the "sweet foods" semantic network in your brain. Because this network also includes things like pie, it's easy to remember *pie* being on the list even though it didn't actually appear there. This is what memory scientists call the *semantic misremembering effect*, and it happens to the best of us by virtue of how the brain organizes memory and information.

Think about this in light of nostalgia. To pull at our "memory," a given brand or advertisement doesn't actually have to tap into our memory directly; it just needs to tap into enough "dots" that our brain is able to connect them on its own. Consider the following advertisement for Internet Explorer.[8] 🔄 It's a charming walk down memory lane for anyone who grew up in the '90s, featuring nostalgic throwbacks like chain wallets ("you had nothing to lose"), bowl cuts ("haircuts didn't cost $60; they cost 4 minutes"), and neon fanny packs ("we still had plenty of storage space"). When you think '90s, you may not immediately think of IE. But now that your memory has been gleefully jogged for all of these items, you're much more likely to misremember IE as having been a big part of your childhood experience.

Probably the best illustration of memory's incredible malleability comes from the lab of UC Irvine psychologist Elizabeth Loftus. Through a series of simple, suggestive inquiries (e.g., "Don't you remember that trip to Coney Island? You were about five years old and it was a bright sunny day . . ."), Loftus and her colleagues actually implanted completely false events into subjects' heads.[9,10] Your brain connects the dots on these familiar pieces from your knowledge bank, and voilà—a memory. And once implanted, the false memory is indistinguishable from other, real memories of experiences you've actually had! Loftus's research has changed courtroom practices by casting some much-needed doubt on the accuracy of eyewitness testimony, especially when the lawyer leading the questioning has a specific memory they'd *like* for the witness to remember. Someone please call Adnan Syed's lawyer . . .

Memory, in other words, is a highly inaccurate reconstructive process, prone to error and fallibility simply by virtue of how our brains store and attempt to retrieve previous events and information. Even people like Bob with superior memory abilities are not immune; research[11] has found that the memories of people with highly superior autobiographical memory are just as prone to these anomalies as the rest of ours!

This matters because our memories of events, either real or imagined, are extremely important. Memory provides the basis for much of our behavior, which means the ability to plant memories isn't just a good cocktail party story. It can also be used intentionally to change our behavior.

Imagine being hunched over in a gas station bathroom, puking your brains out after just having eaten a pork sandwich from the fast-food restaurant next door, tasting the cheap pork and synthetic bread coming up with each heave. Gross. If this had actually happened to you, you'd be unlikely to ever eat at that restaurant again—and probably wouldn't eat a pork sandwich again in your life, either. These are exactly the kinds of scenarios Elizabeth Loftus has gotten people who are desperate to lose weight and can't stop eating unhealthy foods to think they've experienced. When people *believe* they've had a horrendous experience with a specific food, they have a natural aversion and cease eating it—just as they would if the memory were real.[12,13] The False Memory Diet is the perfect example of the authority of memory over reality. It is the memory itself—not the details of the actual experience—that has the greatest impact on the rest of your life.

With the rise in virtual technologies, the creation of false memories is only becoming easier and easier. In a 2009 Stanford study,[14] children were brought into the lab and given an immersive, virtual experience of swimming with dolphins. When they were brought back to the lab a few weeks later, a significant portion of the children had a memory that they had actually swum with dolphins. The technology had merely planted a memory.

As VR and AR technologies continue to proliferate and find application within the consumer world, it will be interesting to see how they not only distort our perception, but our memory as well. Yet we don't need sophisticated technologies to fundamentally alter our understanding of the past. When it comes to memories, a little change in context can go a long way.

CONTEXT CHANGES EVERYTHING

However inaccurate, our memories are vast and detailed. If you were to download your memory digitally, there wouldn't be a hard drive large enough to fit it. We have literally millions of past experiences that, in principle, we can recall at any given time. And yet this lifetime's worth of memories never floods back to us all at once. Why do we think of certain memories at certain times? By and large, we don't get to pick and choose what to remember from our vast bank of imperfect memories. Our context picks for us.

As we saw in chapter three, when a memory is encoded, we take in much more information than we think we do. We also absorb the context associated with the memory. In fact, all memory is contextual. If you play a popular song from your youth that you haven't heard in a while, chances are you'll be flooded with old memories that you haven't recalled in years. This is because the brain packs the details of our experiences in with our encoded memories. When a specific song is played, or a specific scent is smelled, the brain may conjure up entire, vivid memories associated with that song or scent.

The same is true not just for memories of experiences, but also for memories that turn into knowledge. If you always study for a test in a certain coffee shop, in the same chair, listening to the same music, your chances of remembering what you studied are improved if you go back to that same coffee shop, chair, and soundtrack. The same is true for more subtle contextual cues like chewing gum, or wearing a particular article of clothing. Experiments have shown that if you study a list of names underwater, you'll be able to retrieve the memory of those names much better underwater than on land.[15]

Other research has found that having distinct experiences in distinct rooms actually distorts your perception of time. If you spend four hours at a party, all in the same room, you will feel the party was longer than if you had spent the same amount of time at the same party but in four different rooms. Switching contexts extends time, or at least your perception of it. Great hosts know how to use context to craft an experience that is not only enjoyable, but memorable, by planning a range of different activities for the evening, each in different spaces: hors d'oeuvres in the living room, the full dinner in the dining room, cocktails on the deck, then cigar smoking and brandy sipping in the study. Using a range of physical locations prevents these enjoyable events from all blending together in guests' minds the next day. Great hosts know this intuitively: control the physical context, and you control the memories.

But context doesn't just impact your memories; it can also push that memory into behavior.

CONTEXT DRIVES BEHAVIOR

One of the primary reasons memory is so inaccurate and prone to error is because, frankly, the brain doesn't really care about accuracy. The human brain is a fundamentally forward-thinking organ, pragmatic in nature. As we've said, memory isn't simply the brain's attempt at connecting to the past; it's the brain's attempt at connecting to the past *to optimize the future*. Looking back at the past can be a great tool, but our accuracy in doing so is secondary to memory's main purpose: giving us a "good enough" under-standing of the past in order to move forward.

As such, memory and behavior are intimately linked. Recall that mem-ory is the jumping-off point for all behavior; without a memory of our-selves, our world, and where we come from, there's no firm ground for future behavior. And so just as memory is sensitive to the context in which it was created, so, too, is behavior.

This can be seen most readily with simple learned associations. In a fascinating study done at Northwestern University,[16] researchers randomly divided participants from the general population into two groups. One group was given white doctor's coats, and the other, plain street clothes. They found that the group in the doctor's coats performed much better on tests of accuracy and attentional focus. Why? Over time, our brain has unconsciously built an association between doctors and a sense of intelli-gence and accuracy. We have a concept of doctors, constructed over time, that features these characteristics. Wearing a doctor's uniform activates those associations and, in turn, alters our behavior: we unconsciously behave in a way that is in line with the characteristics of that learned con-cept (e.g., intelligence and accuracy).

This is perhaps why we play better, or at least have the confidence to play better, when we wear the jerseys or branded shoes of our favorite athletes. Even with something as simple as clothing, a familiar context with learned associations can significantly impact our memory, attitudes, and ultimately our behavior.

Think about this for music. Next time Lil Jon's "Shots" comes on at the bar, mind the context. You can hate the song and still appreciate the genius behind playing it at a bar. Every time it comes on, customers are more likely to think of, and thus more likely to order, shots. In other words, playing the song triggers a behavior that makes bars money: buying shots.

An equally genius execution of using pop music context to drive behavior involves the Chainsmokers' "Selfie." Each of the song's verses (if you can call them that) consists of the stream of consciousness of a hyperbolized Valley Girl that ends with her wanting to take a selfie. Here's the Nobel Prize–winning (not) first verse, in case you're unfamiliar. Picture a girl fixing her makeup in the mirror of a nightclub's bar, saying:

> *How did that girl even get in here?*
> *Did you see her?*
> *She's so short and that dress is so tacky*
> *Who wears cheetah?*
> *It's not even summer, why does the DJ keep on playing "Summertime Sadness"?*
> *After we go to the bathroom, can we go smoke a cigarette?*
> *I really need one*
> *But first (PAUSE)*
> *LET ME TAKE A SELFIE!*

This song is to selfies what Lil Jon's song is to ordering drinks. The song provides a context that drives a behavior: taking a selfie. And of course, club owners love this song because it provides the venue free publicity. The song comes on, the "adulting is hard" crowd starts taking selfies and tagging the club in their posts. It's a win-win.

You can find context-driven behavior all around you: examples of contexts that drive particular behaviors, and especially purchasing behaviors. State fairs and funnel cakes. Baseball and hot dogs. Movies and popcorn. Peanut butter and jelly. Pizza and beer. Work break and cigarettes. Yacht Week and trust funds.

For brands, the brain's natural pairing of context and behavior is an opportunity to exercise behavior design. An oldie-but-goodie example is Kit Kat's classic jingle: *Give me a break, give me a break, break me off a piece of that Kit Kat bar!* What Nestlé (parent company of Kit Kat) sneakily did here was link the *context* of taking a break with the *behavior* of having a Kit Kat. At your lunch break at work? Have a Kit Kat. Need a break from studying? Have a Kit Kat. The earworm quality of the jingle made this context–behavior pairing doubly effective. Once you hear it, you can't get it out of your head. And whenever someone says, "Hey, time for a break," guess what tune comes to mind? (Side note: Jingles are one of media's endangered species worth saving. Laugh tracks, however, can die.)

Kit Kat's contextual success didn't withstand the test of time, but this next brand's did. Do your best to imagine the following scenario in your mind: *You're on vacation, someplace warm. The temperature is perfect. The setting is serene: no cars, no crowds, just the sound of the ocean waves crashing near you. You can smell the crisp beach air and feel the sand on your toes.*

Take a minute to really imagine being there. Done? Okay, now imagine a waiter asking if you would like a beer. Which beer comes to mind? Chances are, Corona. Over decades, Corona has *Inception*ed you, firmly associating itself with the beach in your mind. (In fairness, we have primed your memory by mentioning Corona in the previous chapter. We have no financial agreement with Corona, but if any execs are reading this, feel free to buy us a round.) This association is no accident. In an ocean of beer options, how can a brand not only stand out, but make the consumer think of it unprompted? By owning a context. Dare you to find a Corona ad without reference to a beach. The not-so-subtle hint as to Corona's context-ownership aims is right there in its tagline: "Life's a Beach."

The power of context to drive behavior, however, can also backfire on a company; products with high contextual association can present a major obstacle to increasing sales. Champagne is associated with special occasions. Think celebration, and you see and hear champagne popping. But many also view champagne as only appropriate for special occasions—even though, aside from it being expensive and fun to spray, there's nothing inherently celebratory about champagne. And in fact, a few bubbly, expensive craft beer brands have successfully penetrated the "celebration" market, getting themselves chosen over champagne as consumers' "pop the bubbly" drink of choice. (Interestingly, they've done this by invoking the same context and behavior associated with champagne, and by being bottled in an identical fashion, just asking to be corked off in celebratory fashion.[17])

With this increased competition, champagne companies have been trying to expand their reach by encouraging champagne drinking at other occasions—they've had to work to overcome their contextual association. The trade group French Wine and Food, for example, deliberately tried to broaden the appropriate context for champagne by appealing to spontaneous enjoyment, as opposed to planned celebrations, in their *Unexpected things happen in the "oui" hours* campaign. One could hardly imagine a more French slogan than that.

CONTEXT DRIVES HABITS, TOO

If you examine the link between context and behavior over a long enough time scale, you can't help but notice the human tendency to fall into regular routines. In other words, humans are creatures of habit—of behaviors we consistently engage in with hardly a thought. And context plays a massive role in shaping these habits. Is there a more context-specific song known to humankind than 50 Cent's "In Da Club"? This song is purely and exclusively a party sing-along song ("Hey Shorty, it's your birthday. We're gonna party like it's your birthday"). No one in the history of humanity has curled up on their couch with their cat on a rainy Sunday and read a novel with this song playing in the background. It's the epitome of an uplifting party track. And when you're not at a party and it comes on, it immediately *feels* like a party, because of everything we've come to associate with it.

Just think of the most context-dependent pairing imaginable: movie theaters and popcorn. A striking study by Greg Burns at Duke University found that people who tend to eat popcorn in a movie theater were almost guaranteed to do so each time they went. They would still eat popcorn when they had just eaten and were completely full. They would eat popcorn even if the popcorn the researchers provided was intentionally made stale! The most fascinating element of the study was that this behavior was incredibly context specific. In other contexts, such as the school library, people who tended to eat popcorn at the movies rejected it when they were full, or when it was stale. Outside of the movie theater context, popcorn's spell was broken.

When it comes to creating or maintaining habits, context is paramount. The most extreme example of this is from the Vietnam War.[18] GIs in Vietnam had alarming rates of heroin addiction. When word of this got back to Washington in 1971, it set off alarm bells. This was the last thing the Nixon administration needed; he had campaigned on a strict, no-tolerance drug policy, and was already fighting a losing battle against negative press from the increasingly unpopular war. He quickly assembled a special council to study these soldiers and their rates of addiction. The study systematically polled GIs on their drug usage, which confirmed the anecdotal reports: 20 percent of American soldiers in Vietnam reported having a heroin habit.

What was shocking, however, was their heroin use after returning to the US. Heroin is one of the most addictive substances known; about a quarter of people who experiment with it become addicted,[19] and of heroin addicts who seek treatment, roughly 91 percent relapse.[20] But the soldiers coming back from Vietnam, who largely didn't seek treatment at all? Less than 5 percent persisted in drug use back in America. The difference? Context.

Even for a behavior like drug use, which has a huge biological component, context changes everything. What's done compulsively in one context may not be done at all in another. Control the context and you control the behavior. How? Repeated context creates memories, which create associations, which drive behavior. But take away the context, the grip of association loosens, and the behavior—the habit—stops.

For most of us, our contexts remain fairly static: home, work, a few favorite stores and restaurants. We're consumers of habit. Nearly half of our purchases—for example, our morning coffee, or our breakfast foods—are repeated regularly and usually made in the same contexts: the same times of day, the same days of the week, the same stores.[21] And consumers tend to buy not only the same brands of products,[22] but in the same amounts.[23] So predictable! Once we've built a habit, we tend to stick with it, since the main aspects of our daily context don't change.

Companies are eager to become integrated into our daily routines, whether it's the phone or the app we check first thing in the morning, the coffee we drink on the way to work, or the streaming service we click on the moment we slump onto the couch to relax in the evenings. Our habits, and the contexts that help create them, are extremely profitable enterprises.

THE IMPORTANCE OF CONSISTENCY

As we've seen, our memory is fallible because of its emphasis on pragmatism over accuracy. It doesn't need to be perfect; it simply needs to be "good enough" to use as the basis for future decisions. This applies to our sense of the past generally, as well as our knowledge of specific previous events. And interestingly, this also pertains to our sense of *ourselves*.

To make decisions and move forward, the brain has to generate and maintain a consistent sense of self; if we're going to make predictions about what is going to be good or bad for us, we have to understand who we are. Memory is key here—it's the glue that keeps our selfhood intact, the means by which our continuity is maintained. In reality, we're constantly evolving and changing. As T. S. Eliot described it, "You are not the same people who left that station / Or who will arrive at any terminus." As a matter of biology, even our very cells completely recycle every seven years or so. Through all this change, our sense of self persists because of memory and its ability to connect us to the past. You wake up every morning as a slightly different physical entity, but memory stitches you together as a single consistent, coherent being.

Importantly, our sense of self—constructed of our memories, creatively remixed—also drives us to maintain the idea of ourselves as a consistent being. When we encounter a new experience, or make a new decision, we're driven to smooth this out to be consistent with this coherent sense of self. Any inconsistency here leads us to what psychologists call *cognitive dissonance*,[24] one of the oldest, most robust phenomena in all of psychology. When there is conflict between beliefs and actions, we experience mental discomfort that drives us to resolve it.

Imagine you're a vegetarian, holding the internal belief that you don't eat meat. Then you and your friends go out drinking. One thing leads to another, and as all good nights do, you end up at the taco shop at 2 AM. And in that context, it doesn't take much arm twisting from your drunken friends for the inevitable to happen: you eat a carne asada taco.

This obviously poses a conflict. *I don't eat meat* does not jive with *I ate a carne asada taco*. Something has to give. The cognitive dissonance must be reconciled. This can be done a couple different ways. You could go the denial route: *I didn't really eat the taco, I just kinda nibbled on it. That doesn't count.* Or, perhaps more rationally, you could own the act and revise your existing belief system and sense of self: *Okay, I ate the carne asada taco. As a general rule, I don't eat meat, but I do sometimes.*

Cognitive dissonance is marketing black magic. It's something brands can architect, by intentionally creating dissonance—forcing a wedge between who you believe yourself to be and what you currently own. This is especially common with lifestyle brands (e.g., fashion, sports cars) that use aspirational ads: messages that remind the consumer of things they aspire to or have not yet achieved.

Take the Nissan Xterra SUV for instance, which launched with an ad[25] where regular people in their mid to late twenties are driving the truck in a not-so-regular way, on and off a series of sand dunes. To get a sense of the choreography, think of something out of a GoPro or Red Bull YouTube channel. Finally, the group decide on a peak, pull out their snowboards, and board down the side of the dune.

The subtext of Nissan's ad is: *Cool kids are buying our car to do cool things like this.* When you see the commercial, you either buy into that claim or not. If not, you are safe (for now). If you do buy in, *and* if you think of yourself as a cool kid, then your brain has to resolve the difference between that belief and you not owning an Xterra. Either you buy the Xterra and retain the belief that you're cool, or you don't buy the Xterra and instead revise your existing belief about your self-worth: maybe you're not such a cool person after all.

Beneath the surface details of celebrity endorsements or clever driving choreography, these aspirational types of advertisements work by pairing their products with positive attributes. They make a subtextual claim: *In order to be cool/attractive/successful, you must have this product.* Every time you implicitly buy into an aspirational ad's claim, your brain is forced to solve the Xterra calculation.

This is especially concerning when it comes to the beauty industry. Maybelline literally has an entire beauty product line called the Eraser. Magazine and print ads for the product line pose a similar subtextual claim as Nissan: *In order to be attractive, you need the Eraser.* Maybelline isn't telling women *overtly* that they are not good enough and that they need Eraser products to be attractive. They don't have to. The cognitive dissonance does it behind the scenes. The strong-willed reject the claim and move on. Others are left asking themselves, "Am I attractive?" If you believe you are, your brain has to resolve it by either going out to buy the Maybelline Eraser or changing your belief: "Maybe I am not attractive after all."

Many people can and do reject the claim of aspirational advertising. But some forms of advertising claims are easier to reject than others. Realizing an ad is just a commercial, in the same way you recognize a movie is not real life, is one way to distance oneself from an ad's claim. Seeing the Rock with his shirt off promoting Under Armour headphones, as impressive as it may be, is not as insidious to consumers if they see it and think, *He's a celebrity, of course he looks like an action figure, headphones or no.*

Celebrities are easy to label as unrealistic aspirational figures; influencers are not. Even the strongest-willed consumer with the toughest mindset has fallen for a moment of dissonance on social media. Influencers on YouTube, Instagram, and the like are harder to tag as unrealistic; you see them as "real people," as opposed to "celebrities." You might be able to ignore Angelina Jolie selling you lipstick, but not so much when Patrick Starrr, the YouTube makeup guru, sells you the same thing.

COGNITIVE DISSONANCE AND CONFABULATION

Accepting the ad and making the purchase is one way that this dissonance can be resolved, but it's not the only one. Dissonance can also be resolved the other way—by bending our psychological reality. This usually means revising our memory: *I only kinda nibbled on that carne asada taco.* In this way, the relationship between memory and behavior can be reversed; in cases like this, behavior drives memory.

One of the most fascinating features of the human brain is its seemingly endless ability to rationalize.[26] This is taken to the extreme in certain types of brain damage, like Capgras syndrome. The symptoms could not be any more bizarre. The patient can recall memories, do math, use language—all of their cognitive functions are preserved—but they also have one, very specific new belief: they are convinced that their loved ones are imposters.

The famous neuroscientist V. S. Ramachandran investigated the reason for this, and it comes down to the very specific brain damage that caused the condition: a severing of the connection between the centers responsible for facial memory and those responsible for emotional salience.

The behavior of those with Capgras syndrome seems odd and nonsensical to us, but to them, it's the only logically consistent explanation. You're used to looking at your parents' faces and feeling a unique sense of warmth and fondness. We hardly notice it when it happens, taking it for granted, but it's always there. But with the connection in the brain between facial memory and emotion severed, that emotional glow is no longer there. The only explanation that makes sense—given this odd state of psychological affairs—is that the person is not their dad, but an exact replica who is impersonating their dad. Our thoughts and explanations bend to accommodate our internal reality.

Patients who suffer a stroke that causes paralysis of one side of the body, and in the process also damages areas near the intersection of the left temporal and parietal lobes (associated with proprioception—the sense of where our body is in space), can suffer from similar distortions. The patient is obviously paralyzed—say, completely unable to lift their left arm—yet they will completely deny it.[27] Asked to move the arm, the patient will offer an incredible range of excuses and reasoning: "I'm too tired." "I don't feel like it." "I would, but I don't want the other paralyzed people in the hospital to feel bad about themselves." In some instances, these patients, to their doctor's astonishment, actually claim that they are moving it and the doctor just isn't paying attention! In other instances still, the patients will exhibit something called *somatoparaphrenia*,[28] where they claim that the limb in question is indeed not moving, but that it's not their limb at all! The confabulations are truly endless.

These examples seem crazy at first glance, but this isn't something that happens only when the brain is damaged. The healthy brain does this all the time. Consider the following experiment published in *Science*.[29] Peter Johansson and colleagues presented people with a simple task: they held up pictures of two very similar faces, and asked participants which one they preferred. They later gave the participants the image they selected and asked them to explain why they made that choice.

In a certain number of trials, however, they gave the participants the *other* picture—the one they didn't choose (the faces looked similar enough that hardly anyone noticed). What was fascinating was their explanations. Their reasoning was persuasive and believable: "I liked this one because it had glasses," or "I like this one because of the hair," or "This one really just popped out to me when I first saw it." The decision-making descriptions were just as convincing and compelling when participants were describing their justifications for choosing a face they didn't choose as they were when describing their justifications for a face they actually did.

There have been similar findings in consumer studies as well. Replace pictures of faces with jars of jam[30] and you get a very similar result. When you trick someone into thinking that they chose the apple jam, when really they preferred the raspberry, they'll stick to their guns and double down on their "choice." They'll sing the praises of the delicious apple jam despite not actually preferring it, reeling off sumptuous descriptions to justify their choice. Maybe marketers are just wasting their time, trying to talk up the features of their product! Customers seem to like whatever they come to *think* they've chosen. It doesn't take much to make us all sound like somatoparaphrenia patients.

This poses lots of implications regarding our decision making. As NYU psychologist Jonathan Haidt describes, "The conscious mind thinks it's the Oval Office, when in reality it's the press office." How many of our "decisions" have we made by mistake, only to rationalize them after the fact? We'll revisit this topic of how in control of our decision making we actually are later in the book. But what's interesting for the moment is our need to explain away our own behavior. Once a "choice" is made, we must make sense of it—it must be "smoothed out" and made consistent with our past behavior and who we believe ourselves to be. Our memory of an experience, and how we explain it, is necessarily warped in order to conform to the narrative we're trying to maintain.

This manifests in the consumer world in a number of different ways. Think about overconsumption. We clearly buy many more things than we realistically need, and deep down, we know this. At the same time, we generally want to see ourselves as reasonable, conscientious people. How to explain this?

The answer is something the marketing world calls *functional alibis*.[31] Researchers at Harvard Business School found that, when it comes to indulgent, hedonic purchases, including a small, utilitarian feature can significantly boost sales. As one of the study's authors, Anat Keinan, told *The*

Atlantic, "You want to feel that you're rational, that you're a smart shopper, that you're not wasting your money, that you're not perceived as the kind of person who buys things just to impress others." Take the Hummer, for example: a $60,000, barely-street-legal tank that gets 4 gallons to the mile. It's brash, big, and expensive. But by including a small mention of its safety features in its advertisements, marketers provide something for the rationalizing mind to grasp. In reality, you want it because it's cool, but you tell yourself, *I'm just buying it to be safe*. Safety ratings were the last thing your purchasing brain thought of, but it's the first thing that comes to your rationalizing mind.

Similar trends have been found with other car brands as well. As Rory Sutherland, vice chairman of Ogilvy Advertising Group, has remarked, "Tesla drivers will wax enthusiastically about the environmental purity of their vehicles, regardless of their initial reasons for buying the car."[32]

CLINGING TO THE PAST

Our drive for consistency can also act as a kind of inertia by keeping us attached to certain elements of the past. We cling to the past in mysterious and, when it comes to decision making, often very *irrational* ways. One example of this is what behavioral economists call the *sunk cost fallacy*. Imagine you bought a used car two years ago, and it has constantly been in the repair shop. Your coworker asks why don't you just buy a new car, and your response is, "I've spent so much money on repairs, it doesn't make sense to buy a new one." This is the sunk cost fallacy in action, and it shows how irrational we can be when we use the past to inform current and future decisions.

Upon closer examination, you can see just how irrational this is. We tend to feel that if we don't stick with something in the future, whatever we committed to it in the past is somehow wasted. And yet, the past is already gone; the time, or money, is already "wasted" in the utilitarian sense, regardless of what we do in the future. Whatever happened with your car before *should* be irrelevant. The money you paid for the repairs is gone. Logically, what's important now is how much your used car is likely to cost versus a new one *going forward*. Yet we have an illogical need to honor our previous purchases and "get our money's worth."

Marketers are particularly adept at using the sunk cost fallacy for lead generation. One of the easiest forms of lead generation is gathering emails, and one tactic for collecting new emails is to get the time commitment first, before asking for the email address. If you've already spent the time filling out the rest of the form, it makes it harder to say no to giving your email address at the end. Next time you come across a form or take a personality test like "Which Harry Potter character are you?" notice when they ask for your email to send you the results. If they ask for your email address *after* you've filled out your answers, then it is a sunk cost design.

If you've been part of a big buying decision on behalf of the company you work for, the sunk cost fallacy certainly impacted the decision. Salesforce is a company that sells software designed to help other companies manage their customers. The software costs from thousands to millions of dollars, depending on the size of your company. Salesforce's tactic is to get a small commitment (*give us your email in exchange for a free e-book*), then a medium commitment (*give me your phone number to do a digital demo*), then a large commitment (*let's do a live demo in person at your office*), before finally asking for the sale. It is harder to say no the more you interact with Salesforce because you've already committed so much time. Car dealerships use this tactic all the time. The longer the car negotiations last, the more time you've committed, and the harder it will be for you to walk away.

Sunk cost fallacy can also help shed new light on why unhappy relationships persist despite one or both partners wanting to leave.[33] Partners tell themselves, *Well, we've come this far.* It's an odd self-justification that sends people into a sort of psychological inertia. Keen marketers often commit us to their products and services by cleverly designing ways for us to invest time, money, or both first. And because of the sunk cost fallacy, once we start along this path, it can be difficult to resist our own inertia. As the famous line in the movie *Magnolia* goes, "We may be through with the past, but the past ain't through with us."

Memory isn't static or stationary. Instead, it evolves over time, thanks to the brain's fallibility, its general pragmatism, and its drive for consistency. In terms of accuracy, our memory is far from a video playback. At best, it is a photograph that is constantly being Photoshopped by our brains without our permission or awareness. Our brains creatively construct the past to plan for the future, and sometimes sacrifice accuracy in the process.

This malleability is important to be aware of, because memory and behavior are intimately linked. Memory, often in tandem with context, drives behavior. And in strange ways, behavior can also drive memory.

As a result, memory is big business. Memory can be used to drive profit, but not in the ways we might expect. Like other aspects of our consumer behavior, the opportunity for brands lies in the strange quirks of our psychology—in how our brains unconsciously fill in the gaps between reality and perception, this time between experience, memory, and behavior. Whether through tacit psychological insight, or through trial and error, brands have figured out how to design marketing campaigns and advertisements to tap into these strange quirks and drive our behavior.

The good news is, we can use these insights, too. Knowing the potency of context when it comes to memory-driven behavior, we can design context on our own terms, to reach our own goals. Knowing the fallibility of our memories, we can adjust our confidence in them appropriately. And knowing our drive for consistency, we can see how we may bend our own interpretation of the past in inaccurate, and even unhelpful, ways.

We'll likely never achieve the incredible depth and accuracy of memory that someone like Bob Petrella has. But we can achieve something arguably more valuable: a keener awareness of the fallibility of memory, how marketers exploit it, and how to be vigilant against the pitfalls of our own remixing.

Chapter 5

OF TWO MINDS

The Role of Impulse in Consumer Decision Making

Imagine you are a soon-to-be-retired CEO and it is time for you to pick a successor. You have narrowed it down to two people, Sam and Kris. Their quotes below summarize their leadership styles. Who would you choose?

Sam says:

* Exceptional leadership is controlled and disciplined.
* Logic is the beginning of wisdom, not the end.
* Control feelings so that they don't control you.

Kris says:

* Intuition, however illogical, is recognized as a command prerogative.
* Sometimes a feeling is all we have to go on.
* I play poker, not chess.

Fans of the original *Star Trek* series might have already figured out who is responsible for these quotes: Sam's are from Spock and Kris's are from Captain Kirk. These fictional characters personify the two primary ways the brain makes decisions: with slow logic versus with quick intuition—or, as described by behavioral economist and Nobel laureate Daniel Kahneman, System 1 (which is slow and deliberate) and System 2 (which is fast and intuitive). Spock (System 1) does not make rash decisions. He exercises deliberate control, slowing down to analyze all available variables before coming to an optimally logical conclusion. Kirk (System 2) is the opposite. He doesn't have time to slow down and think about what he *should* do; instead, he uses intuition to do what he *needs* to do.

Much of why we make the decisions we do comes down to control—control over our own deliberate thought processes. Either we are aware and in control of our decision making, like Spock, or act on intuition, like Kirk.

The Kirk model of decision making is like driving a car with an automatic transmission. You don't have to think about anything that's happening under the hood; you just drive. The Spock model of decision making works more like driving a car with a manual transmission. Here you must actively think about the engine speed, speedometer, current gear, and so forth. Decisions made in manual mode are slow, rational, analytical, and deliberate.

Kirk mode is our brain's default; Spock mode is the exception. But both modes of decision making are vulnerable to marketing tactics designed to influence what, when, and how much we buy.

THE DEFAULT STATE

Recall from chapter two that our conscious attention is severely limited; as a result we use simple shortcuts to arrive at a reasonable "best guess" at reality that informs our behavior. This same dynamic is magnified when it comes to decision making. We're always operating with less than all the relevant information when making a decision. If we go to an ice cream shop, we don't take the time to try, or conjure up memories of, every single flavor. And we're not carefully and deliberately evaluating the short- and long-term benefits of strawberry versus chocolate. If we did, we'd be there all day. Instead, after a quick scan, one of them will look "good enough." And the human brain loves "good enough."

Not only is our attention limited, but we also prefer not to think deeply about the information we do process. All things being equal, the brain prefers less thinking to more thinking. If there's an easy way to arrive at a solution, the brain will take that route every time. This is such a stable characteristic that it's referred to as a "law": the *law of least mental effort*.

But what about people who love Sudoku, crosswords, and jigsaw puzzles? Don't they actually like thinking? Yes, some people genuinely find specific types of thinking and intellectual stimulation intrinsically enjoyable. But on a regular, day-to-day basis, when a task requires thinking that isn't itself enjoyable, even puzzle lovers' brains prefer less thinking over more. That is the law of least mental effort.

This, of course, has major implications for our decision making, as was famously illustrated in an experiment by Shane Frederick and Daniel Kahneman,[1] and described in Kahneman's book, *Thinking, Fast and Slow*. They asked participants to respond quickly to the following scenario:

A bat and a ball cost $1.10.
The bat costs $1.00 more than the ball.

How much does the ball cost?

If you're like most of the people in the study, you likely arrived at $0.10. This experiment was done on undergraduate students from MIT, Princeton, and Yale, and roughly 50 percent of them came up with that same solution. But a quick bit of arithmetic reveals that this is actually incorrect: $0.10 for the ball, plus $1.10 for the bat (which costs a dollar more than the ball), costs $1.20, not $1.10. To meet the requirements of the scenario, the ball must cost $0.05. This would make the bat cost $1.05, which is $1 more than the ball, and would let the bat and the ball together total $1.10.

For most first-time readers of this scenario, an intuitive-sounding response—the ball is $0.10—arises in the mind and that's that. The brain is satisfied enough with the answer that it doesn't switch to manual mode for further analysis—even though the answer is wrong. As Kahneman writes, "The ease with which we are satisfied enough to stop thinking is troubling." The brain's laziness makes stopping to think—switching to manual—easier said than done.

As you might imagine, this default state of ours, in which deliberate thinking is low, is highly suggestible. Unless something drastic happens that requires us to take manual control of the situation, we're happy to go with the flow.

The brain's adherence to the law of least mental effort, coupled with its preference for driving in automatic, explains a vast amount of human behavior. Think about how you use a search engine. When you're googling something, how often do you go to the second or third page? Chances are you stay on the first page. Most of us would rather try a new search to find what we want over clicking to the second or third page. Even on the first page, how often do you read *every* single one of the ten search results *before* clicking? Chances are you click the first result that sounds good enough, then the second and third. Your behavior searching on Google is representative of the way people browse in general—for speed, not accuracy. Just as your brain prioritizes consistency over accuracy in memory, it prioritizes speed and ease over accuracy in decision making. It's no wonder we're such fallible creatures.

Being accurate when googling would mean having to analyze each search result on each page *before* clicking. In theory, this would maximize your chances of finding exactly what you're looking for—but doing so would require your brain to switch to manual mode. Your brain would rather scan quickly and guess wrong than read meticulously and guess correctly. The back button further feeds the brain's laziness, as it effectively erases any wrong guess and lets you try again. The consequences of a quick wrong guess are almost nonexistent.

The consumer world happily obliges our dislike of thinking by making buying decisions as easy and thought-free as possible. This is probably seen most clearly online. Take web design, for example. When browsing the web, English speakers naturally scan the page in an F pattern. Adept web designers conform to this natural, automatic preference by mimicking this pattern, placing the things they most want us to see along the lines of the F. The main navigation elements of websites are placed either across the top, horizontally, or down the left side, vertically.

Interestingly, a flipped F pattern going left to right is the norm in most Middle Eastern countries.[2] Why? Because languages like Farsi, Hebrew, and Arabic are read right to left. English and most languages spoken throughout Europe are read left to right. Reading is an automatic process, and so conforming a web page's design to this natural tendency makes browsing it as frictionless as possible.

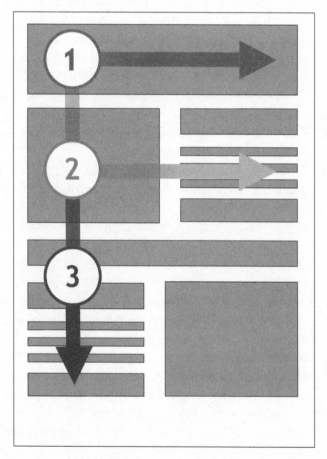

When browsing the web, English speakers naturally scan the page in an F pattern.

Digital design elements on the web are also optimized for scanability. Icons replace words wherever possible because it takes less mental effort to see 🛒 than to read the words *shopping cart*. When websites do use words, the paragraphs tend to be shorter. Text is broken up by multiple titles and subtitles, bullet points are commonplace, and important words are often bold.

We are not usually aware of our brains' explicit preference for the above design elements. However, we often get a good "feeling" from a website, mobile app, or piece of software. You may love the feel of one mobile app, while hating the feel of another so much that you stop using it altogether, like your authors and Snapchat circa 2018.

In your digital life, there's more to be thankful for than complain about when it comes to companies architecting for the brain's automatic mode. After all, the value of technology is truly realized with its ease of use. However, some sneaky companies use their knowledge of our automatic mode preference to *create* friction instead of remove it. They use the law of least mental effort to their advantage by placing anything they don't want you to see or do behind a wall of mental effort.

Think about your favorite e-commerce website. Chances are, it has been optimally designed to make checking out as fluid as possible. What if you want to return something? The return policy is usually harder to find. In theory, harder-to-find return information reduces the number of returns.

For Facebook, saying privacy is an issue is an understatement. Facebook makes money from your data. What you like, share, comment upon, and view is sold to advertisers in aggregate so they can better target their ads—which is why liking, sharing, commenting, and scrolling on Facebook is a frictionless experience. Where you need to go to complete said actions is obvious, automatic, and even natural. If, instead of liking, sharing, and commenting, you want to change your privacy settings to make it harder for Facebook to use and make money from your data, well, that's not so obvious. Where exactly do you go? You may vaguely guess top right, but then what? Your lazy brain is forced to switch to manual mode, and it doesn't like it.

When websites require you to switch to manual mode, it isn't coincidental. It's because the company has an incentive to make something harder for you to find.

DEFAULT SETTINGS

With a global user base of more than 1.3 billion, YouTube currently stands as the second-most-visited site on the whole of the internet, one place above Facebook, and one place behind its parent company, Google.[3] Worldwide, over a billion hours of user time are spent on the site every day, despite YouTube still being banned in the massive Chinese market. Michael Scott of *The Office* famously declared, "When I first discovered YouTube, I didn't work for five days." Looking at how YouTube taps into our automatic default mode, it's not difficult to see why.

With more than four hundred hours of new YouTube content uploaded every minute, there is no shortage of novel content for users to watch. To appease your default mode as much as possible, the site has developed an increasingly sophisticated "suggested videos" function. These machine-learning algorithms tap your search history, viewing history, and demographic information to find the perfect next video to keep you watching.[4]

For example, having just watched "Charlie Bit My Finger" for the first time, YouTube might suggest "Top 10 funny baby videos" for you next. And after you've watched that, it will push you toward the famous "Evil baby face compilation." And so on. Before you know it, you've convinced yourself Kim Kardashian's baby is with the Illuminati . . . when all you came for, four hours ago, was to see that one video everybody was shocked you hadn't heard of. With its army of engineers predicting with razor-sharp precision the perfect next video for each visitor, it's little wonder the average time on the site has been growing a whopping 60 percent year after year at the time of this writing.

As if that wasn't enough, in 2014 YouTube introduced the autoplay feature to its main site. Now, instead of having to actually click on the next cat video, the video will play automatically after a brief countdown. This may seem like a small adjustment, but by creating the autoplay feature, YouTube effectively created a default setting, and because of our brain's tendency to go with the flow, we default right along with it.

Shortly after YouTube's implementation of autoplay, Netflix adopted a similar "Post-Play" option, which made watching the next episode in a series the default option. Like YouTube, Netflix was already a successful platform, but this adoption drove their viewership to new heights. As

Adam Alter, author of the book *Irresistible*, points out, this is literally when the binge-watching phenomenon was born: Google Trends reports that the phrases "binge-watching" and "Netflix binge" began appearing in January 2013, just months after Post-Play's implementation.[5] Netflix's own research found that over 60 percent of adults reported binge-watching in 2013, and that most people who have finished a show on Netflix completed it in binges over just four to six days.[6] Not surprisingly, automatic play has become an industry standard, with Amazon and HBO quickly following suit.

Default options like this are powerful because they allow us to carry on naturally with a safe, ostensibly risk-free status quo. Autoplay features increase engagement because the default option is to continue watching, and it requires conscious action to *stop*. To refuse the default requires forcing your brain out of automatic mode and into manual mode—which, as we know, the brain likes to avoid.

This isn't just true with video. Consider signing up for auto insurance. There tends to be a range of options for how extensive the coverage should be: Do you want to cover just the other driver in case of an accident, or to cover yourself and your car as well? It turns out that what is included already as the default option has a profound impact on what new insurance customers ultimately choose. If "hurricane protection" is listed as a default option, one that we have to choose *not* to enroll in, we're likely to wind up with it. But if we have to opt in, we're unlikely to bother.

The taxpayers of New Jersey and Pennsylvania felt the brunt of this firsthand in a real-life experiment in 1992.[7] Both states switched that year to a no-fault insurance regime where consumers could save money by limiting their right to sue for tort damages, but the way the option was framed differed by state: New Jersey made limited right to sue the default option, while Pennsylvanians were presumed to select full right to sue, unless they opted out. This small change in the status quo had a profound effect on their behavior: 75 percent of Pennsylvania consumers paid to retain full tort, while only 20 percent of New Jersey consumers did.

Similar effects have been found with many other kinds of behavior, including student loan repayment[8] and even, interestingly, willingness to donate organs. In countries such as Austria where donating is the default, donation rates are roughly 90 percent. For opt-in countries, such as the US or Germany, the rate is only 20 percent.[9]

Default options can and are deliberately designed to influence your behavior in the consumer world. Think about the last time you were in New York City, perhaps the last American city where taxicabs outnumber Ubers and Lyfts. Ever since NYC first mandated its cab drivers accept credit cards in 2007, the payment system has come with an intelligently designed set of default options for tipping: you have the option of 20, 25, or 30 percent. What if you want to tip 10 or 15 percent? Well, then you have to go away from the default, run through additional steps, and calculate the dollar amount, all by your lonesome. Back when cab drivers were paid in cash, the average NYC taxi ride tip was 10 percent. After the new set of credit card defaults, it rose to 22 percent. Three options netted cabs an additional $144 million per year! Similar effects have been found when default options are presented on electronic registers such as Square.[10,11] These initial defaults, usually completely outside our awareness, can easily send us in the direction their designer prefers. And once we're off, it can be difficult for us to resist our own inertia.

THE DEFAULT OF CONVENIENCE

When you hear the term *convenience store*, something like 7-Eleven comes to mind, right? The authors humbly disagree. The biggest convenience store in the world is Amazon. Over the past twenty years, Amazon has grown to become one of the world's highest-valued companies by making shopping there as convenient as possible. Part of the reason is that Amazon is exceptional at designing for automatic mode; 2-Day Delivery, 1-Click Ordering, and their Subscribe & Save program are all ways in which Amazon removes friction and doubles down on keeping your brain in automatic mode. Studies have shown that when it comes to an enjoyable retail experience, convenience and ease of purchasing is seen as the most important factor—outranking even the quality of the product itself.[12] Jeff Bezos, founder and CEO of Amazon, uses this as the philosophy that drives Amazon forward.

Technology such as smartphones and smartwatches have made it easier than ever to buy in automatic mode. This mode looks for the path of least resistance between impulse to decision, and technology acts as a lubricant. A 2019 report by NPR found that almost 80 percent of Americans shop online,[13] and a 2019 Statista Report revealed that more than 40 percent of

American digital shoppers buy online multiple times a month.[14] You used to have to get in your car, drive, park, peruse the aisles, and *then* buy. Now, all you need is a thought in your head and a connected device.

Companies are continually coming up with new ways to make giving them your money easier, because gliding along in automatic mode keeps you from stopping and rethinking your purchase. Amazon's Dash Buttons are each synced to a product of your choice. Whenever you want to buy this product, push the button and voilà! It arrives at your doorstep in two days or less. Compare that to the friction-heavy experience of opening your laptop, logging in, opening your browser, going to Amazon, searching for the product, adding it to your cart, and clicking through the digital checkout (soooo 2018).

If even pressing a button is too much for you, fear not, our efficient friend. Smart speakers like the Amazon Echo and Google Home Assistant are for you. Simply say the word (well, words), and Amazon's Alexa will turn your impulse into a purchase quicker than you can say *hot diggity dog*. And with marketers clamoring to find ways to advertise on the Echo and Google Home,[15] this type of one-thought shopping will be easier than ever.

Automatic mode is good for business. Manual mode (typically) is not. Imagine being visited by the Ghost of Shopping Past, who made you revisit all the times you pushed the BUY NOW button last year. How many of those purchases would you take back?

MANUAL MODE

Most of the time, as we've seen, our brains prefer to go with the flow, cruising along in automatic mode. But there are times when exerting the mental energy to take manual control is necessary.

Situations in which manual mode and automatic mode are put into direct conflict result in something called, in scientific terms, the *Stroop phenomenon*. In the classic paradigm, the Stroop phenomenon is elicited by having people look at words for different colors and say out loud what the color of the ink is. This is easy enough when the word and the color of the ink match (e.g., when the word is *blue* and the ink color is blue), but when they don't (e.g., when the word is *blue* but the ink color is red), we're much slower to respond, since we have to override our prepotent response to read, and instead do the manual, unintuitive thing of naming the ink color.

The Stroop phenomenon isn't just an experimental paradigm. It happens in real life all the time. If, for example, you grew up speaking only English—even if you have some proficiency in other languages—it's automatic for you to respond in English, even when you're speaking with someone who doesn't speak English or you're traveling in a non-English-speaking country. A charming example of this can be seen with NBA player Timofey Mozgov, a native of Russia. When being interviewed by an NBA newscaster in English about his recent performance, he went off for about twenty seconds in his mother tongue before realizing his mistake! If you've ever wondered what a seven-foot-tall Russian center looks like when he blushes, check out the video.[16] 🖥

Your automatic system needs to be overridden by your slow, deliberative one. You have to actively decide to think deeply about something, and not just "go with the flow."

How we behave in automatic mode in a given circumstance is determined by the environment in which we grow up and to which we become accustomed over time. And it is only when we go outside of that environment that we realize just how automatic our behavior actually is. If you were to be transported from, say, the US, where you grew up, to the UK, you would instantly experience all sorts of difficulty. And we're not talking about the culture shock of clotted cream and soccer (sorry, football!) hooliganism, but something much simpler—just walking around. When we're in a familiar town or city, we cross the street largely on automatic mode. As we do so, our minds can wander onto other things; we can even multitask by holding a conversation, listening to music, or (sometimes!) even texting on the phone. As a US-to-UK transplant, we lose that ability to use automatic mode. In the UK, traffic comes from the other side of the street. The automatic tendency to first look left to see if a car is coming no longer matches your environment. You have to take a manual approach—deliberately override your automatic response and instead *think* about which direction to look for traffic in order to keep yourself safe. What previously felt effortless now feels arduous, because the brain is now functioning in manual mode.

It's not as simple as it sounds to switch into manual mode. The switch itself doesn't happen automatically; it needs to be done manually. We have to literally fight off the impulse to go with the automatic response: fight off the natural impulse to read the word instead of name the ink, to speak in our native language, or to always look left while crossing the street. Exerting cognitive control is being a salmon swimming upstream: everything is pushing us in the direction of automatic mode, and we're forcing ourselves to go against it.

The thing that makes it possible for us to shift from automatic mode—in which we are susceptible to impulse—to manual mode—which we use to resist impulse—is something neuroscientists call *cognitive control*. Cognitive control isn't the absence of impulses, but rather the ability to keep impulses in check. We all get the urges for certain things, like "eat that delicious burger" or "watch TV instead of study." The difference between those who do these things and those who don't is not the absence of the urges, but the ability to not act on them.

Manual mode is our mental armor against impulses. It lets us evaluate the consequences of following our impulses versus delaying gratification. Which route provides the greater reward? Do we go out partying and enjoy the moment, or do we stay home and study so that we can graduate with a higher GPA and get the best job possible after graduation? Do we eat that juicy, delicious bacon cheeseburger, or do we choose the salad? Do we spend that $5,000 holiday bonus on a vacation, or do we put it in our 401(k)?

One could argue that there aren't right answers to any of these questions. But in the absence of any control over our impulses, we'd always pick the most immediately appealing option—the party, the burger, the holiday. Only when we exert cognitive control via manual mode can we stave off our initial impulses in favor of longer-term reward.

The science of impulse control is fascinating. The classic example is the Marshmallow Test, in which young children are brought into a lab and given a simple scenario: "Here is one marshmallow. You can either decide to eat it now, or, if you wait ten minutes, I'll give you two marshmallows!" Video from these experiments is golden. The marshmallow is placed in front of the child, the experimenter leaves the room, and all that lies between the child and this delicious snack is a thin veil of cognitive control. Their reactions are priceless: squirming in their seat, drooling at the marshmallow, agonizing over it. There is naturally a wide range of performances in this setting. Some children give in after a few minutes, while some wait out the full ten minutes and enjoy the second marshmallow with little issue.

The original Marshmallow Test suggested a fascinating link between a child's ability to delay gratification and a range of important outcomes later in life: children who held out for the second marshmallow showed superior SAT scores and job outcomes decades later. Despite some warranted enthusiasm, these findings have proved difficult to replicate, partly because it takes decades to measure the long-term effects, but also because it's hard to tease out the precise contribution of cognitive control to these long-term outcomes.[17] At the very least, the Marshmallow Test provides an important analogy for understanding the role of cognitive control in resisting our impulses.

Of course, controlling our impulses is the exact opposite of what most companies want us to do. Cognitive control can be kryptonite to many types of commerce. Take, for example, impulse shopping—an incredibly big business. In a poll by CreditCards.com, 84 percent of Americans[18] admitted to having made at least one impulse buy in recent memory, while 54 percent of consumers[19] admitted to spending at least $100 on an impulse purchase, with 20 percent having spent over $1,000. Because impulse buying is so useful to companies, they design both to keep you in automatic mode, where you're more susceptible to giving in to impulse, and to put you in automatic mode even when you're trying to be in manual. In fact, there are several reliable ways in which cognitive control, and the ability to shift into manual mode that comes with it, can be worn down.

HUNGER

One of the best ways to ensure you're wielding your full cognitive resources is to focus not on the brain, but on the stomach. That's right—a full meal (particularly one high in glucose, discussed hereafter) can be key to deliberative thinking and fighting impulses.

The reason we're so averse to thinking is because it is physically draining. The brain's manual mode is a physical process that requires physical energy, in the form of glucose, to sustain itself. If you've ever studied for long hours in the library, you likely noticed that you were physically tired and hungry afterward, even though you'd just been sitting the whole time. Your brain, though stationary, was busy working overtime.

When your metabolic energy is low, the default option in any decision becomes more attractive, because it requires less effort. Imagine coming home from work late at night, exhausted. You drop your work bag at the door and slump down on the couch. You can barely muster enough energy to find the remote. In this state of mind, what are you more likely to want to watch? A mind-bending French psychological thriller? Or . . . *Fast and Furious 8*? No offense to Vin Diesel's "family" and friends out there, but one option clearly requires more mental energy than the other. And when you're mentally exhausted, you just want the option that's quickest and easiest, while still being enjoyable.

In this brain state, you are much more likely to purchase things on impulse, and companies have designed for this. Think about the setup of the average supermarket. There's a reason why checkout aisles are filled with alluring "impulse buys" like candies and other unhealthy snacks. Say you've been a really good grocery shopper. You picked low-sugar, low-carb, healthy foods. You skipped ice cream and potato chips. You utilized manual mode by practicing self-control and saying no. The good news is, you exerted control over your cravings. Killing it! The bad news is, self-control is like the gas tank of a Hummer: quick to empty. And now you're faced with rows upon rows of tasty treats. Ordinarily, you'd have the cognitive fortitude to forgo that delicious-looking candy bar. But tired and hungry after a long shopping experience, with your self-control tank depleted, you're powerless to resist.

The negative effects of hunger in particular on decision making are both common and very real.[20] Even judges, people trusted with some of society's most important decisions, are surprisingly swayed by hunger. When reviewing parole applications, judges were significantly less likely to grant parole the closer it was to lunchtime.[21] Why? Because granting parole requires careful deliberation, and when judges are hungry, they're much more likely to make the less strenuous decision (e.g., just stamping "no"). Just like that, your appeal for that speeding ticket is decided by a hangry stomach.[22]

One company has repeatedly optimized their marketing specifically for hunger-driven impulse buying: Snickers. It's hard enough to avoid impulse gratification in the grocery store checkout line; with Snickers, you have to also combat a marketing message that speaks directly to your struggle.

Hungry? *Why wait? Grab a Snickers.* The Snickers tagline is a disturbingly perfect fit for what they are selling and when the consumer is most likely to buy it—when they're hungry. The updated slogan doesn't steer far from the original: *You're not you when you're hungry.*

STRENUOUS PHYSICAL ENVIRONMENTS

Physical environments can also wear down our self-control. And when you think of physical environments for shopping, you can't help but think of the mall.

For US readers, it is difficult to imagine a time before the American shopping mall. However, the mall is a relatively new "invention." It came to prominence in the 1960s, pioneered by Austrian architect Victor Gruen. Gruen designed the American mall not as a commercial hub, but as an important node in American suburban life—a place outside of work and home for families and friends to spend quality time with one another.[23] He theorized that good design equated to good profits: if he designed an enjoyable space, people would want to spend their time there, and while there, they would naturally spend money.

Gruen was half-right. Malls and modern retail spaces alike do encourage spending, though not by making customers appreciate their aesthetics. To the contrary, retail spaces are deliberately designed to be dizzying, over-stimulating, and disorienting—because the more exhausting the shopping environment is, the less able mallgoers are to control their impulses, and the more money they end up spending.

Nothing about the layout of a mall is intuitive. That moment of instant disorientation you feel when you set foot in a retail space even has a name: "the Gruen Effect," named for the original mall architect, who railed against these techniques. (In his later years, Gruen became an ardent critic of what the American mall had become, claiming in one speech, "I refuse to pay alimony for these bastard developments."[24]) The retail environment is designed to force us into manual mode—hard, deliberative thinking—and keep us there for as long as possible, depleting our finite manual-mode resources.[25]

The disarming sensory overload of the Gruen Effect is just the beginning. Malls are deceptively comfortable places: they're air-conditioned, clean, and filled with smiling people ready to welcome you into their stores. But beneath the surface, malls are deliberately laid out in ways designed to wear you down.

The mall's labyrinthine layout. (Photo by Victor Xok on Unsplash.)

Mall designers know, for example, that people often come for a single item—say, a pair of shoes. And while they're happy to sell you that pair of shoes, they know they can usually get you to buy more than that. This is why shops selling shoes tend to be dispersed at opposite ends of the mall, rather than clustered together in a more convenient fashion. As you walk to and fro, you're exposed to dozens of other mall stores trying to pull you in with various items (who can say no to "free" samples?). All that walking also wears you down physically. You'll notice that the escalators in malls are often designed using this more-walking-is-better principle: if you're trying to go from floor 1 to floor 3, you'll have to take the escalator up to floor 2, walk all the way around to the other side of the floor, and then take the escalator going up to floor 3. They take "shop 'til you drop" literally!

Once they have you worn down and disoriented, the retail stores themselves cleverly nudge you to the most expensive, highest-margin items.

This is done by placing such items at eye level—your default field of vision, the easiest possible place to look without strain.[26] If the law of least mental effort had a physical location, right in front of you at eye level would be it. Companies pay retail stores a premium to shelve their products at this spot.

You might wonder why retailers are often so quick to offer extremely good deals on specific items—for example, a TV from Best Buy for only $50, or a set of knives from Walmart for $30. If these companies sold these so-called doorbusters and nothing else, they'd lose money. The point of the offer is to get people through the door, because retailers are confident that once you're in, you'll buy much more, at full price.

Interestingly, people are actually much more impulsive in store than they are when shopping online. A 2013 Global Study by LivePerson found that, while impulsive decision making is common everywhere, it's almost twice as likely to happen at a store than online.[27] A deliberately exhausting environment, paired with glucose depletion, can go a long way!

EMOTION

Perhaps the biggest opponent to our cognitive control is emotion. When you're extremely angry, sad, happy, or experiencing other strong emotions, you may act in ways that make little sense, even to you once you come back to baseline. There are people currently serving life sentences for making a single emotional decision—one that, had they waited for their emotions to subside, they might not have made. This is not to say that cold, calculating decisions are best. Indeed, emotions can contribute in significant positive ways to our decision making, like how pride in one's education can drive one to finish a master's program or how love for one's children influences the kind of environment one provides them. Should you marry your long-time boyfriend or girlfriend? Considering your emotional experience with the person, and the emotional implications of this decision, are both rational and necessary.

Yet emotion generally influences our decision making for the worse—and our ability to control whether we act on our emotional impulses heavily impacts the decisions we make. If our cognitive control is all fueled up, we're able to recognize our emotional impulses and make a more deliberative decision whether or not to act on them. But if we're low here, we're much more prone to just go on impulse. And just like using manual mode to resist other impulses, constantly suppressing our emotions can wear down our cognitive control. If we are bombarded with emotional stimuli we're trying to resist all day long, we're more likely to fall back on using automatic mode when we shouldn't—like when we're shopping.

TNS Global found that more than half of Americans admit to regularly using shopping as a means to cope with their emotions, or as "retail therapy."[28] Similarly, most people report having purchased something to cheer themselves up, and a quarter had made a major purchase as a form of celebration.[29]

Overall, marketing that appeals to our emotions is extremely effective because of how easily it overcomes our cognitive control to direct our behavior. Just ask the ACLU. In 2017, reports surfaced alleging Donald Trump's real estate company had practiced gross racial discrimination in the rental and purchase of apartments dating back to the 1970s. If you are the type of citizen to be appalled by this behavior, you are primed to act. The strength of that emotion can sidestep your cognitive control and send you back into automatic mode. The ACLU encouraged that increased likelihood to act on impulse by using the following image to urge people to donate:

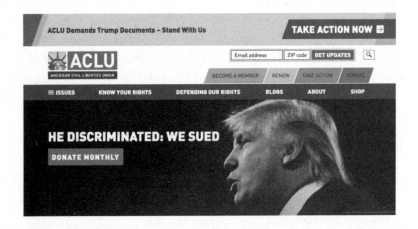

The result was $24 million raised in a mere forty-eight hours.

Emotion-laden advertising is extraordinarily common—and extraordinarily effective. In a sweeping review of nearly nine hundred case studies, researchers at the Institute of Practitioners in the UK directly examined the persuasiveness of "emotional" versus "rational" appeals in advertising campaigns. It wasn't even close. The report clearly found that the more emotional viewers perceived the campaign to be, the more persuasive it was. Further, the *most* effective advertising campaigns had little to no rational content at all.[30] Not too flattering regarding our rational capabilities!

OF TWO MINDS—THE K FACTOR

Of course, we don't live binary lives where all of our decisions neatly fit in one of two categories, impulsive or resistive, automatic or manual. Reality is closer to a spectrum. We move between these two extremes using cognitive control. And in neuroscience, the measure of how well you can resist an impulse is called your *K factor*.

There's an experiment that behavioral scientists use to look at something called *intertemporal choice*: the degree to which time influences our psychological valuation of money. Think about it like the Marshmallow Test for adults, with a little added math. It tests our response to different monetary options of varying amounts and timescales. Participants choose between two options: "Do you want $10 now, or $12 in two days?" Participants respond to a long series of these questions, each involving slightly different amounts of money and lengths of time. After about fifty or so of these questions, you can see a discernable pattern in how much an individual values immediate reward over long-term investment. This pattern, averaged over many trials, reveals your K factor.

Everyone has a K factor. It is where you stand on a scale of impulsivity versus control. High-K individuals are able to delay immediate gratification and therefore better optimize for long-term interests. Low-K individuals give in to immediate impulses, often at the expense of longer-term rewards. A helpful way to think about the K factor is in terms of automatic versus manual mode: a high-K individual is very manual-mode oriented. A low-K individual typically goes with the default automatic mode.

We can easily see how being low K can hinder our longer-term best interests. Consider the famous Ultimatum Game paradigm. You and another person are given a sum of money (say $10) and are tasked with dividing it between the two of you. One person is randomly designated to decide how the sum should be split (e.g., $7 for me, $3 for you). They have to be cautious not to be too greedy, though, because the other person decides whether or not the bid is accepted—and if they decide not to accept, neither player receives anything. (Importantly, the two participants play each other only once, to prevent any long-term collaboration or strategy development.)

We'd all agree that any amount of money is, logically, better than no money at all. However, in these experiments, non-zero sums of about $3 or lower are consistently rejected! In our mind, we can't help thinking, *$3?! How dare you! Well, I'll show you . . .* We're willing to forgo money just to spite a complete stranger we'll never interact with again. We'll even do so to spite a computer algorithm! Our choices in the Ultimatum Game largely come down to our K factor. Participants mostly reject unfair non-zero bids, choosing to take nothing rather than allow their opponent to benefit more than them—though there is cultural variation.[31] If your first impulse would be to reject an unfair bid, you're in good company; it's only human that we experience this urge to punish the greedy person across from us (or the computer we're interacting with). But, interestingly, the degree to which we are able to suppress that urge to punish ends up determining our ultimate response. We know this because individual measures of participants' self-control are highly correlated with their willingness to *not* reject a bid, even when it's unfair. And perhaps a more emphatic source of evidence is that when people are given alcohol prior to playing this game, they're significantly more likely to reject unfair bids.[32] Anyone who has ever witnessed a bar fight emerge seemingly out of nothing can tell you that alcohol is kryptonite to cognitive control.

At any given time, our cognitive control is somewhere along this spectrum from high K (controlled, deliberative, System 2 oriented) on one end to low K (impulsive, automatic, System 1 oriented) on the other. And while we each have a constitutional position on the K scale—our default position—the contextual factors reviewed here, such as emotion, satiety, and environment, can move us along this spectrum in either direction. Our position on the K spectrum (i.e., how much cognitive control we have) at any given moment is crucial to our decisions as consumers: what leads us to a purchase when we're low K may not make much of a dent if we're in a high-K state.

LOW-K SALES TACTICS

Marketers benefit from catching consumers in moments of weakness, of low K, because it's easier to sell them products they might otherwise reject. Constitutionally low-K consumers are a marketer's dream, and low-K-friendly marketing tactics are ones that catch us at our most reactive and then— often by pressing fast-forward on our decision making—double down on our impulsivity.

"Flash sale" companies feed on low-K automatic mode. Gilt is one of the pioneers of flash clothing sales, all of which function off the same blueprint: items on sale have an expiration, and the expiring clock is prominently displayed, counting down by the second. The fact that the deal is only available for a "limited time" drives the fear of missing it—a strong emotion—therefore pushing your brain to make the decision in automatic mode.

Research has revealed that 42 percent of clothing purchases[33] made by people aged 13 to 24 are impulsive, unplanned acts. Seems consumers don't get wiser as they get older: 25- to 34-year-olds exhibited the same impulsive behavior as teens. Even at the theoretically wisest age, 56 to 70, over a third of clothing purchased is impulsive. Flash sales are the crystallization of the low-K sales strategy: elicit an impulse in the consumer, then make executing on that impulse as quick and frictionless as possible.

Amazon has its own set of flash sales under the names Gold Box Deal of the Day, which lasts all day; and Lightning Deals, which are only available for a few hours and cover limited items in stock. The few items that come incredibly cheap on Prime Day work in a similar fashion—they're e-commerce's version of doorbusters. Amazon's Lightning Deals come with a timer countdown and an inventory meter, which approaches 100 percent as other customers buy the flash inventory, further intensifying the sense of urgency that flips us into automatic mode.

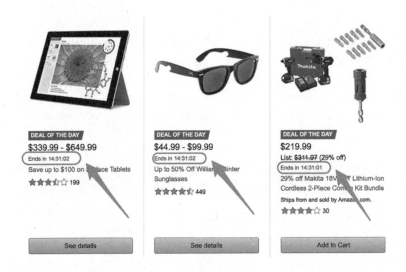

Another low-K-friendly marketing tactic is offering free shipping and free returns. On the surface, these benefit the consumer. However, they are also the features that most encourage consumers to purchase more products online.[34] These promotions are designed to keep you from pressing pause on your impulse to buy. After all, it costs you nothing to try it out!

The distracted mind is also a low-K mind. Sarah Getz and colleagues[35] had subjects participate in a classic intertemporal experiment (e.g., would you rather have $10 now or $12 in two weeks?), except certain participants were also given a task to perform. They were told a long series of digits (648912) to remember and repeat back at the experiment's end, forcing them to continue to rehearse this information in their mind while considering the researchers' questions. These participants were much more likely to choose the immediate reward. As we saw in our discussion of deliberate versus automatic thinking, the inhibition of our automatic thinking takes work. We only have so much mental energy, and when it is being expended on other tasks, we're less able to delegate it toward inhibiting our impulses for immediate gratification.

The clearest example of mentally taxing design in the consumer world is casinos. Most people know that casinos lack clocks and that their interior design is purposely confusing to keep you "lost." But just as with malls, the psychological reason a confusing interior works so well is that it's mentally taxing. Because the casino's layout is difficult to remember, spatial tasks such as finding a bathroom, a bar, or a specific game table all tax your memory. And after your mental energy has been sapped, you are more likely to make impulsive choices. When it comes to impulsive decisions, the house always wins.

One group in particular has been noted as making much more impulsive decisions: poor people. People living below the poverty line use less preventive health care[36] and tend to overspend on luxury items beyond their means.[37] Instead of buying groceries and vegetables, they often go for the immediately gratifying burger. It would be easy to assume that these tendencies—an intrinsic low-K factor—are what lead to poverty in the first place. However, research by Jiaying Zhao and colleagues found this was not the case.[38] Instead, the mental state associated with poverty—high stress, and the accompanying mental exhaustion—was the primary culprit. Having poor individuals think about their finances eroded their ability to make economic decisions more in line with their long-term best interests. These findings were replicated with farmers, who undergo a yearly cycle of stress related to their crops: the same farmer shows diminished cognitive performance right before harvest, when poor, as compared with after harvest, when assets are more plentiful.

In other words, contrary to popular thought, poverty doesn't compel people to buy fast food because it's the cheaper economic decision—in many cases, it's not. Instead, poverty compels people to buy fast food because, due to economic stress, their brain's decision making is biased toward immediate enjoyment, and away from longer-term solutions. As Dr. Zhao describes, "For years, people thought poor people were poor because they made poor decisions which led them to be poor. But what we're finding is that the opposite is true: Being poor in itself leads to making poor decisions."[39] And this unfortunately perpetuates a vicious cycle: poor people experience chronic stress and hunger, which lead them to make poor, impulsive choices, which in turn keep them poor.

Would giving poor people money change impulse buying for the better, then? Early results suggest so. In one of the largest experiments exploring the effectiveness of a Universal Basic Income to date, Zhao collaborated with the Vancouver government to provide a group of one hundred homeless people a direct, no-strings-attached lump sum of $8,000 each. A cynic might guess that the first thing they did was use the money to go out and have a good time. The results indicate that was not at all the case. The experiment is still in progress as of this writing, but so far the findings point to a promising insight: relieved of the mental burden of poverty, and so better equipped to make sound economic choices, participants in the study did so.

HIGH-K SALES TACTICS

Maybe you score high on K factor. What then? Are you immune to marketing? Not at all. The strategy marketers use to sell to you is simply different. Low-K marketing strategies speed the consumer up, whereas high-K strategies do exactly the opposite by slowing them down.

Why use high-K marketing at all if low K works so well? Turns out, low K doesn't work well for the type of buying decisions that force us into a manual model, because what's being purchased is more expensive or more complicated, or the purchase is being completed over a longer period of time. High-K tactics are most effective when a consumer must make a complex decision requiring additional information or further justification.

Progressive Insurance was, well, progressive, when it launched its comparison engine. It was the first major auto insurance company to provide quotes not only for their own insurance products, but also for their competitors'. Why? Well, which auto insurance to buy tends to be a fairly analytical decision, because making it requires us to consider several factors of multiple policies, such as risk, probability, coverage, out-of-pocket costs, and premiums. It can also be a fairly expensive decision, which we're extra-motivated to get right. Moreover, the insurance you buy also tends to be for the long term; you're not just deciding how best to spend $125 now, but which insurance company you should pay $125 to every month. Progressive gave comparison shoppers a reason to come to their site (and only their site) versus competitors' because they positioned themselves as a one-stop shop for quotes.

The comparison quotes slow the consumer down, giving them data to chew on before making a decision. The buyer gets to feel smart for comparing prices, and that comparison gives them a logical justification for their eventual choice of insurance. By playing into the mode of thinking that was most natural for their customers, Progressive prospered. Their stock price doubled one year after releasing their comparison-shopping tool.[40] Progressive knows customers are shopping around already, so why not be transparent and friendly, and let customers do all of their System 2 thinking without leaving their site?

Our context-specific desire for a high-K buying experience explains the ubiquity of metasearch travel sites. Kayak does this very well, appealing to manual mode by providing quotes for flights, car rentals, and hotel bookings from hundreds of other sites all in one place. They give you more data points to help you slow down and make a rational, comparative decision—but do so more quickly and easily than if you had to visit all those sites individually.

Instead of using an expiring price or a limited quantity to speed up our decision making, high-K designs slow us down and play into the kind of deliberative thinking that customers are likely doing already for this type of purchase. What do companies get out of this? Consider them as adopting an "if you can't beat 'em, join 'em" policy when it comes to System 2 thinking. If you know your customer is going to be thinking about your product, you can take advantage of this by directing them to think about the "right" things—the things that will lead them to purchase from you. A website's features can play into this by giving the customer something specific to think and deliberate about.

Evernote's sales page is a great example of this. They understand their customer base well enough to know that power users do not buy a subscription note-taking application on a whim, and that customers want to know exactly what they are getting. Their sales page lists sixteen features available in the vertical column and adds the pricing plans horizontally across the top: Free, Pro, and Enterprise. (Evernote even gets bonus points for using the aforementioned reference tactic to draw the user to the middle choice.)

Plans & Pricing		Free	Pro	Enterprise
		For: Personal Use, Casual Enthusiast	For: Small Businesses, Social Media Professionals & Consultants (from $9.99/month)	For: Businesses, Organizations, Agencies & Governments
		Get Started Now	Get Started Now	Get Started Now
Social Profiles	?	Up to 3	50 included*	Unlimited
Enhanced Analytics Reports	?	Basic	1 included*	Unlimited
Message Scheduling	?	Basic	Advanced	Unlimited
Team Members	?	None	1 included*	Up to 500,000
Campaigns	?	2 included	2 included, up to 8*	Up to 18*
App Integrations	?	Basic	Basic	Unlimited
RSS	?	Up to 2	Unlimited	Unlimited
Hootsuite University	?	Optional	Optional	Included for all seats
Security	?		✔	Advanced
Vanity/Custom URL's	?		Optional	✔
Enhanced technical support	?		Optional	✔
Professional services	?			All inclusive
Custom Permissions	?			✔
Brand Protection	?			✔
Risk & Policy Management	?			✔
Dedicated Account Rep.	?			✔
		Get Started Now	Get Started Now (from $9.99/month)	Get Started Now

Just as we discussed in the introduction to K factor, people are neither all System 1 nor all System 2. And when you're a site that wants to appeal to all kinds of people, and sell products that lend themselves to impulse buys as well as deliberative thinking, you want to cover all your bases. Amazon is a great example of this, in the way it caters to both automatic and manual modes. Initially, Amazon Prime was offered for a one-time annual fee. Over time, Amazon switched to providing two options: a month-by-month choice (for quick automatic deciders) and an annual choice (for deliberate manual deciders). There's something for everyone.

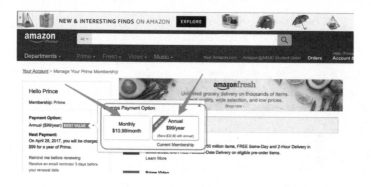

THE QUEST FOR CONTROL

All of this is fine and interesting, but how can we maintain a more controlled, deliberative style of thinking in our own decision making? Aside from remaining aware of these factors (and keeping a full belly of glucose-rich foods!), are there practical steps we can take to exert more cognitive control? The question of self-control goes well beyond the scope of this book, but one approach to better decision making that seems particularly effective is planning.[41] If you know you have a hard time resisting ice cream, don't have ice cream in the fridge. Plan ahead to make it as difficult as possible to give in to your impulses. Instead of forcing yourself to resist this temptation, expend less cognitive control by switching to manual mode up front to guide your future self. The Kitchen Safe is a great example of a product designed to help you do this. It's a simple contraption that can be used for anything tempting, from candy to your iPhone: you put something inside that you don't want yourself to be able to access, close it up, and hit the timer. It won't unlock until the timer goes off.

We saw how poverty primes people to lean heavily toward automatic decision making. Similarly, financial planning is difficult for people whose bank accounts are empty or overdrawn. One series of experiments showed that something as simple as a telephone prompt that asks people to slow down and think can change their financial behavior. In the studies,[42] credit card call-in systems were altered so that they not only read the participant their due balance, but also asked them when they intended to pay that balance off. This simple change dramatically increased the likelihood that the balance would be paid, and the vast majority were even paid off within the time window the person specified on that call. Prompts like this push the listener into manual mode long enough to curb automatic thinking, and help them act more deliberately.

Long-term financial planning can be challenging regardless of socio-economic status. ING Bank did an excellent job of designing for manual mode in a way that benefited both themselves and their customers. Before asking customers to commit to the amount they would automatically save each month, ING asked a set of customers to think for a moment about all the positive things that would happen in their life if they saved more. Controlling for all other variables, ING saw a 20 percent increase in 401(k) enrollment in that group compared to similar customers.

The best thing we can do to help ourselves out is make long-term plans while in the right, high-K state of mind—when we're fully availed of all of our cognitive resources. And then, once that plan is made (e.g., don't eat cookies, save 10 percent each month for retirement), carry out a plan of execution that does not rely on constant thinking to be maintained. That 10 percent is going to be deducted automatically each month, without you having to conjure up the System 2 resources every time to make it happen. Ironically, the best thing we can do with System 2 is make a decision that doesn't require System 2 to get involved. Thinking = depletion of cognitive resources = more impulsivity. Think once, make the best decision possible, and then outsource the execution of that decision to some external system you never have to think about again.

Whether it's resisting impulses, delaying gratification, or maintaining our wits in a retail environment, cognitive control is key. The amount of control we have and the degree to which we can maintain it ultimately determines how we act in a broad range of scenarios. Are we in control, or are we driving in automatic?

Automatic mode isn't always a bad thing, even in decision making. There are times when the benefit of speed trumps the benefit of a thoroughly examined decision. That's as true in the consumer world as anywhere else. But the more in control we are of our buying decisions, the more likely we are to optimize for success, especially long term.

In the real world of science *non*fiction, a low-K buyer like Captain Kirk would be a marketer's fantasy. High-K Spock, on the other hand, would make the ideal consumer's consumer—relentlessly rational in his calculations, and immune to impulse. Embodying a bit more Spock while shopping just might be what we need to *live long and prosper.*

Chapter 6

PLEASURE – PAIN = PURCHASE

How Pleasure and Pain Drive Us to Buy

I magine trying to add up all of the physical objects you own—everything you've bought, everything you've received as gifts, the furniture in your house, the items in the closet, the pictures hanging on the wall. Even the sentimental stuff: the old letters and love notes, graduation certificates and postcards. How many items would that be? And how long would it take to count them all?

In 2001, Michael Landy owned 7,227 objects. Over several months, he counted everything he had accumulated during the course of his thirty-seven years, down to the pesky receipts.

Landy quantified his possessions with one specific goal: to destroy them all. Everything. Between February 10 and February 24, 2001, his entire inventory of personal belongings—from his car, to his computer, to the sheepskin coat his father gifted him—was publicly destroyed. All of the items were brought to a large warehouse, tagged, put in yellow containers, and funneled along a conveyor belt to where Landy, along with twelve assistants, stripped, shredded, crushed, and dismantled the objects as an art project called "Break Down."[1] After it was all over, Landy was left with nothing but the blue workman's jumpsuit he was wearing.

Perhaps the most interesting aspect of Landy's work was the reaction of onlookers who saw the process unfold. It triggered an emotion nothing short of horror. James Lingwood, the curator for the project, told the BBC that onlookers were "deeply unsettled and sometimes appalled . . . to see the destruction of personal mementos, letters, photographs, works of art. That is deeply disturbing."[2]

At the other end of the spectrum, there are people who hoard literal tons of worthless objects, and can't part with anything they've brought into their house. Hoarding behavior is strikingly common, noted to exist in 2 to 5 percent of American adults.[3] Entire houses can be literally filled with seemingly meaningless objects. Yet despite these piles taking over their lives, hoarders get incredible anxiety at even the thought of parting with so much as a pen they've never even taken out of the packaging.

From Landy to hoarders, how can we understand this incredible spectrum of attitude and behavior toward owning things? The explanation comes down to two extremely rudimentary motivations: pleasure and pain. We navigate life by making decisions that maximize pleasure and/or minimize pain. The formula as applied to our consumer lives is simple: *pleasure minus pain equals purchase.*

In one fascinating fMRI investigation, Stanford neuroscientist Brian Knutson and colleagues[4] found that a purchase could be predicted largely by the difference in activation between the brain's pleasure center (nucleus accumbens) and the pain center (insular cortex). Pleasure was measured when the product was presented, and pain was measured when the price was presented. If activity in the brain's pleasure area was stronger than the activity in the brain's pain area, a purchase was extremely likely. Similarly, if pain outweighed pleasure, a purchase was not likely. In other words, pleasure minus pain equals purchase. (Or technically, *if Pleasure − Pain > 0, Purchase*, but that's not as catchy.)

Put more broadly, if the anticipated pleasure of a thing is greater than the pain of obtaining it, we act. For Landy, the pleasure of a possession-free life (or of staging the art installation!) was higher than the pain of burning his possessions. For hoarders, the pain of ridding themselves of their possessions is higher than the pleasure of a clean home.

Smart brands optimize for the ways we are driven to maximize pleasure and minimize pain. But that's not an easy task. For one, the ways in which we experience pain and pleasure are anything but straightforward. Also, the ways in which our behavior is shaped by pleasurable and painful experiences is not always straightforward, either. The result is a strange consumer world.

CHASING PLEASURE

On the one hand, pleasure is intuitive. We know it when we experience it. We enjoy it and want more of it. But we're actually surprisingly oblivious to how it impacts our long-term mood, behavior, and sense of happiness. Let's take a closer look at the quirks of pleasure.

PLEASURE QUIRK #1: IT'S FLEETING

> Willy Wonka: But Charlie, don't forget what happened to the man who suddenly got everything he wanted.
> Charlie Bucket: What happened?
> Willy Wonka: He lived happily ever after.

It would be great if we were built like this. Unfortunately, Mr. Wonka's parable isn't supported.

Pleasure is notoriously fleeting. Think about the last time you ate a delicious piece of cake. You see it there in front of you, the frosting glistening, the anticipation of its flavor exciting your taste buds. You stab your fork in and bring the first bite to your mouth. The pleasure is here. It is everything you hoped and more! You even close your eyes to savor the flavor. Pause and ask yourself: How long was the actual pleasurable experience itself? How much time elapsed between when you experienced the pleasure . . . and when you started thinking about the next bite? One second? Two? Almost as quickly as we experience pleasure, we're already looking for more.

At the biological level of the brain, pleasure climbs and peaks at the moment *just before* our first experience of a thing. The first bite of a cheesecake, the first drive in a new car, the first jog in a new pair of running shoes.

The pleasure then rolls downhill with every additional bite, drive, or jog: the second gives less pleasure, the third even less, and so on.

On the surface, this is strange. Why does the brain reward you for wanting something and then take the reward away as soon as you have it? Put in the context of our evolutionary drives, the brain is motivating us for survival. Many things that give us pleasure are also key to our survival. We need to always be seeking out vital things like sex, food, and the like in order to survive. If we were suddenly content when we got what we want, we wouldn't feel a need to seek out and obtain more of it. The carrot needs to be kept dangling. Satisfaction and contentment—at least of the longer-term variety—is at odds with survival. This is why the brain experiences satisfaction and pleasure all too briefly—or, more accurately speaking, why the brain experiences less pleasure the moment satisfaction is reached. Evolution built this mechanism to push us to always want more.

Daniel Nettle puts it best in *The Science of Happiness*: "Happiness is a handmaiden to evolution's purposes here, functioning not so much as an actual reward but as an imaginary goal that gives us direction and purpose. [Thomas] Jefferson's fundamental right, after all, was not happiness itself, but the *pursuit* of happiness." We are driven forward toward future anticipation of pleasure.

Our unending drive for new and more and different provides the consumer world with myriad opportunities to sell us things. But this strange quirk of pleasure sets us up to be unhappy with our purchases in the long term.

It's like when you were a kid and begged your parents for months to buy you a new bike. Christmas came and you got it. Your world felt complete. But after a few days of playing with your bike? The world was incomplete again. The pleasure you felt from the idea of the bike peaked the day you got it. Your eyes have already wandered to the next toy. Psychologists call this the *hedonic treadmill*—the process of pursuing, achieving, and then moving on to the pursuit of the next thing after an initial burst of pleasure.

Not a whole lot changes for us as adults, except we no longer need to beg our parents to finance our ride on the hedonic treadmill. We can pay for it all on our own! The consumer world happily obliges our fleeting sense of enjoyment with what we already own by constantly reminding us that what we have is old and outdated, and getting us excited about "the next big thing."

Apple's iPhone model-release schedule, for example, is planned hedonism. Until 2015, each new iPhone was released in a planned two-year cycle. The first year of a new model, the phone was all new, sporting a new exterior design. The second year, the iPhone S year, the phone sported the same exterior design, but now had powerful new internals. You had either an outdated interior or an outdated exterior within a year of owning any iPhone. The third year, well, you got a completely redesigned iPhone and the process started all over again.

Interestingly, it turns out that our physical dexterity becomes as attuned to this schedule as our wallets. In a fascinating study from Columbia Business School, researchers found that you're much more likely to be careless with your phone if there's a newer, better version of the product available or soon to come.[5] The researchers looked at a dataset of over three thousand lost iPhones, and found there was a curious spike in losses right before a new model was released. This was further supported by a survey of over six hundred self-reports of iPhone neglect and damage, which, again, showed a huge uptick right after a new model was announced. Even if we feign disappointment that we drop our phone, or leave it in a cab, we may unconsciously just be giving ourselves an excuse to get the latest model!

The sports video-game industry provides another great opportunity for planned hedonism. Electronic Arts' FIFA franchise of soccer (or "football"—sorry again!) video games is the world's favorite sports game, having sold more than a quarter billion copies.[6] In the USA, three of the top-five bestselling games of 2017 and 2018 were sports games. Unlike Apple's two-year strategy, sports video games release a new product every year—one only marginally tweaked to include recent roster changes and extremely minor but nonetheless heavily hyped gameplay updates. Despite the only minor changes, hedonic treadmillers fork over more than $60 year after year (your author Matt has been caught on this exact hedonic treadmill). The anticipation is rewarded by pleasure-inducing dopamine that starts evaporating the moment you start playing the game.

PLEASURE QUIRK #2: WE ENJOY RANDOMNESS

The dissipating nature of pleasure has another massive consequence, one that goes well beyond our subconscious desire for the newest, shiniest gadget. Fifty years before Steve Jobs unveiled the first iPhone, another Bay Area figure interested in Zen philosophy was making his mark: Alan Watts, the British-born philosopher renowned for his wit and wisdom, who has been largely credited with importing Eastern ideas to Western society. During the 1960s and '70s, he would host large dinner conversations and give lectures and workshops at various universities. One evening he was entertaining a series of questions from the crowd when he was asked, "What is the meaning of life?" No pressure, Alan! His reply did not disappoint:

> You have to try and find out what you want, and so I went into that very thoroughly, what do I want to happen? And of course as soon as you ask yourself that you begin to fantasize, and our amazing technology is of course an expression of human desire, desire for power, for what we want to achieve. So I simply set myself to thinking through how far we could go. And so I soon found myself at a great push-button place, where I had a fantastic mechanism with buttons available for every conceivable thing I could wish. So I spent quite a bit of time playing with those . . . you press one button and here's Cleopatra . . . and press this button and symphonic music, in sixteen-channel sound . . . all possible pleasures are available . . . You suddenly notice there's a button labeled "Surprise." You push that, and here we are.

What Watts artfully distills here is another fundamental driver of human behavior: a deep, hidden love of randomness. Pleasure is best served on a plate of randomness.

This preference for randomness can be seen deep in the brain. In 2001, neuroscientist Greg Burns looked at how predictability influences our experience of pleasure[7] using fMRI. The setup was simple: participants lay flat in the scanner with a tube in their mouths that administered small, pleasurable bursts of juice at various times. In one study condition, the juice came at regular ten-second intervals. In the other condition, the same overall amount of juice was given, but the timing of the administration was random and unpredictable. They found that activity in the nucleus accumbens was significantly higher when the juice was dispensed unpredictably than when it was dispensed in a predictable fashion. Moreover, they found that participants' pleasure response deflated rapidly as more and more juice came—but *only* when it was dispensed in predictable intervals. When you know what reward is coming and when, you begin enjoying it less and less. It's the pleasure that we *can't* predict that endures, fresh each time.

Random pleasures can be deliberately baked into the consumer experience to great effect. Research has found that participants were three times more likely to buy a coffee mug when they were told that they were *randomly* selected to receive a special discount.[8] Rapidly growing sandwich shop Pret a Manger empowers employees with a fund to comp random customers of their choosing, a plan their CEO affectionately calls "random acts of kindness."[9] Zappos, a company with one of the highest customer service ratings in any industry, is known to catch its customers off guard with pleasurable surprises.[10] They once went door to door through the entire town of Hanover, New Hampshire, surprising each customer at the door with gifts like warm gloves and scarves.[11]

We're willing to go out of our way to give ourselves the best chance at receiving a random, unexpected pleasure. Would you rather have a 100 percent chance of a 50 percent discount on an item, or spin a wheel to get a random discount of anything from 0 to 100 percent? Even when the overall expected value is the same, most people choose to go with the random discount over the sure thing. Observations like this have also led to the development of unique, lottery-like savings accounts.[12] When you put your money in a savings account, instead of getting a steady 1 percent interest rate, you get a randomized return—which can result in gains of anything between $0 and $10,000. It's essentially gambling with your savings yield. The allure of this potential random pleasure is enough for many consumers to forgo a traditional savings plan.[13]

PLEASURE QUIRK #3: WE'RE BAD AT PREDICTING FUTURE PLEASURE

How happy would you be if you got free ice cream for thirty days? Daniel Kahneman provided an exploration of this exact question through an experiment in which he had participants eat ice cream (free of charge) every day for thirty days. At first, participants were understandably enthusiastic. Everyone predicted that their enjoyment of the ice cream would increase day to day, and by day thirty, they would be in ice cream bliss. This couldn't have been further from the truth. People were begging to drop out of the study by day ten, and those who did make it to the end felt miserable. The idea of ice cream every day was great. The reality, not so much.

Some of this miscalculation, no doubt, was because the "pleasure" of ice cream, usually a once-in-a-while treat, became predictable. But because we derive more pleasure from wanting something than from having it—because the brain engineers pleasure only in the chase—our desire for something in the present is *always* far greater than our actual enjoyment of it will be in the future. Humans don't calibrate for this, and it makes us terrible predictors of what will actually make us happy. Behavioral economists call the ability to predict how you will feel in the future *affective forecasting*, and we're horrible at it.

PLEASURE QUIRK #4: MORE CHOICE ≠ MORE PLEASURE

Choice is a prime example of how humans struggle at predicting their future happiness. Choices are good because the more options you have, the more likely you'll get what you want. Right?

You may feel like you want choices, or the freedom to re-choose, if you regret your first choice. But in fact, too many options can lead you down a path of miserable ambivalence.[14]

This is known as the *paradox of choice*, and it was made famous by something called the "jam study" in 2000.[15] On one day, shoppers at an upscale food market saw a display table with twenty-four varieties of gourmet jam. On another day, shoppers saw a similar table, except with only six varieties of jam. People who saw the twenty-four-variety display were significantly less likely to buy than the people who saw the six-variety display. More choice also did not lead to more enjoyment. As it turned out, the customers who *did* buy from the twenty-four-variety display were less satisfied with their jams than those who bought from the six-variety display.

These days, something as simple as "I need a new pair of jeans" or "I want to buy a BMW" turns into a mountain of choices for you to make.

Here are your options if you want to buy a pair of Levi's: eight cuts, six colors, three options of stretch. Altogether, that equals 144 different disparate choices. If you want to buy a BMW, you must choose from one of ten models, manual or auto transmission, rear or all-wheel drive, at least two engine options, twelve colors, six choices of wheels, five interior trims, eight leather options, and another eight possible add-on packages. This adds up to a total of 1.8 million possible car options.

Understandably, there was a lot of excitement about paradox of choice when the jam study's findings first came out. However, attempts to replicate the findings have yielded mixed results. A greater number of choices isn't always associated with greater anxiety, and directly reducing choice only sometimes results in a more enjoyable experience. The devil, as they say, is in the details.

A meta-analytic review[16] of over fifty studies found that it's not really the *number of choices*, per se, that affects your mood. Rather, it's the actual *act of choosing*. Especially for products that we want, as opposed to those we need, choice is tiring.[17] What's more mentally taxing—thumbing through a menu of ten items, or thirty? The act of choosing forces your brain out of its default, automatic mode, and into manual mode, as discussed last chapter. Remember the law of least mental effort: all things being equal, the brain prefer less work as opposed to more. Choosing makes the lazy brain work.

As you might imagine, the extra effort involved in evaluating an abundance of options affects your decision making in another way: you make riskier decisions. In investment terms, you're apt to pick a high-risk, high-yield junk bond over a much safer but lower-yield blue chip stock. One experiment found that people faced with larger numbers of options not only did less research per option but also ultimately chose options that were much riskier. Choice can easily overwhelm us, leading both to discomfort and poor decision making.[18] Not exactly a recipe for happiness!

People want options, in order to feel empowered, and companies want to offer them. But the act of choosing can be mentally burdensome. How companies resolve this oxymoron is by turning the pain of choosing into the pleasure of abundance.

As the number of buying options has multiplied, companies and customers have converged toward simplified, seamless shopping experiences.[19] Companies that can simplify the act of choosing are handsomely rewarded. Research suggests that brands that successfully simplify consumer decision making—say, by providing an easy, user-friendly way to see all of the product offerings—are 115 percent more likely to be viewed positively and recommended to a friend.[20]

It is easy to forget, between its origins as a bookstore and its current existence as the "everything store," that what originally made Amazon great was its incredible ability to aggregate options. Amazon put books in a warehouse rather than on store shelves, which made it easy to carry a larger selection. However, a large selection is only good if you can find what you're looking for in it. Amazon's answer to that problem was A9: the search algorithm that powers not only searches for books but also "Search Inside the Book" and Amazon's recommendation engine for non-book products. Introduced in 2003, the A9 algorithm made the act of searching and choosing a lot easier in a world where search engines were still in their infancy.

A platform with a similarly large inventory, Netflix, likewise turns the pain of choice into the pleasure of abundance. In 2018, Netflix carried over 13,000 streaming titles.[21] And over the years, Netflix has largely succeeded at creating an algorithm so intelligent that search has become secondary to recommendation. You never have to search through Netflix's deep library of titles for something you'll like, because everything you could want to watch (according to the algorithm) is already there on your home screen.

The way we choose in the consumer world mirrors more generally how we choose in life. Harvard psychology professor Dan Gilbert tested the broader impact of choice on happiness with undergraduates. Gilbert presented students with a series of black-and-white photos, and had them pick the two they liked best. Of those two, one they got to take home, and one they would donate to the lab as proof they had done the experiment. One group of students were told that their decisions were final. Another group was told they could come back anytime and exchange their pictures for the ones they gave to the lab. A month later, Gilbert's team asked everyone how happy they were with their photo choices. There was no contest. Participants who didn't have the choice to return their item were almost twice as happy as the group who could exchange anytime.

These results have been replicated in other studies, some involving chocolates instead of photographs.[22] Ultimately, people who had no choice but to live with their decisions were significantly happier with their selections than those who received an out and didn't experience "closure" in their decisions.

Examined through the lens of consumer experience, this has significant implications. Think about return policies, for example: a window of time in which choice lingers. Research shows that you'll be happier with your decision if you didn't have one. (Why, then, do companies have them? Because customers want them, even if the policies ultimately make them unhappy in the long run.)

Applying this to relationships is fascinating. Research shows[23] that 6 percent of arranged marriages (not forced marriages) end in divorce, sharply lower than the global divorce rate of 44 percent.[24] One possible explanation is arranged marriages don't have a refund policy, so to speak, whereas love marriages do. But are arranged couples happy? Dr. Pamela Regan's research comparing love and arranged marriages in the US found, unexpectedly, that ratings of love, satisfaction, and commitment in arranged marriages were equal to those in their love-marriage counterparts.[25]

FROM PLEASURE TO PAIN

There are many ways to look at pleasure and how it drives our behavior, but pleasure is only one half of the equation. Remember, Pleasure – Pain = Purchase. Things get zanier when pain enters our consumer lives.

NUMBING THE PAIN OF PAYING

What's the most painful part of a purchase? Despite what Lil Wayne would have you believe, making it rain is difficult. The most painful part of a purchase is the payment itself.

People generally dislike parting with money. When neuroscientists looked inside the brain in the act of making a purchase, they found that paying is literally a pain. Experiments using fMRI imaging have found that thinking about the price of a product, especially when that price is high, is associated with activity in the brain's insular cortex, the same region that is active when we feel physical pain or experience feelings of disgust.[26]

One way to alleviate the pain of purchase is, of course, to drop the price. Parting with $5 feels much less painful than parting with $50. But for businesses, that strategy makes neither sense nor cents. Dropping prices means reduced revenues. Plus, recall from chapter one that in high-class industries, a drop in price can also mean a drop in perceived quality. So instead, companies focus on a second method of pain alleviation: reducing the pain of the payment *process*, by tapping into human quirks in pain perception.

As you saw in chapter five, marketers try to make consumers' decisions as quick and easy as possible. The same is true for payment: the quicker and easier (in other words, the less painful), the better. If "don't make me think" is the strategy for product selection, "don't make me feel" would be the mantra for payments. Businesses want to garner the largest payments possible, while making the payment process feel as innocuous as possible.

The most painful way to part with money is actually, physically handing over physical bills. One second you're holding money in your hand, relishing in its power, and the next moment, it's gone and out of your life. It's the opposite of being broken up with: it hurts way more in person than over the phone or text. The more concrete the financial loss you experience, the more painful it is.

Unsurprisingly, then, the more abstract the payment experience is, the less it hurts. This is part of the reason why Vegas is so dangerous. You exchange your cold hard cash for chips, and since it's a trade, it doesn't feel like you're losing anything. But you feel much less attached to these chips than you do actual bills. You feel the pain of losing them less and less—and keep on gambling more.

Credit cards take this to the next level. Consumers spend significantly more when shopping with a credit card than when using cash.[27] They also spend more often: Visa processes over 100 billion transactions every year, or about 3,500 per second![28] When you use a credit card, it simply doesn't feel like you're spending money the same way. You're swiping a card, which you then keep, instead of physically handing something over. There's nothing visceral about the monetary loss.

Even less visceral? Digital transactions. So it's no surprise that their use has grown so quickly. In 2020, they're expected to number 728 billion[29]—and that's transactions, by the way, not dollars. Back in 2000, PayPal killed the pain of pulling out your wallet and filling in the credit card info online. Typing PayPal credentials too painful? Apple's Touch ID lets you pay with your thumb on both laptops and mobile devices. Too much of a calorie burn for you? Apple's FaceID lets you pay by just looking at your phone. What will they think of next? Maybe Amazon Super Prime, where the algorithm and payments are so fluid, you receive the package two days before you order it. Time-traveling Prime Shipping—make it happen, Bezos!

Speaking of time . . . when it comes to the pain of payment, time is the great equalizer. If someone were to offer you $10 to dance to Rick James's "Super Freak" in front of a crowd, would you do it? In a series of studies,[30] George Loewenstein of Carnegie Mellon University was able to convince people to agree to exactly this (yes, to this precise song). What he found, though, was that if he asked them to do it right then and there, very few agreed. Many more agreed if the dance was to take place several days later, but then would renege (having to give back the money!) on the day of. We'll agree to do things in the future that would otherwise be unthinkable, or at least mildly out of character, to do in the present moment. Why? Because imagining something happening in the future numbs its emotional impact on us. Think of this as the less tasty reverse of Kahneman's ice cream study—we're just as bad at predicting future pain as we are future pleasure. It's easy to feel embarrassed about doing something in front of your peers when they're right there in front of you. It's much more difficult to imagine that embarrassment in your head.

The same is true with payments. Credit cards—whether physical or saved in your phone for use with Apple Pay—serve as the ultimate time warp. Credit cards have the abstraction feature found in casino chips, but pass both chips and cash in convenience. What could be more convenient than buying something before you pay for it? In Marshmallow Test terms, using a credit card is like getting both marshmallows up front. Instead of delaying gratification until you have funds to cover the purchase, credit cards expedite gratification: you acquire things now by paying for them in the future. *Buy now, pay later* dulls the pain of payment by muddying up the financial exchange of a purchase. You feel the majority of financial weight when you have to pay the credit card off later, not in the moment, when you're swiping.

The same principle is at work in Airbnb's payment options. Historically, guests had to charge the entire amount up front when they booked. Then Airbnb made a change. Now, guests have the option of paying half now, with the other half being automatically charged a few weeks later. And unlike layaway systems, this delayed payment doesn't come with additional fees. So what's the difference? When you pay only half up front, you don't feel the pain of paying to the same extent.

How do you want to pay for this trip?

○ **Pay in full**	$395.15

● **Pay less upfront** The rest ($197.57) will be charged on Nov 29. No extra fees. Learn more	$197.58 now

No additional fees for any of these options

Pay less upfront

When you use a credit card or PayPal to book an eligible reservation, you'll have the option to pay part of the total now, and the remaining amount closer to the check-in date, with no additional fee.

Pay the rest before check-in
Your default payment method will be automatically charged on the second payment date.

Payment is automatic
We'll send a reminder 3 days before the next payment. If there are any problems with this payment, we'll email you. If we are unable to collect the remaining balance, the reservation will be canceled, and you'll be refunded based on the host's cancellation policy.

Read the Pay Less Upfront Terms.

Got It

Airbnb's checkout system, with the option of delaying the pain of payment

It's interesting to examine the history of payments in the context of pain. Furs were a pain to carry, so humans started using silver and gold coins as currency. Gold eventually became a hassle, so we turned to promissory notes, which you could take to the bank and exchange for gold. Over time, the promissory notes turned to cash, and we ditched the gold standard completely. When cash got too inconvenient to carry, we started writing checks. (Those of you who still do, please stop.) From checks, we went to plastic cards. Then we introduced chipped credit cards to take away the additional pain of sliding and signing. Next came tap credit cards; to reduce the pain of pushing the card inside, you just tap. Slide it, push it, tap it. Now you can make payments with a simple fingerprint scan, or even with a quick glance. Each technological innovation has made the payment itself easier, more abstract, and ultimately less painful—and in the process, helped companies' bottom lines.

USING THE PAIN FRAME TO DRIVE PURCHASING

While the psychological pain of *payment* may give us pause before hitting the buy button, pain in general can play an important role in driving purchasing. By tapping into our unique sensitivity to pain and loss, marketers can align consumer behavior in their best interests.

Which of the following hits harder: losing something or gaining something? Turns out, pain hurts more than pleasure feels good. While anticipated pleasure is a strong motivator, the pain of losing something we already have is one of the strongest sources of motivation there is. What Landy did to himself deliberately in destroying all his possessions, most people would pay large sums of money to prevent. In fact, they already do—the entire insurance industry is predicated on our fear of loss.

Behavioral economists call this particular drive *away* from pain "loss aversion." The clearest example of this comes from examining how we treat money. Consider the following question: you have a 50 percent chance of receiving $150 and a 50 percent chance of losing $100. Do you take the gamble? From a mathematical standpoint, you should take this bet every time. Our manual-mode model Spock would! It results in a net positive of $25: (50% chance of receiving $150 = $75) – (50% chance of losing $100 = $50) = $25.

However, the brain doesn't run simulations this way. Potential losses are weighted much heavier than potential gains. The fear of losing already drives us to make decisions aimed at avoiding this outcome. It makes evolutionary sense: hunter-gatherers felt the pain of missing a meal more strongly than the pleasure of gaining one.

Work by Daniel Kahneman and long-time collaborator Amos Tversky found most people do not take the proposed gamble. We don't play to win;

we play not to lose. In the soccer (football!) game of life, we are Chelsea Football Club, known for their strategy of "parking the bus." Once they're in the lead, players focus only on preventing the opposite team from scoring, putting almost zero effort into scoring more themselves. To the dismay of sports fans who prefer full-throttle, risk-heavy gameplay—which is, admittedly, more exciting to watch—this proved an effective strategy, and has become the backbone for much of Chelsea's success in the last decade.

So while risk aversion might not be the most exciting philosophy—either in sports or in life—taking only the most calculated risks is ideal from the standpoint of survival. You can't lose what you don't risk. And from an evolutionary perspective, protecting ourselves and what we already have is more important than any potential gain.

In the consumer world, brands operationalize the science of loss aversion via a tactic your authors call the *pain frame*: emphasizing the avoidance of loss, to persuade loss-averse individuals.

Some may call this fearmongering. Others call it politics. The most blatant uses of pain as a persuasion tool involve playing with fear, and clever politicians and their marketing teams exploit our fear of losing what we currently have to great effect through pain framing. By emphasizing what we stand to lose by not voting for a candidate, an ad can terrify us into voting for the candidate as the "safe" option. And this kind of marketing is especially effective in a zero-sum game like the US winner-take-all two-party political system.[31]

A blatant example of pain framing is an oldie but a goodie. Before the 1964 US presidential election, the campaign of incumbent Lyndon B. Johnson used fear marketing in a TV ad named "Daisy." It opens with a three- or four-year-old child counting up with each petal she plucks from a daisy—one, two, three . . . As she reaches ten, a megaphoned man's voice overtakes hers, this time counting down from ten to one. At zero, the scene cuts to a nuclear explosion. The call to action after the explosion? "Vote for President Johnson on November 3rd."

On the surface, the ad inspires fear, but what it is really doing is serving up a dose of pain: the pain of losing loved ones to nuclear war. As soon as the pain is felt, the antidote in the shape of a product is presented immediately. In this case, the product is the candidate—hence the immediate call to action, "Vote for President Johnson on November 3rd."

The pain frame was especially evident during the 2016 US presidential election and the 2016 Brexit referendum. Take a look at the victors' slogans. In the presidential election, Donald Trump reused Ronald Reagan's slogan from 1980, "Make America Great Again." In the referendum, Team Leave used the slogan "Take Back Control." Both slogans speak to a loss—specifically, recovering a loss. Trump's campaign claims America has lost its greatness, so let's make it great again. Team Leave says the UK has lost control of its own destiny, so let's take it back. Both slogans use as their frame the pain of losing something.

Pain Framing Versus Gain Framing

To better understand how pain framing works, let's look at an alternative approach to framing: a gain frame. Consider the following two questions:

1. Could you live on 80 percent of your current income?
2. Could you give up 20 percent of your current income?

These two questions are fundamentally the same. Whatever your current income is, both questions ask whether you would be willing to live on the same amount of money. But they don't *feel* the same, because they aren't framed the same. *Living on 80 percent* frames a gain, whereas *giving up 20 percent* frames a pain. The latter triggers feelings of loss in a way that the first question doesn't. As a result, we are much more likely to say yes to the first question than to the second.[32]

Products can be marketed in exactly the same way—through either a gain frame or a pain frame. Which of the following messages hits home for you?

1. Our multivitamin provides increased strength and better endurance.
2. Our multivitamin prevents loss of strength and loss of energy.

Even though the products' effects are the same, the frame makes a massive difference in how you view the product and whether or not you ultimately buy it. Especially for those of us who are particularly loss averse, pain frames tend to be much more compelling. As the Taoist teaching goes, "Between the All and the Void is just a difference in name."[33] Our perception of a product can be shifted significantly by how it's framed.

The Power of FOMO

Losing something can be extremely painful. This pain, and our drive to avoid it, extends to the loss of opportunity—losing what you could have had—and this also holds marketing power.

Research by Daugirdas Jankus at the ISM University of Management and Economics confirmed this.[34] For an e-commerce website, the team tested loss-framing offers via temporarily reduced pricing against other forms of psychological features, such as bandwagon techniques (*250 people have already bought this item*) and use of gain frame (*the quicker you order, the sooner you'll receive it*), and the control/default (neither of the above). Turns out, the offers framed to maximize FOMO (fear of missing out) resulted in the highest online sales, especially eclipsing the control/default group.

Loss-framing marketing might as well be called FOMO marketing. Marketers optimize their offers and messages to trigger this fear:

- "Limited Time Offer!"
- "Act Now!"
- "Don't Miss Out!"

This is an additional reason why the Gilt flash sales and Amazon Lightning deals discussed in the last chapter are so potent. Not only do they push you to think in automatic mode; they also amplify FOMO via loss framing.

One "brand" in particular that has made shrewd use of FOMO marketing is Swedish House Mafia, a bestselling DJ group that helped usher in the first generation of pop electronic dance music in the US. The group announced they would be breaking up in 2011. Unlike the Beatles, who didn't monetize their breakup, SHM designed a whole tour around theirs. The tour was scheduled to span the globe—Russia, India, South Africa, Stockholm, Buenos Aires, and many more. The tickets sold out within minutes.

The breakup tour ended up lasting two years, with the group method-ically adding new dates. Within a year of concluding the tour, the group released a documentary of said breakup. Then, soon after the documentary release, the group announced a reunion tour. Michael Jordan had a more convincing retirement from the NBA, and he left twice! After all of that, you might doubt the authenticity of SHM's breakup, but you cannot doubt how powerfully fear of loss fueled ticket sales.

Can a loss frame be powerful enough to make even a failed product successful? In the case of McDonald's McRib, the answer is a hard yes. You may recognize the McRib as a seasonal product, but that wasn't always the case. When the McRib first came out, it was meant to be a new staple of the menu year round. It did not sell well; the sales were poor enough, in fact, that McDonald's soon pulled the plug. However, when they reintroduced the McRib as a seasonal product, sales skyrocketed. McDonald's is careful not to market it as seasonal, despite its return every fall, because this label doesn't optimize for pain of loss. Saying "The McRib is back for a limited time only!" on the other hand, does exactly that.

All Introduction to Marketing courses hammer students with the four Ps of marketing: price, product, place, and promotion. What is of deeper importance are the new Ps of consumption: pain, pleasure, and purchase.

Our purchasing behavior is heavily driven by our relationship to plea-sure and pain, and their relationship to each other—and as we've seen, those relationships are far from straightforward. Pleasure is elusive, best achieved via its own pursuit, driven by randomness, and difficult for us to predict. And while we make purchases based on what we think will bring us pleasure (despite often being wrong), even more, we make purchases based on the avoidance of pain. Whether by directly instilling fear, or framing a product in terms of loss, tactics that play on the human drive to avoid pain are oft-used tools in the marketer's tool belt.

Looking at the roles of pleasure and pain this way, you'd be justified in seeing the modern consumer world as a pretty disturbing place. What worked in an environment of hunters and gatherers is less effective in the current environment of swipers and searchers. Now we live life one iPhone at a time, waiting for the annual surge of pleasure brought to us by Apple's magicians. The mountain of choice keeps growing every year, and we keep climbing it. Yet, at the same time, we are terrified about losing any of it.

Choosing to step off the hedonic treadmill might just be the ultimate mixture of pain and pleasure. Suddenly Michael Landy's behavior doesn't seem so odd after all.

Chapter 7

ADDICTION 2.0

Monetizing Compulsive Behavior in the Digital Age

Three out of four regular caffeine users are addicted to the substance.[1] One out of eight people worldwide is addicted to nicotine.[2] Addiction is big business. Even after the lawsuits, the public awareness, and the increasingly graphic surgeon general's warnings, in 2018 the tobacco industry's annual global revenue still surpassed half a trillion dollars.[3] But cigarettes are only part of the first generation of addictive products, and in a way, they play nice. Consumers can touch, feel, and taste products that contain nicotine. They know the potential for addiction up front, so they can make an informed decision.

There's a newer wave of addictive products that do not provide these niceties. Thanks to technology, companies no longer need a substance like nicotine to get you addicted. And unlike the companies selling coffee and cigarettes, this second wave doesn't want you to pay for the product. At least not with money. Instead, they want you to pay with your time and focus. Your attention has become the currency itself. Welcome to Addiction 2.0.

In a very real sense, our time is money. Popular platforms like Instagram and Facebook are free of charge in the classic sense, but we pay for them indirectly through our attention. There's no return policy for losing three hours binge-watching or right-swiping or feed-surfing. The longer a site or app can keep you online, and the higher your engagement, the more advertisements it can sell. In this "time-on-site" business model, the longer a platform can keep users active, the more advertising revenue it can generate.

Companies operating in this space love to use the term "engagement," but that's really just a euphemism for addiction. And for a company that thrives on the attention of its users, what could possibly be more desirable than a platform to which users are literally addicted? Your attention is for sale and it's worth billions.

The way these platforms monetize our attention is through digital advertising. Companies pay platforms like Snapchat, Instagram, and Pinterest to access their users, the same way companies used to pay to advertise in newspapers and magazines. Since the early 2000s, digital advertising has ballooned into a massive industry. More than $72 billion was spent on digital ads in 2016 in the US alone . . . with $10 billion of that going to Facebook, where users spend on average about fifty minutes a day. While Facebook currently stands at the top of the pack, it is of course not alone in this fiercely competitive new attention economy. Platforms that compete in the attention economy—some of which have a social element, and some of which don't—compete for our attention and the ad dollars that follow.

Americans spend over three hours a day on their cellphones, with the average Snapchat user opening the app an alarming eighteen times a day. As a result, companies that operate in this space are some of the most profitable organizations in human history—despite having no physical product that the consumer buys and takes home. Consider the top five most visited websites in the US as of October 2019: Google, YouTube, Facebook, Amazon, and Reddit. Only one on that list, Amazon, has an actual product or service that consumers pay for.[4] The customer has become the product; companies are now buying and selling us.

Social media companies in particular have come under heavy pressure recently for simply being too good at operating within the attention economy. They have successfully converged on technological features that exploit psychological vulnerabilities in pursuit of profit. Online platforms have the unique distinction of being the only industry in which its most influential creators are simultaneously its most vocal critics. Facebook's first president, Sean Parker, Google GChat creator Justin Rosenstein, and many other original technocrats have sounded the alarm about how these platforms rob us of our attention and hijack our psychology. Even Steve Jobs, a godlike figure in the world of technology, famously limited the use of iPhones and iPads in his own home. Marc Benioff, CEO of Salesforce, said on record, "I think that, for sure, technology has addictive qualities that we have to address, and that product designers are working to make those products more addictive and we need to rein that back." [5]

What all of today's addictive technologies have in common is their success at tapping into something fundamental—the experience of pleasure itself—and using it to drive users to behave the way the platform wants. To understand addiction, we need to dive even deeper into pleasure—not just what it feels like, but how it shapes us.

PLEASURE AND BEHAVIOR

We saw in the last chapter how our experience of pleasure is a key part of our decision making. Pleasure is also inextricably linked to our behavior, including, at the worst of times, *compulsive* behavior.

Let's start with the basics. The simplest way in which the experience of pleasure can drive our actions is through *behavioral reinforcement*. If we go to a new restaurant and enjoy a delicious meal, our brain learns there is a relationship between going to the restaurant and pleasure, so we naturally seek to return to the restaurant soon. Our enjoyment of the meal *reinforces* the behavior of going to the restaurant.

Experimental psychologist B. F. Skinner pioneered the science of reinforcement learning (which he termed *operant conditioning*) at Harvard in the 1960s. The general mechanism is incredibly intuitive. Every dog owner knows that having a stash of tasty treats is key to shaping the behavior of a new pup. Rover relieves himself outside instead of on the floor—give him a tasty treat. Rover sits on command—give him a tasty treat. And so on. Over time, Rover slowly learns a relationship between his actions and these delicious reinforcements.

Like dog owners, technology companies like Apple, Facebook, and Google are in the business of shaping behavior to keep users on sites as long as possible. Could their addictive nature be as simple as behavioral reinforcement? Are we all refreshing our Facebook News Feeds to get the tasty treats of entertainment and social gratification?

Recent data from the mobile app Moment suggests that this is not the case. Moment tracks application use on smartphones, including which apps consume the most of their users' time. Weekly, they ask users which apps they enjoy using the most, and compare this with their actual usage. If simple reinforcement drove behavior, we'd find that the most pleasure-inducing apps would be the most popular and well subscribed, but in fact, the opposite is true. An aggregate report of 2017 data shows that a higher amount of time spent on an app is consistently associated with *un*happiness: the apps we use most often are the ones we enjoy the least, and the ones we wish we spent less time on. Though to be honest, this should be obvious to anyone who has looked at the person across from them on the bus or subway as they stare endlessly into their phone. The facial expression of the now classic "mindless Instagram scroll" falls far short of pure ecstasy.

Clearly, something more complex is at work than simple behavioral reinforcement. Which isn't surprising, really. For organizations that spend billions of dollars to shape our behavior, simple operant conditioning is mere child's play. Were Facebook a dog trainer, it would make Cesar Milan the Dog Whisperer look like a kindergartner. And what separates the everyday dog owner from elite animal trainers isn't how much reinforcement is given, it's the manner in which it's given.

PLEASURE AND DOPAMINE

Recall from chapter six that the experience of pleasure is quirky. Our experience of it is fleeting in nature, optimized for its pursuit, not its acquisition. We enjoy it more when it's random and unpredictable. Feeling pleasure is crucially important to us, but we're generally bad at predicting how much pleasure we may experience in the future. There are also several quirks to how pleasure shapes our behavior. All of these quirks have to do with how the brain processes pleasurable experiences.

Scientists also know quite a lot about what pleasure looks like in the brain because of a specific region near its center, also discussed in chapter one, called the nucleus accumbens. When this area is stimulated directly using deep-brain electrodes, people report "feeling good." When monkeys are given the choice to press a button that stimulates the nucleus accumbens via such electrodes, they will do this to the point of exhaustion, choosing this self-stimulation over food, water, and even sex. When you stimulate the nucleus accumbens in people with severe clinical depression (those beyond the help of psychiatric medication) who have muscular atrophy due to a lack of smiling, it produces a smile on their faces.

In other words, the nucleus accumbens is as close to a pleasure center as there is. It proves to be a keen fortune teller as well. Researcher Greg Burns and colleagues[6] wanted to see if they could predict the success of pop songs. During the experiment, they examined brain activity in test subjects as they heard a new pop song for the first time. Pleasure proved to be a reliable predictor of the song's success: the more the nucleus accumbens fired during listening, the more popular the song turned out to be when it was released to the general public. Fascinatingly, people's subjective reports of how much they enjoyed a given song didn't correlate with its eventual success at all. Our nucleus accumbens reveals our deep enjoyment of popular guilty pleasures like "Despacito," Nickelback, Backstreet Boys, and Drake.

The nucleus accumbens contains a high concentration of neurons that communicate via dopamine—millions of them, in fact. Given this, dopamine is often called the pleasure molecule. But dopamine is more nuanced than that. Recall from the previous chapter that your brain is always driving either toward something (pleasure) or away from something (pain). Dopamine is the key player in the drive toward something; it is the *want* molecule. If you've ever felt the joy of anticipation, that is your brain releasing dopamine. What dopamine is not is the *have* molecule, meaning your brain releases dopamine when you want something—or more specifically, when you anticipate it—but not once you've acquired it. Dopamine responds to the sizzle, not the steak.

Dopamine is one of the primary reasons why wanting and pleasure are biologically distinct. Dr. Daniel Z. Lieberman and Michael E. Long, in their book dedicated to dopamine, *The Molecule of More*, do an excellent job of distilling this: "Dopaminergic excitement (that is, the thrill of anticipation) doesn't last forever, because eventually the future becomes the present. The thrilling mystery of the unknown becomes the boring familiarity of the everyday, at which point dopamine's job is done, and the letdown sets in."[7]

Think about electronic music genres like dubstep and electro house that feature a lot of buildups and drops. The buildup is as enjoyable as it is tense. This was taken to hilarious extremes in the *Saturday Night Live* skit titled "When Will the Bass Drop?," where an electro house song builds for what feels like eternity until it eventually crescendos to the long-anticipated drop—at which point the tension is finally released. This is exactly how dopamine works: the more you anticipate something occurring in the future, the higher dopamine climbs. The anticipation of pleasure is intrinsically rewarding to your brain. It would be accurate to call dopamine the *future molecule*, but calling it the *drop-the-bass molecule* is more fun.

Think about how these principles play out in dining. Taste via the tongue is only the proverbial tip of the iceberg when it comes to the pleasure of a good meal; what lies beneath is anticipation and expectation. This is particularly true of new food and wine pairings. You have a general impression that the food and wine will taste good together, but having never had this combination before, you can't know for sure. This positive but uncertain feeling leads you to anticipate that future pleasure. When a sommelier pairs a bottle of Côtes du Rhône with your lamb dish, say a *gigot d'agneau pleureur*, the mental machinery of anticipation kicks in. Without a single taste of either, you are already experiencing pleasure.

We experience dopamine based on anticipation, but we get an extra kick when our expectations are exceeded; this is why random pleasures are the best pleasures. Pairing red wine with red meat is fairly predictable. What if we instead order a fusion dish like, say, a Nutella lasagna? Unlike the wine pairing, we don't have a context for Nutella plus lasagna. Solely because it is new to us, the pleasure we get from anticipating it is already higher than it would have been with the wine pairing. The brain also sets a level of expectation for the dish. The more handsomely something exceeds our expectations, the more pleasure we experience. When the lack of context for Nutella lasagna is met with a surprisingly delicious result, a surge of dopamine is released into your brain, amplifying the pleasure. It's the pleasure we don't predict *and* that we anticipate the most that gives us the strongest mouthgasms.

This also helps explain why pleasure is inherently fleeting in nature—why once we have experienced something, and therefore have informed expectations for what that experience is like, the joy we derive from it can fade. Anyone who has been on a tropical vacation knows this all too well. Lying on the beach sipping mai tais is heavenly at first, but even the nicest white sand beaches get old after a few days. Sooner or later, you need to experience something else before you can enjoy the beach again. What is at play here is a phenomenon called *attenuation*, or the tendency for a psychological experience such as emotion or attention to fade naturally over time. And when it comes to pleasure, this phenomenon may be hardwired into us by evolution. Bliss is simply not a sustainable state. With enough repetition, even bacon gets boring.

PLEASURE, PREDICTION, AND SURPRISE

We are constantly making predictions about what's coming next. If we go to a restaurant, we're predicting how good the food is going to be. If we think the food is going to be so-so, but it ends up being amazing, this is what scientists call a *positive prediction error*: you were wrong, but in a good way. That happy error, as you just learned, launches dopamine into action. We love to be positively surprised.

One common strategy for building in this kind of positive surprise is to carefully manage expectations. Seeing Zappos employees at your front door with a pair of free gloves is pleasurable in large part because you didn't expect it to happen. In fact, if a consumer experience doesn't exceed our expectations, we're likely to move on, seeking out new pleasures—hence the business idiom "underpromise and overdeliver."

Zappos's success has been built on employing this, especially early on, in their shipping strategy. Before Amazon bought it, Zappos was a scrappy start-up. It was one of the first companies to prove to the world people are willing to buy shoes online. Online shoppers during the early years of e-commerce associated it with slow delivery. "Four to five business days" was the established expectation. Zappos deliberately chose to ship items using two-day delivery without telling their customers. Why? Because the customers expected to see their Nikes in a week, and when this expectation was violated with a two-day delivery, the joy of receiving new Nikes was amplified by surprise.

Zappos isn't alone in using expectation to craft positive experiences for its customers. Imagine your flight is scheduled to arrive in San Diego at 2:30 PM, but over the intercom, the captain giddily announces that you'll be arriving at 2 PM instead! Everyone on the airplane is happy. Ever wonder why your airline seems to arrive early a little *too* often? Well, so did researchers at the Kellogg School of Business.[8] The researchers found that published flight times had increased over 8 percent in the past twenty years. But this increase was due not to changes in the time it actually takes to get from point A to point B. Rather, they found that this extra time was "strategic padding." Airlines intentionally reported flight times as being longer than expected so that they could positively surprise customers in flight when they announced the early arrival time (which was actually the real estimated arrival time all along). On-time or ahead-of-schedule flight arrivals result in happy customers. And our idea about what is on time or ahead of schedule has everything to do with the expectations that are set.

This approach has its limitations, however. If an airline "surprises" its customers by being exactly ten minutes early each and every time, people catch on. The next time they go on a flight, their expectations will have shifted. Their prediction error, and therefore their level of enjoyment, will be smaller, thanks to their elevated expectations. Dopamine is what lets us recalibrate our expectations; with each additional data point regarding our anticipated pleasure versus our actual pleasure, our prediction error narrows. Dopamine is crucially involved not only in the *anticipation* of pleasure, but in *learning* about pleasure and when we can expect it.

OPRAH AND OVERDELIVERING

How do you apply "underpromise and overdeliver" to people with extremely high standards? How, for example, would you pull this off for a party you're hosting for, say, the Obamas, or Oprah? Could you tell Oprah, "Hey, it'll be a pretty fun party but don't get your hopes up," while secretly planning to blow her away? This is the exact scenario Debi Lilly has been faced with, multiple times. She has hosted a number of high-profile events for Oprah, including her fiftieth birthday celebration on live TV, which included guest appearances from none other than John Travolta and Tina Turner. "In these stakes, that phrase goes out the window," says Lilly. However, the value of surprise persists: "It's amazing how powerful small, surprising gestures can be—having someone show up to your table at an event with something thoughtful or surprising. Or being surprised by a locally made gift bag."[9]

Lilly and her team were behind perhaps one of the most quoted television events of all time, Oprah's massive car giveaway in 2004.[10] *YOU get a car, and YOU get a car, EVERYBODY gets a car!*[11] Ⓢ Even if you've seen it countless times before, it's hard not to be swept up in the emotion. The reason? Joy, anticipation, and surprise are built in and maximized at every opportunity.

First, Oprah *randomly* selects eleven people from the audience to come join her onstage, under the ruse that they are getting special recognition for being teachers. If the event had ended right there, these eleven people would have gone home happy with just that. However, Oprah was just getting started. "I've been lying to you," she tells them. "I admit right here and now. All of you share a wildest dream. All of you are in desperate need of . . ." (cue the dopamine) ". . . a brand-new car!" The eleven people are over the moon. And the audience erupts in applause and joy, sharing in their delight. But this was just the warm-up act.

After the crowd calms down, Oprah reveals that she is lying again, telling the audience that there is one more car to give away. The crowd hums and gasps in *anticipation*. And now Debi's team springs into action. They go through the aisles passing out small, silver boxes tied with bows as Oprah explains, "Don't open it now, but in one of these boxes is a key to the final Pontiac G6!" The *anticipation* builds as every member of the crowd wonders, "Could I be the one?!"

Oprah literally cues a drumroll (more dopamine!), then tells the audience to "Open them up." Of course, the *surprise* is that EVERY box contains the key. Each person opening the box thinks THEY are THE winner. Each person is not only happy to be getting a G6 but also experiencing a sense of *surprise* and feeling special that THEY, out of everyone in the audience, were the lucky, random winners.

With everyone experiencing this special injection of random, personalized pleasure, the collective audience is an eruption of pure joy. Then slowly, people begin to look around and see that everyone is holding a pair of keys. And then Oprah delivers her famous line: "You get a car, and YOU get a car. Everyone gets a car!" Possibly the only thing better than being the lucky winner of a car is to feel this final jolt of pleasure, the feeling of knowing in that moment that you're part of a once-in-a-generation moment in TV history.

It's worth reflecting on just how important this incredible layering of pleasure is. Had Oprah come into the studio and immediately announced,

"You get a car, and you get a car. Everyone gets a car!" this would no doubt have resulted in an incredibly happy audience. But by layering in the surprise and maximizing the dopaminergic response, the show took the experience to an almost otherworldly level.

Even in situations where expectations are naturally high—as in a car giveaway on *Oprah*—surprise can still be incorporated into the design. Great event designers know this intuitively: an unexpected gift is a great start, but it isn't just the gift that matters—it's how the gift is given. Not only do we enjoy pleasures more when they're unexpected, but the repeated violation of our expectations—in other words, randomness—significantly impacts our behavior.

RANDOMNESS AND BEHAVIOR

The importance of randomness in driving behavior was first uncovered in the 1960s by the seminal research of behavioral psychologist Michael Zeiler, who compared how pigeons respond differently to variations in the timing of rewards.[12] Like dogs, pigeons are quick learners. If they peck on a lever and food comes out, they will quickly pick up on this and do it again and again. Pigeons have nearly insatiable appetites, so simple kernels of corn make for a profound reward.

In Zeiler's experiment, the pigeons were allowed to pick freely between two levers. One lever consistently gave them food each and every time they pressed it. Pressing the other lever also provided food—but only 50 to 70 percent of the time and at unpredictable intervals. The results seem easy to predict. Naturally, pigeons should select the option that gives them a tasty treat each and every time. But the pigeons' vote was decisive. They spent almost twice as long pecking when the reward was not predictable.

This result has been replicated hundreds of times, across a variety of species including us humble humans, and the results are amazingly consistent. We're eerily drawn to inconsistency.[13] When it comes to reinforcing a behavior, a variable reward schedule—you know a reward is coming at some point, but you don't know when—is much more potent than a consistent reward schedule.

If we find something enjoyable, why would we want it more when it's inconsistent? As we saw last chapter in Greg Burns's juice-squirting experiments, inconsistency is just more pleasurable, on the level of the brain, than consistency is. Recall that anticipation itself is rewarding. And so is that moment when, our expectations lowered by inconsistency, we are surprised by pleasure. "Is the juice going to come now? How about now? Now? Ahhh, finally!"

This high level of variability also compels us to return again and again. When we can't predict what's going to happen next in response to an action we take, we're more likely to repeat that action, in an unconscious effort to understand this elusive relationship. It creates compulsive behavior—what some (including us, for the purposes of this chapter) would call addiction.

The peculiar activity of dopamine is why the floors of Vegas casinos are stocked full of hopeful slot machine enthusiasts. Despite their minimal gains over time, like the pigeons in Zeiler's experiment, gamblers pull lever after lever (or push button after button) in the dopamine-lubricated hope that *this* time, they'll get the big payout.

In terms of addiction, social media platforms have more in common with gambling than, say, nicotine. Each time we visit our Facebook News Feed, we pull the lever on the social media slot machine. We anticipate that doing so will be generally rewarding—that we'll see a new video, find out our friend is getting married, and so forth. But the degree of pleasure we receive is unpredictable and random. Every post doesn't blow our minds. Some posts are boring, others are annoying, and some are even offensive. Nonetheless, we keep scrolling, because we feel as if the sweet reward might be just beyond the next post.

Sean Parker, an early Facebook investor and its first president (played by Justin Timberlake in the movie *The Social Network*), understands this all too well. Facebook designed for the activity of dopamine in the user experience. According to Parker, "We need to sort of give you a little dopamine hit every once in a while because someone liked or commented on a photo or a post or whatever."[14] Because the experience is dynamic, and we never know when or from where the pleasure is coming, we keep returning again and again. Just like Zeiler's pigeons, the variability keeps us guessing, which keeps our dopamine levels in constant flux.

THE EVIL GENIUS OF THE NEWS FEED

The News Feed is so powerful and so familiar these days that it's difficult to imagine a world without it. As the infamous origin story goes, Facebook was launched as a Harvard-only networking site in 2004, and slowly branched out to other colleges and universities before eventually becoming available to everyone. Even in its early days, Facebook was an agile platform that evolved quickly. Your personal profile page changed and became more refined through time, as Facebook adopted a barrage of new features: first, the ability to blog; next, to add photos; and then, to tag friends. Facebook's user growth was healthy, accruing its one millionth user before the end of 2004, less than a year after its initial rollout to Harvard students. Only two years later, Facebook was estimated to be worth over $1 billion.

Despite this rapid evolution, the structure of the site itself was still much simpler than it is now, consisting only of personal pages—your Wall. This made for a very different user experience. The social element was protracted. You could "friend" (and "unfriend") at will, but if you wanted to see what a friend was up to, you had to actually visit their individual page and scroll their feed, like a barbarian. Life before the News Feed in Facebookville, population 10 million, was simple: a poke here, a poke there. If you were really lucky, someone would write on your Wall.

A virtual trip down memory lane:
Facebook circa 2004 (left) and 2005 (right)

On September 6, 2006, everything changed. Facebook made its most significant change to date when the company launched the News Feed, an expression of Mark Zuckerberg's vision of Facebook as a juiced-up form of transparent, social email. Zuckerberg himself had predicted the future of the internet would be a set of curated streams. The News Feed, the first real social stream, embodied this concept.

Surely Facebook citizens loved it, right? The reaction was universally negative, causing an upheaval of angry responses. Ruchi Sanghvi, the product manager behind the News Feed, was burned at the digital stake; following the News Feed launch, the fastest growing Facebook Group was "Ruchi Is the Devil." The morning after the launch, angry reporters and users actually gathered outside the Facebook headquarters in Menlo Park in protest.

Despite the rancor, an analysis of user time on the site revealed something remarkable: while feedback was almost completely negative, people were spending more time on Facebook than ever. Sanghvi herself documented this[15] in her own Facebook status (emphasis added):

A lot of folks wanted us to shut News Feed down. And most other companies would have done precisely that, especially if 10% of their users threatened to boycott the product. But we didn't . . . News Feed was actually working. Amidst all the chaos, all the outrage, we noticed something unusual. Even though everyone claimed they hated it, *engagement had doubled* [emphasis added].

That's right: User engagement doubled. Variable reinforcement—like with Zeiler's pigeons—had officially arrived on social media.

As users got more used to News Feed, the negative hysteria slowed, and engagement and user activity only accelerated. With every new update, Facebook began to shape the News Feed into what it is today: a masterpiece of attention hacking. In 2009, the Facebook News Feed got an update that killed chronological order. Instead of Father Time, a new magical algorithm began deciding which posts you would see and when. The update was a major win for randomness, as it took away the last piece of control users had over posts: the order in which they were seen.

The "News Feed model"—where platforms deliver an experience that is generally pleasurable and yet variable in its delivery of that pleasure—is now commonplace in the world of social media. Instagram and Snapchat employ something almost identical. Even LinkedIn, long thought of as the old, boring, buttoned-up social media platform, implemented a news feed to monumentally increase its users' time on site. A 2012 study by *Adweek*[16] found that the average LinkedIn user spent a laughable twelve minutes on the site *every month*. After it implemented a news feed the following year, its engagement shot up over 45 percent, with almost half of users spending over two hours a week on the site.

THE FEELING OF UNFINISHEDNESS

Another way to look at the potency of pleasure delivery in driving behavior is through the psychology of completeness. Human beings have a natural mental drive for completeness. Imagine your best friend telling you a suspenseful story . . . only to walk away right before the ending. You'd be understandably dissatisfied, and it would be difficult to focus on anything else until you finally got that resolution.

This fixation on things left unfinished is referred to as the Zeigarnik effect. Named after its discoverer, Lithuanian psychologist Bluma Zeigarnik, it states that once we become engrossed in something and focused on completing it, we hate being interrupted. In instances when we are unable to finish what we're doing and get the resolution we crave, our behavior is affected in a very specific way: the discomfort of the unfinished task captures and draws our attention until we can find closure. We get stressed, we fixate on the task, and our memory for where we left off is intensified.

Some of the earliest demonstrations of the Zeigarnik effect were in a classroom setting, related to memory.[17] When students are given the task of memorizing a list of words but are interrupted halfway through by another task, they remember the words far better than if they'd been able to "complete" their memorization. Furthermore, regardless of how boring the task is to them initially, interrupted students express a strong desire to complete it as soon as they are given the chance.

Human nature is to finish what we start, and if we cannot, we experience discomfort. This creates an unmet need we feel compelled to meet at the earliest opportunity. Platforms in the attention economy are keen on creating that unmet need, providing us with a drive to continue in search of a completion that simply never comes—because the longer you spend in an insatiable search for completion, the more money you generate for these platforms.

ZEIGARNIK IN THE WORLD OF CLICKBAIT CONTENT

Using the Zeigarnik effect to keep consumers' attention has been taken to an extreme in the Addiction 2.0 era. But its use isn't new. Local TV news broadcasts have used it for decades to keep you coming back after a commercial break with phrases like, "How one resident became best friends . . . with a drone. That, *and more,* after the break." Sports news shows like *SportsCenter* use asking a trivia question before a commercial break the same way. The trivia question without an answer is classic Zeigarnik. By leaving you with these cliffhangers, they increase the chances you'll stay tuned.

Netflix's Post-Play feature employs a particularly strong dose of the Z. With the introduction of Post-Play, walking away after watching the first episode of *Stranger Things* feels as if you're leaving in the middle of a seamless, eight-hour movie. But *Game of Thrones*, the hit HBO show based on George R. R. Martin's series of novels, did a Zeigarnik even without the Post-Play. How? It had many developing story lines covering dozens of characters. The sheer scale of unfinishedness kept viewers and readers begging for more.

Perhaps the master of the large-scale Zeigarnik effect in storytelling is Marvel Studios' Marvel Cinematic Universe (MCU), which as of late 2019 is the highest-grossing movie franchise of all time, with $22.8 billion (and growing!) in sales from the films alone.[18] The Zeigarnik effect is triggered not only by the films' mid-credit and end credit scenes, but by the interweaving of a universal story line among its (to date) twenty-three separate films with thirty-two superhero characters. The sheer scale of characters, plots, subplots, and sub-subplots provide a healthy dose of unfinishedness that can only be sated with a new Marvel film.

So while use of the Zeigarnik effect predates modern technology, today's digital marketing has turned it into an art form. Today's "clickbait" articles use a teaser format—snippets of information that create a need for resolution—as bait to encourage site visitors to, well, click.

It is unlikely the average web surfer has heard of Outbrain or Taboola, but they have definitely seen the "sponsored content" these companies are responsible for placing at the bottom of web articles. *What she looks like now will amaze you!* Sound familiar? Never mind how inappropriate such an article might be, placed under an article on the Syrian Civil War.

Outbrain and Taboola are the silent giants of this kind of sponsored content ad, which blatantly abuse the Zeigarnik effect: "Three Amsterdam Locals Walk into a J. Crew Shoot . . ." "Here's Why Guys Are Obsessed with This Underwear."

In 2014, Time Inc. signed a deal with Outbrain worth $100 million.[19] CNN, Bleacher Report, Slate, and ESPN are all clients of Outbrain. At the time of writing, Taboola and Outbrain are exploring a merger that would set their value at over $1 billion. Hate them all you want, Mr. and Ms. Web Surfer, but the awkward "Hot Baseball Wives" ad under that Syria story isn't going anywhere.

There's another company well known for using the Zeigarnik effect to deliver what most journalists would call pseudo-news: BuzzFeed. It's hard to argue with their results: nine billion monthly content views, a quarter billion unique monthly visitors, and a valuation of $1.7 billion.[20] How'd they do it? Their article titles are mini Zeigarnik cliffhangers meant to induce a sense of unfinishedness that only clicking on the article can resolve. Journalistic integrity be damned, just try and resist these headlines: "*24 Times Tom Hardy Ruined Other Men For You.*" "*This Might Be The Scariest Trail In The World. But You'll NEVER Guess Where. Unbelievable.*"

CAN'T STOP WON'T STOP?

Clickbait ads work by creating a sense of incompleteness, which then compels us to click on them to reach resolution. However, once we click, that resolution is generally provided. That's not the case with today's online platforms, especially social media. Their addictive technology works by denying us completion, creating an ongoing need to return to it for that ever-elusive resolution. This is why it's physically difficult to pull yourself away from the infinite scrolling of Instagram and Facebook. By failing to provide any clear "end," these apps effectively put you, the user, in a box of unfinishedness. Welcome to digital hell. Or more accurately, welcome to Zeigarnik purgatory, where the seeds of compulsive behavior are planted.

In everyday life, we're generally able to accommodate our need for closure, by dividing our lives into satisfying "chunks." When we're reading a book, we can finish the chapter we're on before leaving the café, and when we're at work, we can finish the email we're writing before going out for our lunch break. But whether it's swipe after swipe on Tinder, or a scroll down into an endless news feed, the user experience has no psychological stopping points—no milestones—nor a finish line after which the user can walk away saying, "Okay, I've completed that." In the case of the bottomless News Feed, we never feel satisfied because there is no point at which we feel we've completed our task.

The "continuous scroll" model, as it is known in the industry, has become popular beyond just social media. Time.com, for example, revamped their website in 2015 to include a continuous-scroll interface. Their engagement improved almost immediately. The bounce rate, the percentage of visitors who leave the site after viewing only one page, dropped 15 percent.[21] Bleacher Report achieved a similar reduction in bounce rate when they killed their traditional front page and replaced it with an infinite scroll design. In 2012, one of the largest digital media companies, Mashable, which covers pop and tech news, redesigned their website for both mobile and desktop to show news articles in a bottomless stream of tiles. Go to Mashable.com and try to get to the bottom of the page. Just don't hold your breath. If the visual of scrolling tiles feels familiar, you've likely spent some time on Pinterest. Pinterest serves up images with a particularly potent combination of randomness and the Zeigarnik effect. Perfectly sized and spaced square tiles are presented for your viewing pleasure, in a seemingly endless stream. No wonder Pinterest was the fastest site in web history to hit ten million users, was able to go public so quickly, and is currently valued at almost $13 billion. Next time you're on your favorite website or app, check to see if it has a traditional homepage—or an endless river of content designed to maximize the Zeigarnik effect.

DIGITAL WELL-BEING

Thanks to our understanding of variable reinforcement and the Zeigarnik effect, we can see how online platforms inspire the behavior they do and have risen to become some of the most profitable and powerful companies in the world. But where do we go from here? Are we doomed to spend increasingly greater amounts of time scrolling through Instagram and swiping through Snapchat?

This is a question Tristan Harris has thought a lot about. Harris, thirty-three, is an outspoken critic of modern platforms hijacking our attention, and has been described as the closest thing Silicon Valley has to a conscience.[22] Harris understands the workings of the attention economy firsthand: he launched an app in 2012 that installed pop-up advertisements on a number of prominent web platforms. The company was acquired by Google shortly after, and Harris was hired to help integrate it into Google's advertising product portfolio.

Harris was in Silicon Valley heaven, which for most people would be a dream come true. Harris isn't most people. He couldn't shake the feeling that there was something underhanded about his industry. Fresh off a weekend at Burning Man, he finally broke and had his *Jerry Maguire* moment. He produced a 141-slide deck, released in 2013, outlining the responsibility large tech companies have to foster an "ethical approach to attention"—to design platforms that don't merely hook users, but also consider their long-term well-being.[23] The document quickly spread to over five thousand Google employees, up to and including C-level management. To Harris's amazement, he wasn't fired; instead, he got a face-to-face meeting with CEO Larry Page and was given the formal title "Chief Ethicist."

Harris has urged technology companies to adopt ethical design principles, but he has also urged consumers to be more vigilant against the temptations and compulsions those companies create. He's teamed up with Joe Edelman, founder of the company that publishes the Moment app, to form the nonprofit group Time Well Spent. The idea behind Time Well Spent is to bring attention to . . . well, attention. More specifically, it aims to empower technology users against mindless and compulsive behavior. The suggestions are deceptively simple, but effective: turn off app notifications, customize your smartphone home screen, and build a daily routine that doesn't start and end with looking at a screen. They also encourage use of a wide range of desktop and mobile applications to monitor the amount of time spent on common platforms, in the hope that showing users just how long they are spending on particular sites will curb usage.

Time Well Spent has gained a following, and a number of tech founders have taken Tristan Harris and Facebook investor Sean Parker's lead in coming out against the products they helped create. Loren Brichter, the designer of the slot machine–like "pull down to refresh" mechanism for mobile devices, said, "Pull-to-refresh is addictive. Twitter is addictive.

These are not good things. When I was working on them, it was not something I was mature enough to think about. I'm not saying I'm mature now, but I'm a little bit more mature, and I regret the downsides."

Nearly a decade after Facebook's introduction of the News Feed, the public began catching on to how potent technological platforms had become. The dam finally broke in 2018. Perhaps it was the Stanford study[24] that suggested taking pictures with a smartphone actually reduced the photographer's ability to form memories of what they were viewing, or the Penn State study[25] that showed a strong link between social media addiction and depression among adolescents. Or it could have been the increasing number of tech founders and pioneers voicing their concerns, a chorus that finally became too loud and disturbing to ignore. Whatever the reason, 2018 was a turning point in the national consciousness of tech addiction. People looked up from their phones and realized their technology was making them addicted and miserable.

The market has been quick to respond to this epiphany. In addition to Moment, perhaps the pioneer of digital detox, several other commercial tools are now available that help provide users with increased awareness and autonomy. Los Angeles–based start-up Boundless Mind, for example, aims to harness the power of addictive technology to steer people toward healthier habits. "We're talking about mind control—oh my God, right?" cofounder Ramsay Brown told Time.com.[26] "But what if we sell you those mind-control tools to help people get off opioids? Or to communicate with each other on a more meaningful level? Why can't we engineer your brain to be who you want to be?"

Outside of digital solutions, probably the most extreme reflection of technology's addictive hold is the proliferation of digital rehab facilities. These come in a variety of forms, from resorts that encourage travelers to "disconnect to reconnect,"[27] or that offer perks to customers who are able to abstain from their phones for a given duration, all the way to legitimate digital-rehabilitation centers. These are exactly what they sound like: physical housing, usually isolated in rural areas, that serve as recovery facilities. Phones, laptops, tablets, and other digital devices are strictly forbidden and must be surrendered at check-in. Washington-based reStart, for example, offers six- and ten-week programs, and has several full-time addiction counselors on staff.[28]

At the time of writing, Facebook has yet to take initiative for driving responsible use of its platform. However, the other tech giants, Apple and Google, responded to the conversation about responsible tech usage in 2018 by making digital well-being apps available in their respective smartphones, the iPhone and the Pixel. The apps are similar, with the iPhone version having the edge in terms of amount of usage data provided. It shows the user which apps take up most of their time, as well as how many notifications the user averages a day and from which apps.

Pessimist Pete might say these smartphone apps are branded Band-Aids, and he'd have a point. Surely you've seen, while driving, those speed-sensing road signs (YOUR SPEED IS 47 MPH) that nudge you to slow down. These signs only work because, in our society:

1. We agree that speeding is bad, and has consequences for the safety of the driver and others.
2. If you speed, you face legal and financial consequences.

Digital well-being apps are like putting a speed-sensing road sign in a country where people don't believe speeding is bad and have zero laws against it. Sure, it may slow a handful of people down, but most of the population will blow right past it. When it comes to tech usage, the general public is still largely unaware of how addictive these design elements are, while lawmakers are only now figuring out that Apple, not Google, makes the iPhone.[29] The only people aware of the impact are the people whose financial livelihoods our habitual app use funds.

Ultimately, time will have to tell if digital well-being apps can be effective. As it stands, making money in the current digital landscape means capturing attention. Companies that have successfully done this have flourished financially. Making your product less addictive is tantamount to making your product less profitable; every minute less the average consumer spends on your platform, the less revenue you generate. And at least currently, consumers aren't demanding or willing to pay for addiction-free versions.

Until consumers value their time and well-being enough to overcome the allure of these "free" addictive platforms, it's difficult for this business model to truly shift. While the likes of Google and Apple can (literally) afford to sacrifice immediate goals like "time on site" in an effort to come across as more ethical than their competitors, other, smaller brands operating within the attention economy either cannot or will not. And if Google (or Alphabet, their holding company) or Apple begin to lose market space to these competitors over time, their shareholders may persuade them to reconsider.

Consumers have a choice: pay with money, or pay with attention. So far, we have defaulted to attention. Here's hoping we go back to good ol' dollars.

THE FUTURE OF ADDICTIVE TECHNOLOGIES

Addiction isn't simply about dependence on a physical product. Digitally, addiction is "engagement"—the focused application of our attention. We have age limits for things like gambling because we know it can lead to compulsive behavior. Yet no such restrictions exist for social media. It doesn't even come with a parental advisory, like music and film do. As more and more of Earth's population starts using these platforms, the price of our attention for advertisers will only increase, and these platforms will only become more adept at hijacking our attention. As Harris has said, "There's a whole system that's much more powerful than us, and it's only going to get stronger."[30]

Our screens are addictive enough in two dimensions. Now virtual reality and augmented reality are beginning to supercharge "engagement" in 3D and beyond. Addiction 3.0 will use VR and AR to enable deeper and more compelling experiences. It is no surprise Facebook spent $2 billion to purchase Oculus Rift, a virtual reality video-game system, or that venture capital investments of nearly as much, $1.9 billion, were made in VR and AR start-ups in 2016 alone.[31] And if the AR phenomenon *Pokémon GO*, which had 100 million downloads in the summer of 2016, is any indication, we are only scratching the surface of AR's potential to transform the attention economy.

It's hard to imagine a world in which people wake up tomorrow and do not feel compelled by technology and online platforms. It is equally hard to imagine a world in which massive technology companies are willing to forgo billions in advertising revenue by making their platforms less addictive.

Technology products are unique in their lack of transparency. You can't pick them up and assess their parts and how they work the way you can with, say, a pair of shoes. The business models of products in this sphere are equally shrouded in obscurity. If you're shopping for a deal on pairs of shoes, "buy one get one" means what it says. If you're shopping for tech products, "free" *never* actually means free. These are businesses, after all. And their products—especially the "free" ones—only succeed if they can alter our attention and behavior to align with their interests.

Fueled by technological advancement, the battle over our attention will only intensify in the coming years, and the stakes could not be higher. Time and conscious attention are the most precious resources we have, and how we choose to invest them dictates how we live our lives. Some of the world's most ancient philosophers, from the Buddha to Socrates, admonished us to treat these resources with care, to remain vigilant in our focus, and to not give in to life's distractions. Aristotle, for instance, famously worried that the advent of writing would lead us astray by taking over our thoughts and consuming our valuable attention.[32] One can only imagine how he would react to the potency of Tinder. Ultimately, it may be wise to heed the words of Epictetus, the philosopher and Stoic: "You become what you give your attention to."

Chapter 8

WHY WE LIKE
WHAT WE LIKE

The Odd Science of Preference

" The Unesco motto is: 'Since wars begin in the minds of men, it is in the minds of men that the defenses of peace must be constructed,' and having just been through a war, the motto was a sufficient incentive for me to get engaged in scientific initiatives that might make a contribution toward preventing future wars."[1]

These are the words of Robert Zajonc, one of the most influential psychologists of the twentieth century, whose contributions are foundational to understanding the psychology of likeability.

Zajonc's personal history is as remarkable as his research. In 1939, he and his parents were forced to flee their home when the Nazis invaded Poland. Shortly after, the building in which they were hiding was bombed, and Zajonc narrowly escaped death. His parents did not. A few years later, Zajonc managed to attend an underground university in Warsaw before getting shipped to a German labor camp. He escaped, but was caught and sent to prison in France, where he escaped again.[2] After the war, he continued his studies in—of all places—Germany, at the University of Tübingen, before coming to the US for his PhD in psychology at the University of Michigan.

Zajonc's early experiences drove him to pursue psychology, and he started off by researching racism and stereotyping. However, he then dedicated the latter half of his career to answering a deceptively simple question: Why do we like what we like?

He discovered that "liking" something is not as straightforward as we think—that we're largely unaware of the factors that shape our preferences. This finding changed the landscape of modern psychology. And even if you aren't aware of his work, it almost certainly plays a role in shaping your preferences in the consumer world.

MERE EXPOSURE

As it turns out, we humans are often completely unaware of the root causes of our preferences. Sometimes, what we like is born out of seemingly unrelated experiences. Zajonc's most consistent finding: humans show a surprising preference toward what is familiar. This preference plays a massive, underappreciated role in shaping what we enjoy and seek out—including in the consumer world. If a company manages to boost your sense of familiarity with their product or service, it can have a major, positive impact on how much you like it.

Fascinatingly, this preference for the familiar appears to operate completely outside our awareness. In one of Zajonc's classic studies, he showed English-speaking participants who did not know Chinese a range of different Chinese characters. There was no task; they were just instructed to look at them and pay attention. Later, he showed the participants another set of Chinese characters—some repeated from the first set, and some not—except this time he asked them to guess what each character meant. Knowing zero Chinese, participants simply threw out words: "dog," "cup," "handsome," "soccer."

From the standpoint of the participant, they were just shooting in the dark. But what Zajonc found was that their guesses weren't random: if a person had seen the character before, even briefly, they were much more likely to assume the word was associated with something positive. They gave these familiar characters meanings like "happiness" and "love," and also rated themselves to be happier after viewing them, compared to after viewing the unfamiliar characters.[3] In follow-up experiments, these effects persisted despite none of the participants claiming to remember having seen the characters before.

The simplest way to breed a sense of familiarity with something is to get people to spend as much time with that thing as possible. Zajonc dubbed this phenomenon the *mere exposure effect*: all else being equal, the more experience you have with something, the more you'll like it.

The implication of this for the consumer world is worth underlining. While it doesn't seem crazy that consumers who are exposed to more Pepsi ads will buy more Pepsi, Zajonc's work illustrated that the impact of exposure is far deeper. Even if you lived under a rock and had never heard of Pepsi or the concept of soda or the English language before, simply being exposed to the Pepsi logo would make you like Pepsi more. Turns out, even a little familiarity goes a long way.

More than two hundred studies across a wide array of domains has replicated the mere-exposure-effect finding: we just plain like things more the more we're exposed to them.[4,5] Similar findings have been noted in animals as well, including in developing chicks still in the egg. Tones of two different frequencies were played to two groups of fertile chicken eggs. At birth, the chicks preferred the tone they had previously heard.[6]

The fact that this effect remains relatively robust across the animal kingdom suggests that it may be grounded in evolution. Being exposed to something multiple times—*especially* if that thing did not make a conscious impact—means that, by definition, the thing must be harmless. And from the standpoint of survival, harmless is unequivocally good.

One of the oldest adages in marketing is the "Law of 7," which states that a customer needs to see your ad seven times before they'll actually want to buy your product. The law originated in the movie industry circa the 1930s, when marketing teams converged on seven as the magic number of ads needed to compel someone to see a new movie. The number seven wasn't researched in any way. And in fact, now that we have user tracking and data analysis, it's been thoroughly debunked. Whether or not someone decides to see a movie or buy a product depends on the individual, the product, the type of advertisement they've seen, what they may have heard from friends, and the like. However, this myth does touch on a fundamental truth of advertising: more is better.

That's why we continuously see advertisements for the most well-known major brands, like Coca-Cola, Apple, and Nike. You've had a Coke; you know how it tastes. So has everyone else we've ever met. Yet Coca-Cola keeps paying for ads and billboards over and over and over. Is there one potential customer somewhere, somehow, who hasn't heard of Coke and whom they're desperately trying to contact? Brand awareness for Coke is already through the ozone. Why continue? Because each repetition *ever so slightly* improves your opinion of Coke.

Recall from chapter one that big companies are in the business of creating positive associations with their brand. Perhaps no one has done this better than Coca-Cola, which has spent tens of billions of dollars associating Coke with the concept of happiness. But almost regardless of that engineered association with happiness, simply seeing the Coke name so many times has increased our preference for it. Coca-Cola spends almost $4 billion on advertising a year.[7] For a global population of 7.5 billion, that's more than fifty cents a year of advertising to each human brain on the planet. Over a decade, that's $5 spent on each of us. Have you bought $5 worth of Coke in the past ten years? Chances are, yes. The character Tracy Flick in the movie *Election* may have said it best: "Coca-Cola is by far the world's number one soft drink and they spend more money than anybody on advertising. I guess that's how come they stay number one."

If you're ever in Los Angeles, walking down 3rd Street Promenade, we recommend playing a little game called "How many Starbucks?" At the time of writing, there are at least five within walking distance of one another. In San Francisco, the game is "How many Walgreens?" on Market Street. Walgreens also owns Duane Reade in NYC, which as of 2019 has more than 400 locations. And the mere exposure effect means that each new location also doubles as a way to make us like the chain more.

Sheer proliferation is a great approach for the dominant name in the market, since they can afford to run a location or two at a loss to stem competition in the area. But for less established companies with smaller capital, it can also be worth the risk. The scrappy upstart coffee house Joe & the Juice has employed the same tactic, targeting populous cities like San Francisco, Sydney, Amsterdam, and London. The cost of renting retail space in these major world capitals makes many locations a financial loss. However, the store's presence in highly visible areas is increasing likeability through exposure, providing value beyond the traditional profit-and-loss statement.

This doesn't just work with storefronts. Companies pay millions each year to advertise on taxi cab exteriors, but car companies get the same kind of advertising for free. Whenever you drive your Honda Accord around town, you are essentially driving a billboard on wheels—even without Honda paying you (you paid them!).

This brings to question the most peculiar of examples, Google. Despite being the largest advertising company in the tech world, Google doesn't spend much money on ads. Google was formed in 1998. Yet their first ad ever was during the Super Bowl in 2010. Their market cap in 2009 was nearly $200 billion, so clearly Google could have afforded to advertise more. With all this talk about the importance of repetition and exposure, what gives? The answer is simple: Google had already built a product so compelling and useful that they didn't need to advertise. Google was getting all the exposure they could ever want through their role in the everyday lives of the consumer. When Google Search is being used 3.8 million times *per minute* on any given day,[8] what need does Google have to pay for exposure? All of a sudden, Coca-Cola's $4 billion makes perfect sense. Its product is the exact opposite of Google—lacking in any real utility.

Tesla followed Google's lead by creating a product so compelling, the exposure is baked in. Instead of Super Bowl ads, Tesla spent money on projects like creating miniature Tesla S's for kids. Naturally, the press loved this and Tesla received exposure through media coverage. You could argue that Tesla's most effective exposure campaign had a $0 budget. The caveat? It required a SpaceX Falcon rocket. When Tesla broadcasted its Roadster flying to space atop SpaceX's rocket, it earned exposure without buying it directly.

This kind of exposure-without-advertising is significantly more effective than traditional advertising. Both seeing advertising from Google and using Google have the same end result—increased exposure to Google. But because you don't think of using Google's site as advertising, this only makes the mere exposure effect stronger. When you know the car commercial is, well, a commercial, its message loses potency. You know you are being sold to, which feels inauthentic, and therefore less powerful. We'll revisit this in the following chapter, when we discuss empathy. Suffice to say for now that when you want a product you are indirectly exposed to, you think it was your idea; research validated this decades ago.[9] It's like the brain is giving brands a financial incentive to be sneaky!

Mere exposure effect does come with a caveat: it only works on things that you initially find at least mildly enjoyable.[10,11] Just because you read the word "Coke" nine times in the past thirty seconds does not mean you will like it more if you were never fond of it to begin with. If you didn't like "Call Me Maybe" the first time, it won't get any better the hundred-and-first time. (Though if you found the first listen inoffensive, you may find it's grown on you significantly a dozen radio plays in.)

FLUENCY EFFECT

The mere exposure effect isn't the only reason multiple exposures boost likeability. Things we've seen multiple times are also easier to bring to mind, and we like this as well. Remember the law of least mental effort—the brain's general aversion to thinking and mental calculation. It takes more effort to process something that's brand new than to reprocess something familiar, so we show a preference for things that come to mind easily over those that are difficult. This is the mere exposure effect's first cousin: the *fluency effect.*

The fluency effect has some surprising effects in the consumer world. Research by Adam Alter of New York University shows the brain's preference for fluency impacts consumer investments in the stock market, for one. Turns out, stocks with more fluent names (like GOOG) robustly outperformed stocks with disfluent names (like NFLX) in the short term.[12]

The fluency effect can also impact our sense of truth. Read the following two sentences. Which sentence *feels* truer?

Option 1: **Baltimore is the capital of Maryland.**
Option 2: Baltimore is the capital of Maryland.

Chances are you chose option 1. Option 1 uses 11-point Verdana font; option 2 uses 11-point Times New Roman font. A study by the Software Usability and Studies Lab investigated the legibility of several fonts and found Verdana to be the most legible and Times Roman to be the least legible.[13] And not only are you more inclined to like a statement that is easy to read, you are also more likely to judge it as being accurate, versus if it were difficult to read.[14] The easier it is to understand something, the more likely you are to believe it to be true. Oh, and fun fact: Annapolis, not Baltimore, is the actual capital of Maryland.

AVAILABILITY BIAS

The ease with which we can bring something to mind influences our sense of its truthfulness in another way: it impacts our sense of how common the thing is. Our tendency to believe information that is easier to bring to mind as being more important is known as the *availability heuristic*, a.k.a. the *what have you done for me lately* bias.

If you were asked about the crime rate in America, whether it's trending up or down, what would you say? Chances are you'd guess it's trending up, and you would not be alone. Multiple polls show the majority of Americans believe the crime rate is rising. However, all the evidence points to the contrary. Crimes per 10,000 people are trending down (and have been for over a decade). Why the disconnect? The availability heuristic.

Let's say you're watching your local TV news one night. Local news programs focus on sensational, emotional stories; reports on car chases and home burglaries are common. While these stories may keep you glued to the TV better than C-SPAN, their frequent coverage tricks your brain into thinking they are actually a common occurrence. Then, still thinking about the report you just saw on a series of local break-ins, you hop on Facebook to check how your friend's vacation was . . . and see similar home burglary stories posted by another friend living in a different state. While the actual number of burglaries near you may be no higher, and might even be lower than last week, your brain now has a grossly inaccurate sense of their frequency, and of the probability that your home will be burglarized.

Studies have found people tend to overestimate the rates of abductions in the weeks following a major child abduction case. Further, the more violent media someone consumes, the higher they think crime rates are.[15] What comes to mind most easily heavily shapes our ideas of the world.

Domino's Pizza found this out the hard way in 2009.[16] Two Domino's employees at a location in Canover, NC, had a bright idea while preparing sandwiches for delivery: put cheese up their noses and mucus on the sandwiches, and break a bunch of other health-code standards. Thinking it would be funny, they filmed their "prank" and uploaded the videos to YouTube. But when Domino's got wind of them, they were far from amused. Hundreds of dollars of food had to be discarded immediately. And the work of the company's PR team got a lot harder.

The videos' damage was immense and far reaching. Sales took a major hit nationwide, and the slump lasted for months. Welcome to an availability-bias-fueled PR nightmare. Within just days of their posting, the videos had been seen over 700,000 times. The top Google search results for Domino's referenced the scandal. The perception of Domino's quality among consumers went from positive to negative almost overnight, according to consumer research firm YouGov. The scandal was so bad that the CEO, Patrick Boyle, had to address it directly in a national commercial.[17] ⑤ Needless to say, the two employees were promptly fired. (The store they worked for later closed due to bad business.)

The actual probability that someone will put mucus in your sandwich—from any store—is extremely low. But this single instance became the first thing people thought of when they thought of Domino's, and their perception of the probability of it occurring at their own local restaurant became skewed. Remember from chapter six that pain hurts more than pleasure feels good. You're especially sensitive to a violated sandwich because of the brain's natural aversion to loss. You may see the data and understand objectively that the chances of something happening to your sandwich are remote. But that doesn't prevent the readily available imagery from entering your mind, and influencing your choice of restaurants.

Given our sensitivity to losses, we mentally weigh negatives like crime and tainted food extra-heavily. But the availability bias applies equally to positives. Think about *The Oprah Winfrey Show*, and the image that first comes to mind is likely a group of fanatically loyal, incredibly enthusiastic middle-aged Americans seated in Oprah's studio. Especially after reading the previous chapter of this book, this image is likely to be of this group being sent into overdrive after just finding out they all were given a free car. Most days Oprah didn't give out cars on her show. But this incredibly salient single event heavily influences your concept of the show and its fan base, because it's so easy to bring to mind.

As the availability bias shows, the relationship between exposure and likeability isn't completely straightforward. In the consumer's mind, a decade's worth of positive exposure can be erased by a single negative scandal. So brands must constantly shape their public perception by driving new positive exposure.

NEW AND SAFE

This is a good place to pause, zoom out, and check in. Have you, by any chance, noticed a contradiction between this chapter and chapter three, on encoding experience?

Recall from chapter three that there is a massive advantage to disfluency: a difficult-to-read font, like Sans Forgetica, forces you to strain your attention, and this helps you remember the information you read. No pain, no gain. This chapter shares how font fluency increases likeability (and truthiness). Adding friction boosts memory, but it doesn't improve likeability. So which one is better? It depends on what you want to maximize: memory or likeability.

But beyond this surface conflict, a much larger contradiction exists. This chapter covers what makes your brain like things. You would be correct to summarize the appeal of familiarity, fluency, and availability as *the brain likes the safety of familiarity.* However, previous chapters outlined concepts that could be summarized as the exact opposite: *the brain likes the newness of novelty.*

Think about chapter two's explanation of why breaking existing associations gets our attention, like the Cadbury gorilla drumming "In the Air Tonight" by Phil Collins. Then there's the science of pleasure from chapter six, which is an ode to novelty: you want something new, but as soon as that new thing becomes familiar, you start wanting something else. Last, there's positive prediction error from the last chapter, which shows we get real pleasure out of the unexpected.

On one hand, a good experience becomes great when it's new and comes as a surprise. On the other hand, what is familiar and repeated increases the probability of us liking it. So what gives? How can the two be reconciled?

In the early 1970s, an ambitious young film director made his directorial debut. The film represented years of hard work, both in honing his craft and developing the courage to take on such a challenging project. The director was wary of the Hollywood mainstream and, in this project, envisioned something completely different. The film was *THX 1138*, which centered on a dystopian future in which sexual intercourse is outlawed and psychedelic drugs are mandatory. It was an abject commercial failure.

The young director was devastated by the response, but persisted. After a flurry of research, he dove almost immediately into another creative project. Producers gave his treatment a dubious reception, but the script was eventually greenlit. It became the first film in the single highest-grossing movie franchise of all time: Star Wars. The director, of course, was a young George Lucas.

The books Lucas read as research are telling—particularly Joseph Campbell's seminal work on mythology, *The Hero with a Thousand Faces*. In it, Campbell details the striking similarities in hero myths, which he argues are shared across disparate cultures because they are part of our innate human endowment. Campbell distilled a common template for "the Hero's Journey," and Lucas found this template paralleled the journey of Luke Skywalker in *Star Wars*. It helped Lucas combine the familiar (the myth of the hero) with the new (space travel and science fiction).

Back, then, to the original question. Do birds of a feather flock together due to familiarity or do opposites attract due to novelty? The answer, it seems, is a bit of both. There are times when your brain wants what is familiar, and there are times when it wants what's new. But what your brain *really loves* is a perfect combination of both.

This insight doesn't come from modern neuroscience, but rather from midcentury American designer Raymond Loewy. Loewy is possibly the most influential person forgotten by history; his design philosophy shaped the entire aesthetic, from furniture to fashion to brand logos, of the 1950s and '60s. At its core, that design philosophy recognized and addressed the tension between our neophilia (our attraction to the new) and our neophobia (our fear of the new). Loewy's philosophy was profound in its simplicity: most advanced, yet acceptable. To help someone like something new, make it feel familiar; to help someone like something familiar, make it a little bit novel. In other words, optimize for the Goldilocks zone between novelty and familiarity—make it *New and Safe*, what we'll refer to as *NaS*.

The success of that first Star Wars film is a striking illustration of the power of NaS. *THX 1138* failed in part because it was pure novelty. The concept was so new, the audience lacked the familiar grounding they needed to help them feel safe. The first Star Wars film injected just the right amount of novelty into an existing template that audiences recognized from countless adventure stories and myths. In other words, *Star Wars: A New Hope* was the most New and Safe science fiction film of its time.

For all the talk of the importance of consistency in branding, there's evidence that it's possible to have too much repetition.[18] A closer examination of the mere-exposure-effect literature reveals that while you like something better the more you see it, repetition has sharp diminishing of returns after roughly fifteen exposures.[19] Indeed, when you look back at the original mere-exposure-effect experiments with Chinese characters, the moment participants became aware that they'd seen the characters before, the effect disappeared.[20] You like things the more you're exposed to them, but only as long as you're not hit over the head with them. It is very possible to overdo it. That catchy pop tune on the radio eventually gets annoying. (Insert any Nickelback song here.)

Just a little novelty goes a long way. Researcher Stewart Shapiro and his colleagues tested this idea[21] in print ads. In these ads, they placed brand logos (familiar) in different areas of the ad (new). Instead of always showing the logo on the bottom left of an ad, for example, the researchers moved it to the top right. The result? These subtle changes to the ad design led to a 20 percent increase in subjects' preference for the brand. Moreover, all subjects claimed not to have detected the subtle differences. Additional research validated this effect in varying forms of advertisements.[22]

Just like in the multisensory experiences in the first chapter, there isn't a magic ratio for familiar to new. The trick is to not overdo either, and to find the perfect balance between the two.

This NaS sweet spot can be seen directly through food trends. What's up with state fairs' obsession with frying random foods, like fried butter, fried Kool-Aid, and fried beer? NaS is. It's also why ideas like honey pizza, mayo-froyo, and peanut butter cheeseburgers are popular.

Think about food pairings. There are established food pairings and experimental food pairings. Established food pairings, like cheese with wine or sushi with sake, have an established context in our brains. They are familiar and safe. But they didn't start out that way. It is easy to forget that today's classics, like Reese's peanut butter cups, peanut butter and jelly sandwiches, and even Red Bull and vodka, were yesterday's NaS. And while specific, experimental food pairings, such as whiskey with dark chocolate or ramen burgers, may come and go, food pairings as a concept is here to stay. Their use of familiar foods in unfamiliar combinations is just the kind of "safe novelty" the brain loves.

NaS IN POP CULTURE, FILM, AND THE MUSIC INDUSTRY

As we saw with Star Wars, NaS is a particularly strong driving force in pop culture. While creating film, fiction, and music is an artistic endeavor, selling them is a business, one that profits heavily off NaS.

The music streaming service Spotify has been a runaway success, boasting year-over-year subscriber growth of nearly 50 percent at the time of this writing. When Spotify first introduced its playlist dedicated to new music, which gave users personalized music recommendations based on their past listening data, the results were as expected. The more data a user had provided by liking, playing, cataloging, and saving music, the better they responded to the recommendations. And then, Spotify stumbled upon NaS.

Courtesy of a mistake by the engineering team back in 2015, the same discovery playlist, packed with new songs, was accidentally mixed with users' most listened to songs—and something unexpected happened. Users with the "broken" playlist that combined new and familiar songs spent more time listening to the playlist! "Everyone reported it as a bug, and so we fixed it so that every song was completely new," CEO Matt Ogle told *The Atlantic*.[23] But when they did, listenership dropped. So they restored the previous version. "It turns out that having a bit of familiarity bred trust," Ogle remarked.

An unforgettable example of NaS made its creator money while changing the behavior of buyers: *Fifty Shades of Grey*.

Before *Fifty Shades of Grey*, BDSM (an acronym referring to bondage and discipline, dominance and submission, and sadism and masochism) was an underground subculture. Play parties and dungeon nights were whispered invites, as opposed to open Facebook events. Only the most exploratory, or perhaps neophilic, of sexual practitioners ventured into BDSM.

Then came *Fifty Shades*. The book began its life as "Master of the Universe," a piece of popular Twilight fan fiction posted on FanFiction.net. For the uninitiated, fan fiction is fiction written by a fan featuring characters and/or story lines from television shows, comics, movies, or books. In "Master of the Universe," the author E. L. James applied "new" BDSM themes to the familiar characters and relationship of Bella and Edward. The end result was a story that made BDSM both new and safe enough first for Twilight fan fiction readers and then—with the characters' names changed from Bella and Edward to Ana and Christian and the text published as *Fifty Shades of Grey*—the general "vanilla" public. The work that started off as "Master of Universe" sold more copies on Amazon UK than *all of the Harry Potter books combined.*

Fifty Shades of Grey and its sequels also gave an incredible boost to sex toy companies, mainly due to first-time customers. UK-based sex toy manufacturer LoveHoney's profit tripled, from $1.1 million the year before the movie's release to $3.39 million by January 2014, based purely on items that appear in the Fifty Shades books, including handcuffs, riding crops, feather ticklers, spanking paddles, and blindfolds. Pamela Doan, spokesperson for Babeland in Manhattan, also reported doubling of revenue in her sex shop following the movie's release. "Customers are really excited. They come in and make references to 'Fifty Shades' . . . Some of these people have never been to a sex shop before."[24]

NaS also explains sampling in hip-hop music production. Kanye West is well-known for sampling songs from genres that don't usually cross over, following the business model of Sean Combs, better (worse?) known as P. Diddy or Puff Daddy. Sean Combs did in the '90s what Kanye did in the 2000s. For example, Combs sampled a David Bowie beat for a Notorious B.I.G. rap song. He also sampled funk group Mtume's "Juicy Fruit" for what became Notorious B.I.G.'s most popular song, "Juicy" (it was all a dream!). Combs and Kanye both created success from taking something familiar and adding novelty to it.

Think of how electronic dance music became popular in the USA. In the early 2000s, EDM was new—*too* new for the majority of American listeners. David Guetta, love 'im or hate 'im, was the ambassador of EDM. He took this new thing and wrapped it up in the safe blanket of pop artists like Usher, will.i.am, Nicki Minaj, Snoop Dogg, Ludacris, and more.

Once EDM became common on American radio, certain electronic music DJs used NaS to further expand the genre. When Avicii premiered the track "Wake Me Up" at Miami's Music Week by bringing live country musicians onstage to play the signature riff, the audience was initially confused. Soon after the song's release, however, people could not get enough of the combination of EDM and country music riffs.

Beyoncé used NaS when she combined the novelty of reggaeton with the familiarity of her pop sound in "Mi Gente," a song featuring reggaeton superstars J. Balvin and Bad Bunny. Rapper Lil Nas X put his own spin on NaS in a twangy collab with country legend Billy Ray Cyrus, "Old Town Road"—with results that topped the summer 2019 charts. The list of artists, in music and other areas, who profit from combining the novel with the familiar goes on and on, and will continue to grow—because NaS works.

You know now that what your brain likes can be architected. On one side, there's the mere exposure effect and its cousins, the fluency effect and availability bias, which power advertising. The advertising industry in general is more accurately described as the exposure industry. The Googles, Facebooks, and MTVs of the world all make trillions of dollars because companies pay them for exposure. Entire industries—from web search and social media, to TV, radio, and print—are built on the effectiveness of the mere exposure effect.

Next time you have to choose from a wall of energy drinks (cost not being an object), the company that you have been exposed to the most consistently, frequently, and recently is the one you will walk away with. Really, the can of energy drink has already been chosen for you; you just like to think it's your idea. Familiarity works.

But so does novelty. Your brain pays attention to things that violate expectations. It rewards you with dopamine for chasing new things, and it amplifies the dopamine reward every time a new thing pleasantly surprises you. Novelty keeps you liking and wanting more.

Your brain is high maintenance. It wants both the newness of novelty and the safety of familiarity. NaS is everywhere—even in the original Zajonc experiment that opened this chapter. None of the participants knew Chinese, which made the Chinese characters *new*. When they had seen the characters before in passing, a part of their brain recognized them as *familiar*, despite that overall sense of newness. And the result was they felt happier after seeing those new-but-familiar characters, and more positive toward them.

NaS reconciles the brain's contradictory preferences, but it isn't without its detractors, especially in the movie and music industries. Critics of the NaS philosophy have described it as "selling out" to the masses. Raymond Loewy wouldn't have considered this a criticism at all. His views on style were proudly populist. When the objective is to maximize consumption, there's no better approach than NaS. The best rebuttal comes from rapper and business mogul Jay-Z, himself an expert in mixing the new with the familiar:

> *I dumbed down for my audience to double my dollars.*
> *They criticize me for it, yet they all yell "Holla!"*

Chapter 9

EMPATHY AND THE HUMAN CONNECTION

The Secret Language of Brands

Put yourself in the dancing shoes of a middle-school girl who, after several weeks of waiting in agony, receives the following reply to her application for admission into the American Ballet Theatre:

Dear Candidate,

Thank you for your application for our ballet academy. Unfortunately, you have not been accepted. You lack the right feet, the turn out, the Achilles tendons, and the leg and torso length. You simply have the wrong body for ballet. With your body, you could be a professional dancer in Vegas. And, at 13, you are already far too old to be considered.

A thirteen-year-old girl was just told her figure is wrong and her body is better suited for a stage in Vegas than a theater stage. How did this rejection letter—a real letter sent to a real thirteen-year-old, incidentally—make you feel? Perhaps angry. Perhaps sad. Likely many of the emotions that the girl herself felt, as she took it in.

Take note of the transformation that just occurred in your mental state: one short paragraph's worth of text transformed your mental state and shifted your mood considerably. This is the magic of human communication.

Communication goes well beyond the acts of reading, writing, and speaking. It goes well beyond language altogether. Communication is the ability to share our deepest internal states—our thoughts, our emotions, our perspectives—with others. It provides the basis for empathy: the ability to assimilate the mental and emotional states of those around us. In short, empathy is the foundation for human sociality.

Fundamentally, communication reflects the human ability to connect. In its most basic form, we connect through communicating information. For example, if a stranger asks you for directions, and you share that piece of useful knowledge in your head, you have connected through that knowledge. We can also connect through communicating on an emotional level. If you see someone smiling ear to ear, typically you can't help but connect to their emotional state, and in the case of a smile, feel a little happier yourself. But less straightforwardly, and perhaps even more profoundly, we connect with others through stories: narratives that communicate complex ideas and perspectives, and are designed to elicit empathy.

There may be no single ability more crucial to brands than communication, because brands are in the business of garnering connection. Branding is about building an informational, emotional, cultural, and personal connection among a company, its message, and its products.

Of course, this is not always an easy thing to do. Human-to-human communication comes with a range of challenges. And when you move from the one-to-one communication humans excel at, to trying to connect on a larger scale of one-to-many as brands must, the challenges compound. When brands do it right, however, they can elicit a connection between their product and the consumer—a connection as strong and transformative as any bond between humans.

THE TENNIS GAME OF COMMUNICATION

To understand how brands and companies communicate, we first need to understand how humans communicate. Let's start with the basic building blocks: how a simple idea is communicated from one person to another.

The longer you study human psychology, the more you inevitably come back to the same conclusion: we humans are pretty dim-witted. We're bad at most things most of the time. We've seen it again and again in this book: our sensory abilities and attention are so limited that, when it comes to how we perceive reality, we more or less make a lot of it up. Our decision-making apparatus is deeply flawed, so much so that an entire field of study, behavioral economics, centers around our irrationality.

Then you turn to communication and it's like a breath of fresh air. When you examine human communication, you can't help but be astonished by just how amazing humans are. First, we have to store an incredibly rich and sophisticated bank of linguistic knowledge. We have to figure out what we want to say on the fly, and then access all of the right words and constructions and combine them in a way that makes sense. Next, there's the physical aspect of communication. We have to coordinate the fine musculature in our throats in order to articulate sounds within the convention of a shared language, which our conversational partner must then understand and interpret. And this is just to communicate a single sentence, much less an idea, story, or complex emotion.

How is this all possible? The growing field of social neuroscience has begun shedding light on this question. By eavesdropping on the brain's activity as communication is taking place, neuroscientists have found that, at the most fundamental level, *communication is the ability of a speaker to plant images and ideas into a listener's head.* When you have an idea in your head that you want to communicate, you are the sender. The person you want to communicate to is the receiver. Your job as the sender is to re-create, inside the receiver's head, your own internal brain state.

Research by Uri Hasson at Princeton University has provided a compelling glimpse of what this looks like in the brain through use of a specialized fMRI technique, inter-subject correlation, which compares how the brains of different people respond when listening to the same story. Not surprisingly, the auditory cortex, which processes basic sounds, reacts very similarly across all individuals as they process a particular story. However, brain states are very different across individuals in more advanced regions of the brain, such as the frontal cortex, which is more concerned with interpretation and meaning. In the brain, we all *hear* something the same way but we don't all *interpret* it the same way. This is why, though we all hear the same notes of a Nickelback song, for some they bring tears of joy, and for others they bring tears of pain—cruel, cruel pain.

Interestingly, there is a special similarity that occurs in the brains of speakers and listeners, which Hasson calls "neural coupling." When you are telling a story, there's a specific constellation of neural activity that represents this story in your brain.[1] Intriguingly, *a very similar array of neural activity is present in the brain of the person listening to your story.* Additionally—and this is key—the more similar you and your listener's brain states are, the better the communication. When the listeners in Hasson's experiments were given comprehension tests on the story they just heard, their scores were highly correlated with the degree of neural coupling they shared with the speaker.[2] The more similar the brain state, the higher the comprehension.

At the level of the brain, *communication is neural coupling* between speaker and listener. We communicate the ideas in our head by transferring our brain state into another person's brain. Effective communication can feel like playing a friendly tennis rally, where the goal is to keep the rally going as long as possible. If you want your partner to be able to return the ball, you need to hit it in such a way that it gets to your partner in stride, on their preferred hand, on their preferred side, and so forth. Likewise, effective communicators are able to frame their messages to best fit the receiver. The better you are at doing this, the better you are able to communicate.

We also subconsciously adjust ourselves as speakers to best "couple" with our communicating partners. You may have noticed that you speak a little slower and softer to your grandmother than you do to a cab driver or a waiter. And you almost certainly speak differently to your closest family members than you do the CEO of the company where you work. You may use different vocabulary, emphasize or deemphasize an accent, or speak at a difference pace or cadence. Just as tennis players learn each other's strengths, weaknesses, and preferences over time, in the rally of verbal communication, so, too, do we adjust ourselves over time to a partner's style of play.

Scottish linguists Martin Pickering and Simon Garrod summarize this phenomenon as what they call *interactive alignment*.[3] Their research shows that over the course of even a few minutes of speaking with someone, our timbre, amplitude, speed of speech, and even our posture will subtly and unconsciously shift to match those of the individual we're talking to, while they also match theirs to ours. This slow, unconscious convergence to a shared intersection naturally facilitates communication; the longer we talk with someone, the more similar our styles become, and the more similar our styles become, the better we understand each other. Watch for this the next time you talk with someone; if you slowly begin to lean back in your chair during a conversation, chances are, the person you're speaking to will do the same. Similarly, if you live in another country for an extended period of time, you may find it's not just a new language you learn. Your speech rate and even your accent may shift to better match cultural differences in speaking styles. All of these verbal and nonverbal shifts are implicit attempts to match our conversational partners, to establish neural coupling, and to increase the efficiency of communication.

Bottom line: The more you can mirror the communication style of your conversation partner, the better the communication and the more persuasive your message.

Adjusting to a new tennis partner takes time, however. The first few attempts can be frustrating—you may spend more time chasing down stray balls than you do actually on the court. We all have our own complex sets of experiences, peculiarities, and associations that can affect how we hear what others say. Effective communication means establishing a common understanding of shared semantics. And that's hard enough with only one listener. As the number of people you're communicating to multiplies, the difficulty only grows.

NEURAL COUPLING (AND DECOUPLING) IN THE CONSUMER WORLD

To sell their products or services, companies need to communicate with current and potential customers. But unlike interpersonal communication, marketing communications must be generated centrally and distributed en masse. It's difficult enough to get our brain to sync with that of the person sitting across from us. Brands are trying to sync up with millions of different people at the same time.

When neural coupling isn't established and certain semantics are merely assumed, trouble ensues. In the summer of 2017, clothing company KA Designs released a line of bright, rainbow-colored T-shirts prominently displaying, of all things . . . swastikas.[4] Their rationale was explained in their Facebook ad: "For thousands of years, the swastika meant something positive. But one day, Nazism . . . They stigmatized the swastika forever. The swastika is coming back, together with Peace, together with Love, together with Respect, together with Freedom."

While it is technically true that the swastika was originally derived from ancient Hindu tradition, where it was a symbol of auspicious good luck, this meaning is, unsurprisingly, lost on the average consumer. Today the swastika is synonymous with hate, Nazism, and genocide. Sure, the designers knew they meant peace, love, respect, and freedom when they used the swastika, but this is clearly not what they generated in their audience's brains. It was a massive failure in coupling. In an fMRI study, the intersubject correlation between KA Designs and a potential customer would be next to zero. Which, coincidentally, is also the T-shirt line designers' chance of future employment.

swastika
$22

PEACE with Swastika
$22

ZEN with Swastika
$20

A sample of KA Design's infamous "Swastika" T-shirt line

The backlash was swift and emphatic. KA's Twitter feed and email inboxes instantly flooded with a torrent of negative comments. To be fair, they did receive one positive endorsement: "I am thankful these hippies are finally getting onboard. I endorse these shirts." This came from Andrew Angling, founder of the neo-Nazi newspaper *The Daily Stormer*. Not exactly the ideal Yelp review. KA Designs backpedaled vigorously, apologizing and then releasing a new T-shirt featuring a swastika—this time with a red line through it. However, the damage had been done.

KA's campaign was so disastrous it seems unthinkable that it even happened. Shouldn't they have known better? Couldn't they have anticipated the response? KA's stumble was extreme, but more modest semantic missteps are far from rare. The year 2017 also featured a Facebook ad for Dove body lotion in which women removed their T-shirts to transform into another woman underneath, ostensibly intended to convey Dove's racially diverse customer base. But Dove was sharply criticized for one of the transitions, from a black woman to a white woman, which looked shockingly close to a literal whitewashing.

However, the Oscar for the best neural coupling mistake of 2017 goes to Pepsi for its infamous Kendall Jenner commercial, in which she played the role of an activist who defuses a tense situation by handing a police officer in riot gear an ice-cold can of Pepsi. In one fell swoop, Pepsi shamelessly commodified images of protest while also marginalizing the racially charged issue of police brutality. The backlash was so severe that Pepsi pulled the commercial almost immediately and issued a formal apology.[5]

The examples of KA, Dove, and Pepsi show how establishing neural coupling becomes exponentially more difficult as a group of listeners enlarges and diversifies. It's like trying to play tennis with hundreds of people at once, each with their own very different style.

BEYOND WORDS

The more you can cater your communication style to that of your intended audience, all else being equal, the more effective your message will be. The same is true for companies. This adds an important nuance to the common business idiom *Know your customer*: it is important to understand not only the preferences and needs of one's customers, but their communication style as well. Sharp brands pay painstaking attention to customer vocabulary. Do people in their target demographic speak quickly or slowly? Do they have a grandiose vocabulary, or a simple one? Do they say *hell* or *heck*? *Oh my goodness, oh my God,* or *OMG*?

Communication style matters. Parents who want to get their teenage children to eat healthier, but aren't having much luck with rational arguments on the long-term health benefits of antioxidants and dietary fiber, may do better by downloading Snapchat and sending messages like *Veggies are like totes lit, fam, and like way delish btw.* Okay, no, they wouldn't. But in all seriousness, it's long been noted that teenagers have far more influence over one another than their parents do,[6] and this may well have something to do with the exclusively nuanced slang that this cohort uses to communicate.[7] The teenage years are defined by a struggle for independence from parents. By linguistically excluding their totally uncool moms and dads, teenagers successfully limit their parental overlords' persuasive power.

Tailoring communication style to the audience is why advertisements for geriatric products tend to be spoken in a slow tone by an elderly person, and why advertisements for teenagers attempt to use teenage slang. But when communication styles are mismatched, the results can be disastrous.

Look no further than Depends, the adult diaper brand, as a case in point. Hashtags have become commonplace on products catering to millennials and Generation Z, but you won't typically see them on products for older adults. Depends was an exception. In 2014, they activated a social-media marketing campaign encouraging customers to post pictures of themselves wearing Depends diapers using the hashtag #DropYourPants to increase awareness about adult leakage.

In case you think you misread, here it is again: Depends' social-media marketing campaign encouraged customers to post pictures of themselves wearing Depends diapers using the hashtag #DropYourPants to increase awareness about adult leakage. It's hard enough explaining to Grandpa how attachments in email work; now you have to teach him how to Instagram his (literal) shit? Never have people been more thankful for a failed marketing attempt.

2017 was when millennials surpassed the $1 trillion mark in consumer buying power. It was also the year millennials became the largest generation in the US workforce.[8] Companies not only want to sell to millennials and Generation Z; they also want to hire them. As is the case with each subsequent generation, there are gaps in communication styles and vocabulary. See the following email from Microsoft, which made a noble effort at emulating their audience's communication style through heavy use of "hip" millennial and Gen Z vernacular:

Hey Bae Intern! <3

Hi! I am Kim, a Microsoft University Recruiter. My crew is coming down from our HQ in Seattle to hang with you and the crowd of bay area interns at Internapalooza on 7/11.

BUT MORE IMPORTANTLY*, we're throwing an exclusive after party the night of the event at our San Francisco office and you're invited! There will be hella noms, lots of dranks, the best beats and just like last year, we're breaking out the Yammer beer pong tables!*

HELL YES TO GETTING LIT ON A MONDAY NIGHT!

(An image of the actual email is available on our resources website. 🖳)

Depends and Microsoft's neural coupling failures are good for a laugh. But when a brand simply can't (or won't) adjust their communication style as their available customer base shifts, it can threaten the business itself. Enter Harley-Davidson. The legendary brand of motorcycles provides a perfect example of how neural coupling can halt a brand completely. Harley-Davidson built its business and brand on the baby boom generation. But with this group quickly aging, the company's primary task for the last decade has been simple: reach out to millennials. On its face, the challenge is easy. Harleys should be extremely marketable to millennials. They're fuel efficient, vintage, and speak to the free-minded spirit of the generation. And "there are plenty of millennials riding motorcycles," Harley-Davidson's CEO, Matthew Levatich, noted in 2017. "It's up to us to inspire them to ride and engage with Harley-Davidson." But their messaging strategy is failing, because their ads don't speak "millennial":

Harley-Davidson is that rare brand you see tattooed on people's calves, arms, and asses because, for a certain demographic, it resonates so deeply. But this legendary American brand's sales have been declining for ten consecutive years, with the stock price steadily slumping from $72 a share to $31 between the summers of 2014 and 2019.[9] Clearly, Harley-Davidson is missing the mark with millennials as they mock their concerns over social well-being, unemployment—and even smartphone culture. This mockery likely endears them further to their existing older audience but has done little to persuade the all-important up-and-coming generation of potential riders.

While Levatich fully acknowledged the strategic necessity of attracting a new generation of buyers, he also insists on criticizing the smartphone usage iconic of millennials: "We have to find riders who are freedom and adventure-seekers, who want to live for real, get out from under their smartphones, and be out on the open road." In other words, they wish millennials weren't millennials.

As of 2019, Harley is mulling the release of an electric motorcycle, a drastic departure from the core of their brand in a last-ditch attempt to appeal to younger riders.[10] Time will tell if this is too little, too late, and whether their inability to speak millennial will be their undoing.

Think of the products, services, and brands you love and defend. How similar are the communication styles of those brands to yours?

Netflix is the perfect example of a company that does this aspect of neural coupling right. Instead of talking *at* the consumer, they talk *to* the consumer. Most importantly, they speak the language of the modern consumer—they speak "internetish." The vocabulary of internetish is filled with memes, GIFs, and references to pop and tech culture. Internetish is what happens when you run the subculture of Reddit users through an NaS filter. One look at Netflix's Twitter and Instagram accounts shows just how good the brand is at neural coupling with their internetish-speaking consumers. They respond to fans with GIFs just as friends do when texting. They've never seen a meme they didn't like. And they make sharp, self-aware cultural references that are witty AF. See Netflix Australia–New Zealand's response to Twitter extending its character limit:

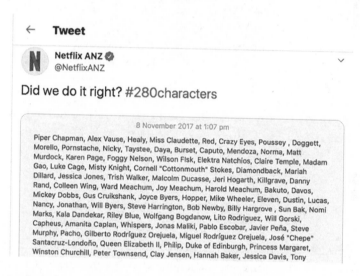

Examples of Netflix's flair for summarizing movie plots:

A typical Netflix response to sassy fans using a meme featuring Queen Bey:

Consumers regard brands like Netflix that do neural coupling especially well as friends. And not only does that serve their communication needs; it also fosters trust and belonging.

MIRROR NEURONS

Neural coupling enables our brains to connect to others' in order to share information. But our tendency to align ourselves with the people we interact with goes beyond the communication of ideas. The people in our environment influence us, and we influence them, through their behaviors and even their simple presence. Have you ever had the experience of yawning upon seeing someone else yawn? Or digging into your pocket for your phone when the person across from you does? We feel compelled to do these things because mirroring others is a core feature of human sociality.

The people in your environment are constantly influencing your brain state, and you're influencing theirs. You're walking down the office hallway and you see the elevator door shut abruptly on a person's shoulder. Automatically, you recoil in sympathy. Or you're watching a football game, and you feel your own heart racing with excitement as the running back takes off on a fifty-yard run. Or you see a woman pick up a steaming, delicious coffee, and you feel warmed by the cozy-looking beverage. You automatically and unavoidably mimic the mental states of those around you.

This innate human tendency is largely the result of a small cluster of neurons in the frontal lobe, appropriately called *mirror neurons*. The mirror neuron breakthrough was made about ten years ago by Giaccomo Rizzolati at the University of Parma. Rizzolati and his team did not set out to discover this fundamental linchpin of human sociality; they stumbled onto it while trying to understand how monkeys produce simple motor movements. Using a single-cell recording device, they monitored the activity of individual neurons in the frontal cortex as monkeys completed several actions. When a monkey reached down and picked up food, specific cells in the frontal cortex would fire. So far, not so impressive; we've known for a long time that frontal regions of the brain are heavily involved in the production of motor movements. What was interesting was the same region—in fact, the same *exact* neurons—also became active when a monkey *observed another monkey* reaching and picking up food!

After additional studies, they found these neurons did not just respond to the *act* itself; they also responded to the *intentions* behind the act. Our mirror neurons are able to detect extremely subtle differences in the *intent* of a motion—way before a behavior is produced.[11] That is, when you see someone reach over and pick up an apple, your mirror neurons can already tell that at that juncture whether the person is intending to then put it to their mouths and eat it, or just place it somewhere. In other words, we have a group of neurons in our frontal cortex that fires both when we intend to do something and also when another person intends to do that same action.[12]

Many studies in humans have replicated and extended these findings. Marco Iacoboni and his UCLA colleagues have concluded that these neurons support the automatic and immediate *internal* simulation of *external* mental states[13]—something that intimately connects us with others. They are what make our noses scrunch up when we see someone take a bite of unappetizing food, and make us wince with embarrassment at a public speaker nervously fumbling their words. Mirror neurons also provide us with a key insight about this mirroring process: we don't merely mimic the actions of others like automatons; we *involuntarily* simulate their mental state and intentions behind the action.

MONKEY SEE, MONKEY DO

Still, mirror neurons are more than a tad overhyped. A quick Google search might lead you to believe they're responsible for everything from autism to the evolution of language to the birth of human civilization itself. Their role in human sociality is much more nuanced[14] than popular culture suggests. But one thing is clear: they are crucial to our ability to represent the intentions and behaviors of others, and to mimic these intentions and behaviors. And eliciting mimicry can be an incredibly potent tool in the consumer world.

When it comes to eliciting mimicry, Coca-Cola proves once again why it's one of the world's top brands. Coke is famous for advertisements showing fun-loving groups of relatable people exhibiting Coke's desired behavior: drinking and enjoying the company's sparkly brown beverage. Take Coca-Cola's "Taste the Feeling" commercial,[15] which regularly plays in movie theaters right before the feature film begins. ⓢ The ad starts with a handful of people buying a Coke and popcorn, sitting down in the movie theater, and singing along to a cheery song while they eat their popcorn and drink their Coke. There are twenty-one people in the theater shot. All are either holding or drinking a Coke while watching a film.

This ad doesn't just model a behavior Coca-Cola wants consumers to engage in—buying Coke. It also models the mental state of people engaging in that behavior. People are drinking Coke and smiling, if a bit excessively. The emotion their smiles symbolize amplifies the action; it drives the viewer to mirror not only buying Coke but also the depicted emotional and mental state once the Coke has been purchased. Through ads that rely heavily on the human tendency to mirror others, Coca-Cola effectively made their products synonymous with happiness well before they made this association explicit in their "Open Happiness" marketing campaign.

Seeing someone similar to you enjoying a product helps the brain simulate the experience of having the product, which in turn leads to a greater desire for it. And there is reason to suggest this is particularly true when it comes to clothing. In fall 2017, women's fashion rental service Rent the Runway came up with a new, down-to-earth, "every woman" way of showcasing their dresses. They asked real women, who had really rented from them, to volunteer their pictures for use on the site. And according to Rent the Runway, women were 200 percent more likely to rent after seeing an article of clothing on women who looked like them, as compared to viewing it on a model.[16]

Other companies quickly followed suit. Lululemon garnered more than two million page views and a million Instagram "likes" when they asked their customers to post photos of themselves wearing Lululemon gear under the hashtag #thesweatlife, and Coach gained over 26,000 posts nearly overnight when they asked their customers to post pictures of themselves casually using their Coach purses in their everyday lives. Katherine Lin, a frequent participant in this trend, told the *Wall Street Journal*, "It shows how much they want to connect with us as consumers . . . It makes it more real to see it on a real person at a real event."[17] Next time you're shopping on Adidas's or Reebok's website, you'll see a "Share how you wear it" section that pulls real-life pictures of products from Instagram to include on the e-commerce pages.

Mirror neurons don't just activate based on what you see. They're also impacted by what you hear. Mirror neurons explain why laughter can be contagious—and why the television laugh track was so popular for so long.

Laugh tracks may have gone the way of the dinosaur, but from their invention by Charles Douglass in the 1950s through the end of the century, they were the true genius behind American TV. The laugh track is the sound of laughter that punctuates a joke, a verbal exclamation mark to comedic writing. But the laugh track did much more than punctuate a joke; it made the joke *funnier*. At the mirror neuron level, hearing other people laugh makes you want to reflect the emotion and action of the laughter. People who previously wouldn't have smiled at a joke chuckle at the same joke with an added laugh track.

Laugh tracks became an endangered species in the 2010s, partly because modern audiences understand the inauthenticity of the laugh track—and this awareness made the laughs a hindrance to the humor, not an addition. And the complex, cinematic nature of today's shows would only highlight this falseness further, unlike the stationary sets of yesteryear. Can you imagine a laugh track accompanying *Game of Thrones'* Tyrion Lannister saying, "I drink and I know things"?

EMPATHY

As we've seen, mirroring is not merely about mental states, but also emotional states—and this is where the phenomenon of empathy comes in.

Study after study confirms humans are biologically built for empathy. If you've ever spent time in a nursery, you know this all too well: when one child laughs, they all laugh; when one cries, they all cry. fMRI studies have found that the same regions activated when we experience pain are also activated when we see others experience pain.[18] We are wired to feel how others feel, and this emotional mirroring is a tremendous human trait. Empathy is the reason we were horrified and sad after watching the Red Wedding in *Game of Thrones* and overjoyed when the evil King Joffrey was finally killed (spoiler alert, by the way).

However, our empathetic system has a major glitch: it focuses on the individual, not the group. We care more about one person than we do about many people. We deeply empathize with the plight of a single child, but the suffering of a large group of children is too abstract to compel our feelings. Given what we know about human evolution, this makes sense. We lived for tens of thousands of years in small, tight-knit social groups. Our circle of care—the people we depended on, and who depended on us, for survival—did not extend beyond these few significant individuals.

Let's revisit the rejection letter from the beginning of this chapter with this quirk in mind. This time, instead of one teenage girl, imagine an entire team of middle-school ballet dancers applying to the American Ballet Theatre academy. Here's how the rejection letter would read:

Dear Candidates,

Thank you for your application for our ballet academy. Unfortunately, your team has not been accepted. They lack the right feet, the turn outs, the Achilles tendons, and the leg and torso lengths. Your team simply has the wrong bodies for ballet. With your bodies, you all could be professional dancers in Vegas. And, at 13, your team members are already far too old to be considered.

Most people feel *less* empathy reading this second rejection letter. But the only difference is singular nouns and pronouns have been changed to plural. Our brains are programmed to feel more empathy for one person, the singular, than for multiple people, the plural. *Empathy does not scale.*

Research led by Paul Slovic at the University of Oregon has systematically explored how this bias, termed *psychic numbing*, influences our judgments and actions.[19,20] In one experiment, he showed an image of a young, impoverished child to a group of undergraduate students and asked how much they would personally donate to help this unfortunate child in need. He asked the same question to another group of students, this time showing two children in need. The group who saw the solitary young child actually donated *far* more than the group shown two children. Follow-up studies have shown, with horrifying precision, that our empathy, and our willingness to help, actually *decreases* as the group becomes larger.

This results in a massive glitch in our moral intuition. If we care about child #1, and we care about child #2, we should care *at least* as much about child #1 and child #2 together than either child alone. Yet we don't. It's the arithmetic equivalent of saying that the sum of 1 and 1 is not only less than 1 + 1, but is *less than 1*. This is even more egregious when we consider that we care about a group of children less than an individual child, even when the group contains *that very same child*! It's as if the empathy we feel for an individual dissipates the moment that individual is grouped with others. Saint Mother Teresa, one of the most empathetic people in modern history, provides the perfect distillation: "If I look at the mass I will never act. If I look at the one, I will."

Events affecting single individuals pull at our heartstrings, and this is mirrored in the amount and type of news in the media coverage certain events receive. The year 1987 was one of the most violent on record; over twenty thousand murders were committed across the nation. However, it was the story of one life-and-death struggle that brought everyone to their knees: Baby Jessica's. On October 14, eighteen-month-old Jessica McClure fell down a well in Midland, Texas. In the two days it took rescuers to bring her to safety, nearly a hundred people (including several children) were killed across the country—yet these masses received hardly a footnote in the news as the world watched Jessica's rescue with bated breath. The story gained global attention and countless hours of nightly national news coverage. When she was lifted to safety, she became an instant celebrity; her story prompted multiple interviews, an ABC television movie, and even an invitation to the White House. President George H. W. Bush declared that "everybody in America became godmothers and godfathers of Jessica while this was going on," and in 2010 *USA Today* ranked her twenty-second on its all-time list of "lives of indelible impact."[21]

The coverage of Baby Jessica was extreme, but stories like hers, where an individual's circumstances grip our hearts, are exceedingly common. From Natalee Holloway's tragic 2004 disappearance in Aruba, to the unforgettable mystery of JonBenét Ramsey's 1996 murder, there are innumerable examples of individuals who become focal points for our empathy and receive national attention as a result. Our empathetic system homes in on the individual. And nothing magnifies that empathy for the individual like a well-told story.

A VEHICLE FOR EMPATHY

It would be reductionist to claim there is one element that underlies the enjoyment we get from stories; people enjoy them for a variety of reasons. However, if we did have to posit a single element, the strongest candidate would be human empathy. The ability of stories to magnify and export empathy is, frankly, amazing. It is natural to empathize with people in front of you, but stories connect us to people with whom we'd normally never interact, in other places and times, and for whom we would otherwise feel no affinity. As the late, great James Baldwin put it, "You think your pain and your heartbreak are unprecedented in the history of the world. But then you read."

Yet not all stories garner empathy to the same degree. One common feature of stories is that they tend to revolve around a single individual. Luke Skywalker carries the plot in Star Wars, Pip is central to *Great Expectations*, Tony Soprano bosses *The Sopranos*, and so forth.

This observation makes complete sense given what we know about avoiding psychic numbing: focusing on a single individual maximizes empathy.

Your authors directly tested this connection between stories and empathy to explore how it affects our consumer experience.[22] We created pairs of stories with believable situations like running through an airport to barely make it on a flight; one story featured a single person doing this, and the other featured a group of people. For example, one set of participants would read a story about a woman named Ellen who was running late for her flight. She asked the TSA to skip to the front of the security line, cleared the scanners in record time, and sprinted to her gate just before they closed the doors. A second set of participants would see the same story, but instead of Ellen, it was a family that was running late for their flight, with the pronouns updated from singular to plural (instead of "*She* ran through the airport," "*They* ran through the airport").

We found, across a very wide array of stories and situations, that stories revolving around a single person generated far higher rates of emotion and empathy than those with families. Empathy is maximized when delivered via an individual, character-driven narrative.

These individual narratives not only drive empathy but also impact purchasing behavior. In the experiment, after subjects read each scenario, they were presented with a *call to action*, marketing speak for the brief statement that tells the customer what they should do next (*Buy Now, Learn More, Add to Cart*). In this case, both variations of the stories were followed by the call to action *Buy Acme Brand Shoes*. Participants were then asked how likely they were to buy the product featured in the story. Scenarios involving a single individual (e.g., the Ellen story) led to a higher likelihood of buying the product than the plural scenarios!

We all love stories. Brands optimize for this fact by using character-driven narratives to exploit empathy and maximize wallet greasing. When you mix the brain's empathetic bias toward individuals with its natural proclivity for stories, the effect is irresistible.

If you reflect on recent advertisements that pulled at your emotional heartstrings, chances are they were commercials telling a story that focused on a single individual. Nike, for example, profiled youth athletes' daily workout routines in their "What's Your Motivation?" series. In one, a teenage boy gets up at the wee hours of the morning and heads to the courts to practice his jump shot, finally returning home at sunset only after he hits the shot he had been struggling so hard to make. It's a chillingly emotional ad, and it's nearly impossible not to empathize with the boy's diligence. It's also hard to imagine having a similar response had the ad focused on an entire high school basketball team all practicing jump shots at dawn.

Along similar lines, one of the most well-received campaigns in recent memory was the English Sports Council's "This Girl Can" campaign, aimed at getting more women to participate in sports. The ads each focused on a single female, who did not fit the typical mold of an athlete, participating in running, kickboxing, or lifting weights to the tune of Missy Elliott's "Get Ur Freak On." *Forbes* named it the top sports marketing campaign of 2015. In that year alone, the Council's inaugural video was viewed over eight million times, and #ThisGirlCan was used on social media over a million times.[23]

Example advertisement from England Sports Council's
#ThisGirlCan campaign

BRANDS ARE PEOPLE, TOO

The fact that empathy orients to a single individual also has deeper consequences: we naturally see objects, as well as complex entities and large groups like companies, as having personalities the same way individuals do. In other words, we personify things we know aren't human.

When our smartphone acts up, we ask it, "Why are you doing this to me?" or claim it "doesn't like me." We name our cars. Test subjects act politely toward computers they interact with,[24] and even exercise politeness toward websites, with the implicit assumption that, as with humans, their consideration will be reciprocated.[25]

This personification naturally extends to how we see corporations. We tend to personify brands the same way we personify our cars, our laptops, and our pets. To our brains, brands are people, too, and we establish relationships with them just as we do with the people in our lives.

Sometimes, brands aid this by creating fictional characters such as Tony the Tiger, the Pillsbury Doughboy, and the GEICO Gecko. Other times, they may use a real-life "character" to tell the company's narrative. Think of Elon Musk and Tesla, Jeff Bezos and Amazon, Arianna Huffington and HuffPo.

Creating fictional characters and hyping up real employees both serve the same branding purpose: they give you a single figure as a focus for empathy and connection. Brands then use this empathy to establish an enduring relationship with you.

The effectiveness of tapping into the brain's love of character-driven narratives and brand personification also explains the millions of dollars brands spend on endorsements. What companies are really paying for here are empathy and connection. Connecting consumers' personification of their brand with the right celebrity not only galvanizes an empathetic connection; the celebrity's positive traits also may transfer to the brand personality. No wonder Wild Turkey and Lincoln Motors use Matthew McConaughey, Uniqlo sponsors Roger Federer, and Dior uses Charlize Theron.

These campaigns require considerable repetition, and often a hefty endorsement check, but they can also be incredibly effective. Market-Watch estimates that the average endorsement deal leads directly to a sales increase of 4 percent.[26] As Kit Yarrow, author of *Decoding the New Consumer Mind*, remarks, "Whether they do so consciously or not, consumers will attribute a personality to your brand in their quest for a shorthand, emotional understanding of your brand's values. The people who represent your brand are part of that perception."[27] As consumers, we extend our preexisting perception of and empathy for an endorser to the brand itself.

Take the example of Under Armour. The athletic-gear industry is a competitive landscape chock-full of titans like Nike, Puma, and Adidas, so when Under Armour came on to the scene in the late 1990s, it was the scrappy new kid on the block. So, when seeking out an athlete to be their first endorser, Under Armour didn't attempt to sign a larger-than-life megastar like Nike did with LeBron James, or Adidas did with Paul Pogba. Instead, Under Armour went another route completely, one very much in line with the company ethos and the brand's "personality." Who did they choose to represent them?

A ballerina.

Yes, a ballerina. Meet the personification of Under Armour, Misty Copeland.

The opening frame of Misty Copeland's first video advertisement for Under Armour, introducing her as their original "triumphant underdog"

Copeland is not just any ballerina. She's the teenage ballerina whose real-life rejection letter you read at the beginning of this chapter. Her Under Armour video ad opens with Copeland standing *en pointe*, balancing on her toes, profiling her toned, sculpted physique. A narrator reads the rejection letter. Copeland ends the ad with another graceful pose as the screen fades to the Under Armour logo and the words *I will what I want.*[28]

Copeland had a rough childhood. She was one of six children under the care of a mother on her fourth marriage, with an abusive stepfather who would often call her racial slurs. Despite all of her hardships, Misty Copeland became the first African American principal dancer at the American Ballet Theatre. And by positioning Copeland as the personification of Under Armour, the company connected her triumphant underdog story with their own and earned a mountain of empathy in less than two minutes and six sentences—empathy that quickly propelled the brand into the American sports apparel conversation.

Communication seems simple, but as we've seen, this "natural" task is anything but. Effective communication is a social game of Tetris where the skill is in the ability to rearrange your message to best fit the listener.

Brands have a direct incentive to communicate skillfully. Brand messaging that connects successfully with consumers via neural coupling fosters deeper communication and connection. Thanks to our natural predilection toward mimicry, we involuntarily mirror the actions, language, and behavior—even the mental and emotional states—of the people around us, even when those people are in ads. The old adage *You are who you surround yourself with* is truer than we ever thought!

The proverbial lubricant in the psychological gears of communication is empathy. And today's advertising only scratches the surface of what's possible in terms of establishing deep connections with consumers. Artificial and virtual realities provide innovative platforms for deeper neural coupling between brands and consumers. Mirroring and mimicry are likely to become more nuanced and powerful, exposing our empathetic bias to greater impact.

For now, though, the most powerful way brands have to elicit empathy, and therefore create a connection with the power to drive your behavior, is still the story. It's for this reason that Tyrion Lannister from *Game of Thrones* justifies his choice for the next king of Westeros by picking the candidate with the strongest story: "What unites people? Armies? Gold? Flags? *Stories.* There's nothing more powerful in the world than a good story. Nothing can stop it. No enemy can defeat it." And no consumer can resist it.

Chapter 10

THE ESSENCE OF
EVERYTHING

*The Science of Essentialism and How It Drives
Attachment (and Sales)*

Creating stencil art is relatively easy. You sketch or print an outline, cut around it, and place it on a surface. Spray some paint and voilà—art. A similarly stenciled painting was created in 2006. A mere twelve years later, in October 2018, it was sold for $1.4 million at Sotheby's auction house in London.

Paying $1.4 million for a sports car makes a certain amount of sense, because you can't create that car yourself. But $1.4 million for a stencil? Humans certainly have a strange way of valuing things.

But the case of this million-dollar stencil gets even stranger. As soon as the auction gavel slammed down, signaling the painting had been sold to an undisclosed buyer, the painting "self-destructed." The frame turned into a paper shredder, pulling the painting down into its blades. Onlookers gasped in horror as the bottom of the frame shredded the painting live, for every auction goer to see. The $1.4 million painting was shredded roughly halfway before coming to a halt. Surely the half-destroyed painting was no longer worth the $1.4 million, right?

The buyer decided to keep the painting. As she explained,[1] "When the hammer came down last week and the work was shredded, I was at first shocked, but gradually I began to realize that I would end up with my own piece of art history." The person responsible for the art piece's destruction was the original artist himself, Banksy, who—unbeknownst to anyone but him—had included the shredder in the frame and set it to destroy the painting as soon as the final bid was accepted. Initially called *Girl with Balloon*, the piece is now retitled *Love Is In the Bin*. Banksy did not destroy a million-dollar piece of art at that auction; he created one.

Banksy's stunt was one of the most-discussed events of the art world in recent memory and has been deemed one of the all-time greatest instances of "performance art." The most ironic aspect of the event (and perhaps part of the point Banksy was trying to make) was that shredding the painting made it *more* valuable. The bidder of the painting kept it. Moreover, should the bidder choose to resell, the new, half-shredded version should fetch an even higher sum![2]

As we've seen over and over since chapter one, we don't experience the world as it actually is. We're a step removed. Rather than experience something directly, we experience the brain's mental model of it. Simple things like our other senses influence our mental model (e.g., a louder "crunch" means a tastier potato chip), as do our beliefs about a product (e.g., expensive wine tastes better) or brand (e.g., Coke tastes better *only* when we know we're drinking Coke). There's a gap between objective reality and our internal subjective experience, space in which our other senses and our beliefs color (and sometimes even alter) our perceptions.

But those aren't the only factors working in that gap. There is a different category of belief that impacts our mental models, one concerning the metaphysical nature of the physical world. As examples like Banksy's balloon girl make exquisitely clear, our perception of any given object is about much more than just its physical qualities.

Beyond the physical is our hidden belief in an object's "soul," or as psychologist Paul Bloom refers to it, an object's *essence*. This essence transcends its physical qualities. Even when the object is physically destroyed, its essence—our underlying beliefs about that object, the story we tell ourselves about it—lives on. And it is an object's essence, as much as or more than the object itself, that we value and find pleasurable. Banksy's *Girl with Balloon* had value to begin with largely because it was *created by Banksy*. Its origin was already part of the stencil art's story—its essence. Destroying the work didn't rid the art of its essence. Rather, the act of destruction *enhanced* its essence—and in the process, increased its value.

The example of Banksy's painting provides an interesting window into the psychology of essence, and why we appreciate art the way we do. But art is not the only field where essentialist beliefs are at play. Companies are eager to instill their products and brands with essence, because in just the same way that they do for art, these essences fundamentally alter our perceptions of those products and brands.

ESSENTIALISM: THE SCIENCE OF MEANING

Before exploring its place in the consumer world, let's first take a deeper dive into the science of essentialism.

Essentialism may be deeply rooted in human development. From a young age, humans must learn to generalize about the world, about how things and people persist despite surface changes over time. Your father doesn't cease to be your father just because he shaved his mustache, and the ice from the freezer box doesn't cease to exist just because it melts. It's only through this essentialist understanding that you can operate in the world with the safe assumption of its stability.

This has a lot to do with the special importance we place on ownership—or, in behavioral economics speak, with the endowment effect: once we have something in our possession, we tend to value it more than we otherwise would, just by virtue of our ownership. Much of this phenomenon has to do with our loss-averse nature; once we have something, it is ours to lose, and we're more motivated to prevent potential losses than to achieve potential gains. But sometimes, there is something else at play: we value objects we own because of the unique history we have with them.

Psychologist Paul Bloom tested this directly by tricking children into believing that he had made exact copies of their favorite stuffed animals.[3] They were then given a choice of which stuffed animal to take home: the original or the duplicate. Despite the physical features being identical, they overwhelmingly preferred the original. In other words, the original teddy bear carries its own specific essence that cannot be duplicated. Just like the sentimental value associated with a game-worn Michael Jordan jersey, the essence transcends the physical.

As we get older, we become more sophisticated in our understanding of the world, but our brains never fully outgrow these essentialist tendencies. And the essences the brain attaches to things impact our ultimate pleasure, our sense of those things' value, and, of course, our consumer behavior.

Think of sports teams. What makes a team someone's favorite? Why do fans like the Los Angeles Lakers? It can't be just the players, since players change often; Magic Johnson's Lakers of the 1980s had zero players in common with the Shaq and Kobe Lakers of the 2000s, let alone the LeBron Lakers of 2020. It can't be coaches or management, because operations personnel change as frequently as the players. It can't even be the city, because the Lakers were originally from Minneapolis, Minnesota. There is also a second NBA team in Los Angeles, the Clippers. If this team preference were driven by allegiance to the city, fans *should* like both LA teams equally. And if the Lakers were to move to, say, Las Vegas, many fans would follow the team despite losing this objective geographical link. In fact, this exact scenario occurred with the Raiders. The NFL team was originally in Los Angeles, before moving to Oakland. As of the 2020–2021 season, they become the Las Vegas Raiders. And many (not all) fans followed the team through these moves. This is because, ultimately, they are following the team's ongoing story—its essence.

THE ESSENCE OF TASTE

Recall from chapter one how, of all our senses, taste is by far the most impressionable; our mental model for taste may as well be made of Silly Putty. This is particularly true when it comes to essence, which is why restaurants work hard to add essence to their offerings.

Think about asking for a wine recommendation to pair with an entrée at a nice restaurant. The sommelier recommends a few options, and you ask what the Chianti tastes like. The sommelier says, "It's soft and fruity at the beginning, jammy and dark-chocolaty in the middle, and woodsy-smoky at the end. It tastes like watching an autumn sunset." Before you can fully grasp all the feelings, associations, and memories (both conscious and subconscious) that description conjures up, the somm moves on to the biography of the winemaker, and how he named the bottle after his eldest daughter who hated red wine until she tried this exact bottle. By providing you with additional details about the wine, the somm is building up the essence of the wine in your head and altering your mental model for it. This, in turn, deeply impacts how the wine actually tastes when you finally drink it.

One test that has demonstrated the strong effect of storytelling and essence on taste, by culinary firm CatchOn, compared the reactions of diners to two dishes.[4] One dish was described via a list of ingredients on a nondescript card that awaited each diner at their table. The other dish was personally introduced by the chef, who also shared a treasured childhood tale that inspired the dish. The group that received the story prior to the dish reported a much better overall eating experience—despite their dishes being identical to those eaten by the non-story group.

In another study,[5] scientists at Cornell discovered that diners' appreciation of their meal could be influenced by where they thought their wine was from. In addition to being served a plate of food, all of the diners were given the same inexpensive Charles Shaw wine (known affectionately to Trader Joe's shoppers as "Two-Buck Chuck"), but half were told it was from Noah's Winery in Northern California, and half were told it was from Noah's Winery in North Dakota. It turns out that North Dakota doesn't carry quite the same gravitas with wine drinkers. Diners who believed their wine was from California rated it as being much more enjoyable. Interestingly, they also rated the food as being more enjoyable, and said they were much more likely to return to the restaurant.

In every dining experience, your brain is digesting sensory information about your food beyond its taste: smell, texture, sound, and visual presentation. But even as you wait for your food to arrive, your brain is already devouring the food's essence: the restaurant's background and founding, the chef's biography, the inspirations for the dishes, the geography of wine, and so on. Your brain tastes the meal before you've had your first bite.

The TV show *Portlandia* hilariously hyperbolizes this in a skit called "Is the Chicken Local?" A dining couple considering ordering a chicken dish ask about the life story of the chicken, his name (it's Colin), his breed, whether he's local, how many acres his roaming area was, who raised him . . . the questions go on. Although exaggerated for humor, the underlying point is spot on: the joy of dining is more than the food's taste, it is the food's *story*.

As Catherine Neville, Emmy-winning host and producer of *taste-MAKERS*, told *Forbes*, "The food industry is no longer solely focused on farm-to-table restaurants, with chefs presenting dishes made with ingredients sourced directly from local producers. Now, people want that type of connection in everything they eat. They want to know who roasts their coffee, who bakes their bread, who pickles their vegetables. They want to feel good about who and what their dollars are supporting and they want connection to their community."[6]

Examples like these are common not only in the restaurant world, but in the food and beverage industry more generally. Does knowing where your cheap 3.5 percent alcohol beer is from really make a difference? If you asked Coors Brewing Company, the answer would be a resounding yes. Nearly every one of their campaigns emphasizes their Rocky Mountains origins. Similarly, Sam Adams recently launched a campaign detailing their "deliberately inefficient" brewing process, emphasizing their traditional manufacture and the human attention that goes into each bottle. Brands take essence, and package and sell it in creative ways. Done right, the brain finds it irresistible.

LIKE WATER FOR ESSENCE

When it comes to consumer products devoid of essence, you can't get any emptier ones than commodity products. Commodities are goods that, physically, are effectively identical from company to company, like gasoline or water. Sure, bottled waters may differ ever so slightly in pH or sodium, but these differences are largely imperceptible to consumers—the product is identical. So what's the difference that makes the difference? Price aside, why choose one brand over another?

These products are fascinating from a branding standpoint because these products can only be clearly differentiated in one way: how they are perceived. And of course, the better a brand is perceived, the greater the demand for it and the higher it can be priced. How do you differentiate a basic good? You give it an essence.

Walk into any grocery store today, and chances are you'll see whole shelves filled with a wide range of different bottled waters—and, depending on the fanciness of the store, some may also carry pretty hefty price tags. If you were to time-travel back to the 1960s, however, and tell someone this, they would call you crazy. In fact, that's exactly what all of the experts, including the preeminent consulting firm McKinsey, told Gustave Leven about his plan to convince Americans to pay a premium for water. After all, why would you pay for something that you could get for free? At the time, potable water was delivered to homes and offices just like the mail.

Leven, the chairman of Source Perrier, had purchased the languishing French company in 1947 after he "concluded that if the [local] people of Vergeze could sell a natural mineral water for three times the price of wine, then the company must have remarkable potential," according to a company history.[7] After seeing moderate success in France, Leven set his sights on America. However, Perrier did not find instant success there. In fact, sales numbers during the first few years proved its critics correct. The fancy French name wasn't fooling anyone; nobody wanted to pay for something they could get for free. That all changed in 1977, when Leven hired marketing guru Bruce Nevins away from Levi Strauss to run Perrier's marketing. Nevins subsequently embarked on a marketing campaign that would change the bottled water industry forever.

Perrier spent an estimated $2.5 to $5 million on Nevins's campaign, which tripled down on the product's origins and hit the essentialist nail on the head. Perrier had one feature that clearly distinguished it from the other waters being sold at the time: bubbles. It wasn't a feature customers were particularly interested in, but through essentialist marketing, Perrier gave that feature depth and bold appeal. Their new slogan? "Naturally sparkling from the center of the Earth."[8] Nevins even flew a plane full of journalists to Perrier's "source" in Vergeze, France.[9] The most iconic Perrier commercial of the era features an Orson Welles voiceover. As the camera pans up dramatically on a glistening bottle, we hear his voice: "Deep below the plains of Southern France, in a mysterious process begun millions of years ago, nature herself adds life to the icy waters of a single spring—Perrier."[10] Take out the mention of Perrier at the end and the commercial could as easily be describing the origin story of a mythological creature.

Sales skyrocketed.[11] In 1975, before the campaign, Americans bought 2.5 million bottles of Perrier. In 1978, the company sold over 75 million!

By 1988, Perrier was selling nearly 300 million bottles a year in the US, nearly 90 percent of all imported mineral water. And before the end of the decade, Perrier had cemented itself as the leading mineral water brand in the world.

Beyond becoming a runaway success, Perrier also opened the door for other companies selling bottled water, both still and sparkling. Within a few years of Perrier's campaign, so many competitors had come to market that New York City appeared to be "drowning in a sea of carbonated waters," as the *New York Times* noted in April 1983. Seagram's, Schweppes, and others jumped at the opportunity to persuade otherwise budget-conscious shoppers to buy their heavily branded, premium-priced product.

The story of bottled water since Perrier is one of constant growth. Bottled water is a booming industry, and the US market is the largest. We spend more than $150 billion a year on bottled water, and in 2017, our bottled water sales volume hit an all-time peak of about 13.7 billion gallons, outpacing milk, coffee, juice, and alcohol. And this is all despite the fact that most of the US is able to get free, clean drinking water straight from the tap. Not to mention that half of all bottled waters carry exotic-sounding names to suggest overseas origins . . . despite the fact that brands like Poland Spring, Pepsi's Aquafina, Coca-Cola's Dasani, and Nestlé's Pure Leaf all come from public sources.[12] They are treated tap water, bottled and branded with an essence.

Looking back on the incredible, pioneering rise of Perrier, the essentialist beliefs about their water that the company was able to instill in consumers through their marketing in the late '70s were key. No "Pepsi Challenge" has been done for Perrier, so unlike Coke, it's difficult to directly measure its brand equity. However, we do have the next best thing. On live radio in 1979, Bruce Nevins reluctantly took part in a blind taste test, in which he couldn't tell the difference between Perrier and other sparkling waters. Radio host Michael Jackson, a critic of Perrier's campaigns, placed seven paper cups on the table. Six were filled with club soda, and one with Perrier. Nevins tried them all and then chose one. It took him five tries to pick out Perrier.[13]

Water is a commodity, after all. The genius was in marketing its essence—which, in the end, tricked even its creator.

Essence doesn't just impact our perception of an individual product;

it can also fundamentally alter how we conceive of an entire product category, even one as ubiquitous as water. When we go to the grocery store and see aisles full of ten different brands of bottled water, we have Perrier to thank. But if essence has the power to create value when it comes to a commodity product like water, how far can it go in driving value in the greater consumer world, where products are *actually* different?

ESSENCE MEETS OUR WALLETS

When it comes to the impact of essence on how we perceive and value things, the food at Michelin-starred restaurants and even bottled water are one thing. They both involve our weakest and most gullible sense, taste. Can essence also add value to everyday objects?

According to the Significant Objects Project, the answer is a resounding yes. Anthropologists Rob Walker and Joshua Glenn purchased a series of ordinary objects on eBay, like rubber duckies, a Pez dispenser, and a small garden gnome. The average price they paid for each was $1.25. They then enlisted the support of professional writers to create a biography for each item. Last, they re-auctioned the items on eBay, using the biographies as the item descriptions. How much did the same objects, now dripping with essence, go for? The average price was well over $100. In total, the project generated $8,000 (which was distributed to the writers).[14]

We see examples of stories that instill essences all the time in the consumer world. The difference is, the stories that instill essences in those items are real.

Ever heard of the 1926 Macallan Valerio Adami? In October 2018, a bottle of said whiskey was auctioned off at a price of $1.1 million, making it the most expensive bottle of alcohol in the world.[15] The essence of the bottle had everything to do with its value.

First, the Macallan brand name is highly respected in the whiskey world. The distillery was founded by Alexander Reid, whose family had been growing barley since before the United States was a country. The alcohol inside the bottle is a sixty-year-old single-malt, single-batch Scotch. Only forty bottles were ever made and each label was painted by hand. The whiskey's namesake, famous pop artist Valerio Adami, created twelve of the labels. None other than Peter Blake, co-designer of the cover of the Beatles album *Sgt. Pepper's Lonely Hearts Club Band*,[16] hand-painted another twelve.

The lore of the bottle transcends the physical properties of the liquor inside. The brain attaches value more to the subjective story than to objective attributes. Fun fact: Only one other bottle of the Valerio Adami has been auctioned on record. It went for $75,000 in 2007. What a steal!

On Etsy, essentialism is baked into the platform itself. "Keep commerce human" is the e-commerce company's tagline. How is it thriving in Amazon's territory while other e-commerce players are barely surviving? Essence. If you want something purely utilitarian, you get it on Amazon. There are product specs, you can read reviews, and your item comes faster and generally cheaper than if you'd bought anywhere else. Etsy offers the opposite of raw utility. A coffee mug from Etsy has value beyond its physical, utilitarian factors. It has essence.

When you buy from Etsy, you can read the seller's biography and what drives them to be an Etsy entrepreneur. You know who made your item, how they made it, and sometimes the inspiration behind its creation. Items can be personalized, customized. They are created *by* someone, *for* someone. Consumers are able to connect to Etsy's sellers in a way that they cannot to Amazon's.

The pleasure derived from an Etsy item is not merely a function of that item's physical components, but a result of its essence. Etsy customers are frequently willing to pay more than they would on Amazon and almost definitely wait longer to receive it. That is the power of essence.

THE ESSENCE OF A COMPANY

Essence isn't just found in individual products, nor is it only found in the way a product is made. The organizations that create those products also carry an essence. Imagine walking into a quaint ma-and-pa Italian grocery that has been in the neighborhood for 150 years. They make everything by hand. The shop, the business, and the recipes have all been passed from generation to generation. Old, dusty black-and-white pictures of family members smile and laugh from every wall. Now imagine walking out of the shop having purchased some of this family's pasta—still with the same label and packaging they'd been using for a century and a half. You bought more than the pasta; you've bought a piece of the store's story, its essence.

Dean Small is the founder and CEO of Synergy Consultants, a food-industry consulting firm that has advised major restaurant businesses such as Buffalo Wild Wings, Macaroni Grill, and Olive Garden for over twenty-five years. He knows the importance of essence firsthand. "The story is crucial in a restaurant," he says. "The origin of the place, the authentic 'why we're here.'" But scaling this to a nationwide chain or brand is easier said than done. "Katz Delicatessen in New York City is a great example of this," Small points out. "Great concept, but difficult to scale and replicate."[17]

Indeed, an authentic, compelling story and a big brand are difficult to marry. But that hasn't stopped some brands, especially older, more established ones, from trying—sometimes embellishing their company stories to instill essence at scale.

One successful example of this comes courtesy of Mercedes-Benz, which is famous for emphasizing its company's history in its marketing. In one dramatic four-minute-long, high-production commercial from spring 2019,[18] they tell the dramatic true story of Mercedes's history dating all the way back to 1888, when Bertha Benz embarked on the first ever long-distance journey via automobile. Another slot, this one only thirty seconds long,[19] provides an equally captivating journey through the company's history. This emphasis on the past instantiates the company as timeless, transcending generation, country, model, and even fuel source.

Macy's has repeatedly dug into its essence to try and stave off the retail apocalypse. Without the convenience of the e-commerce giants who were overtaking the market, what else could they turn to but their storied history? They released the "150 years of Macy's" commercial,[20] which included small clips from popular culture throughout the years that mentioned Macy's. It's hard not to be impressed. Macy's is name-dropped in everything from *I Love Lucy*, *Miracle on 34th Street*, and *The Dick Van Dyke Show* to *Seinfeld* and *Family Guy*. The ad even included a clip of a jovial Kanye West dancing through its aisles. The commercial ends with, "Only one star has been a part of your life for 150 years."

Wells Fargo utilized a similar tactic in a 2018 attempt to rebrand itself after a series of high-profile scandals, the most egregious of which involved employees who, driven by aggressive sales targets, had opened as many as two million deposit and credit card accounts on customers' behalf without their knowledge or consent.[21] The commercial plays out like a mini-documentary, depicting the bank's history from the time of the California Gold Rush.[22] "Back when the country went West for gold, we were the ones who carried it back East. By steam, by horse, by *iron* horse . . ." It goes on to describe, using footage in black and white and then color, its storied history as America's trusted bank. Then, in dramatic fashion, the lights go out—"Until, we lost [that trust]," the narrator says—before the commercial shows smiling modern faces and continues, "But that isn't where the story ends." It goes on to address the changes Wells Fargo has made—including an explicit mention of ending sales quotas—to win back consumer trust. It ends by marrying the history with the modern: "It's a new day at Wells Fargo, but it's a lot like our first day." 🅢 *Don't let the recent scandals fool you,* the commercial says, *we're still who we always were.* In other words, their original essence remains intact.

Several older companies have gone to even greater lengths to commemorate their history and instantiate their essence. IKEA, for example, opened up their own museum in their native Sweden, decked out with rotating exhibitions, documentary viewings, guided tours, and educational events for schools. Rolls-Royce has done something similar for their storied brand by opening up several historical showrooms both in their native UK and Austria.[23] You won't find any Swedish meatballs there, but you will get a fascinating glimpse into the company's history. Some trivia: Co-founder Charles Rolls was an aviation enthusiast and the first Briton to be killed in an aeronautical accident involving a powered aircraft. And the famed Rolls-Royce hood ornament, the "Spirit of Ecstasy," carries with it the story of a secret affair between Baron Montagu of Beaulieu, a pioneer of the automobile movement, and the model for the emblem, Eleanor Velasco Thornton.[24]

Art museums help artists by showcasing their catalogs of work, laying out their histories, and exhibiting their essence—all of which drives up the value of their work. Why not use the same approach for brands?

ESSENCE AND US

Every company, product, and object we encounter has a story—an essence. But so, too, do we. Recall from chapter four that we humans—and really, all living things—are in a perpetual state of physical change, with bodies that completely renew every seven years or so. A life is more than just a series of experiences. It is also the story we tell ourselves about those experiences—the glue that binds them all together. And this story glue is arguably more important to our happiness and well-being than all of our individual experiences added together. The ultimate impact of stories and essence is on our own lives.

The "personal story" helps make sense of an odd finding in research on the science of happiness. In one of the largest studies on happiness to date,[25] Daniel Kahneman had one thousand women in Texas fill out a daily questionnaire detailing everything they did and how happy they were at the time. He found that the activities that made the participants happiest were things like sex, socializing, relaxing, praying, and meditation. Seems like a perfectly reasonable list of enjoyable items . . . until you realize what it's missing: spending time with children. This is a remarkable omission, considering that children are consistently reported as the greatest source of life satisfaction.

This pattern—this disjuncture between what gives us immediate enjoyment and what gives us longer-term fulfillment—comes up again and again. People report being happier with their car the more expensive it is. But if you ask people to report how happy they are when they're actually *inside* their car, live in the process of their daily commute, this correlation flatlines. It seems that the enjoyment we derive from a car rests not in the actual experience of driving it, but in the abstract idea of it—yet another example of how what makes us happy in the moment is not the same as what gives us the most long-term life satisfaction.

Kahneman is arguably the world's foremost expert on happiness and how we value things. After dedicating his career to this research, what does he ultimately conclude? "I gradually became convinced that people don't want to be happy. They want to be satisfied with their life. People don't want to be happy the way I've defined the term—what I experience here and now. In my view, it's much more important for them to be satisfied, to experience life satisfaction, from the perspective of 'what I remember,' of the story they tell about their lives."[26]

It's the story we tell about our lives that is the source of enduring happiness. The story we tell about ourselves fills in the gaps between individual moments, and in the process makes us *us*.

The stories of objects and companies impact how we value them. And in the same way, the story we tell about ourselves impacts how we value our own lives.

As we've seen from the outset of this book, our beliefs about something influence how we perceive it. If you believe a wine is expensive, or if you drink it from a fancy glass, you'll actually enjoy it much more. If you're led to believe that a pair of sunglasses is expensive, you'll report that they're actually better at blocking the sun.

The beliefs we have about an object go beyond worldly, physical qualities like its features and its cost, and extend to more abstract types of value. Think of your wedding ring, or a gift you received from someone who has since passed away. These objects carry sentimental value that goes beyond the physical. If you were to replicate your wedding ring, atom for atom, it would be identical *physically*—and yet its value to you would drop precipitously. Or imagine catching a home run ball hit by your favorite baseball star, a memento you've kept in a glass case since childhood. If a thief broke into your house in the middle of the night and replaced it with a replica, you'd never notice. And yet, if you knew the original ball had been replaced, its value in your mind would plummet to zero. We're strange, sentimental beasts.

Our natural tendency to see the hidden essences in things provides a massive opportunity for brands, which can infuse otherwise ordinary objects with incredible worth, in the process fundamentally altering how we think of and value them. Even the most trivial products can be given essences that take them, in the consumer's mind, well beyond the sum of their physical parts.

Just as we're drawn to the essences of objects, we're drawn to the stories that weave them. Storytelling can be described in the same way Nobel Prize–winning physicist Richard Feynman describes physics: "It's like sex:

sure, it may give some practical results, but that's not why we do it." Simply put, we're suckers for stories.

Stories, and their ability to instill essence into the otherwise banal, gives the consumer world a magical, almost otherworldly quality. Consumerism aside, a carefully crafted story that provides depth and meaning to an ordinary item is an incredible thing.

When is a door not a door? When a marketer has told you a great story about it.

Chapter 11

MIDLIMINAL

The Science of ~~Sub~~Midliminal Marketing

Maybe you've heard this story before. The year is 1957. Halfway through a routine screening of the classic film *Picnic,* an entire theater of moviegoers suddenly gets an urge for popcorn and cola. This overwhelming urge seems to come from nowhere. The theater crowd looks around at one another, confused, before heading to the concession stands in droves. As reported by theater owner James Vicary, sales skyrocketed, resulting in an 18 percent rise in cola sales and a 58 percent rise in popcorn sales.

What caused this sudden craving for popcorn and Coke? According to Vicary, carefully embedded hidden messages added within the film. Right when actress Kim Novak was about to kiss Clifford Robertson in the park, the screen flashed "Drink Coke" and "Eat Popcorn" for a fraction of a second. The flash was too quick for anyone to notice—the advertisements were subliminal, or below the threshold of sensation or consciousness. These subliminal messages, Vicary claimed, embedded specific wants into the audience's subconscious and compelled them to the concession stands.

However, this event didn't actually take place. Vicary later confessed to making the entire story up as a publicity stunt to help bring attention to his ailing theater.[1] He was a marketer, after all. But his "experiment," such as it was, sparked important questions: Is it possible to speak directly to a consumer's subconscious, completely bypassing their conscious attention? And if you could, should you? The concept of *subliminal priming* was born.

This sounds like a science fiction concept, but its mechanisms are fairly straightforward. For a piece of marketing to qualify as truly subliminal, it must be objectively outside the consumer's awareness. For example, we need at least about 50 milliseconds (ms) to be able to process a piece of visual information; we are not consciously aware of seeing anything that flashes in front of our eyes faster than that. A true example of subliminal marketing would be flashing the word *PEPSI* for 30 ms every time you opened your smartphone. Whether an advertising tactic is subliminal or not is as binary as black and white. If the message captures the consumer's attention, it is not subliminal.

In the decades since Vicary's publicity stunt, subliminal priming—the neuroscience underpinning subliminal marketing—has been studied in labs around the world. And while that research doesn't exactly suggest that Vicary's story was plausible, actual controlled studies have illustrated that subliminal priming is a genuine phenomenon that operates similar to Vicary's original description—minus the hyperbolic mind control.

In subliminal priming, some *thing* (scientists call this a *stimulus*) is introduced, without your conscious awareness, through one of your senses. Then, later, this *thing*—this stimulus—affects your behavior in some way (scientists call this a *response*). In other words, subliminal priming is when exposure to sensory stimuli influences you, potentially affecting your future behavior, all without your awareness.

In one study, people were shown a series of ordinary photographs on a computer screen—simple scenes like a woman doing the dishes, or a kid eating a sandwich. They were asked after viewing each image whether they thought the person in the photograph was in a good or bad mood. Simple, right? However, right after each photo, another image flashed on the screen for 30 milliseconds, below the brain's threshold for visual awareness.

These subliminal images were not nearly so subtle in their content; they were either extremely negative (e.g., a rotting corpse or a burning house), or extremely positive (e.g., ice cream or puppies). When a positive image was subliminally flashed on the screen, subjects overwhelmingly reported that the person in the dishwashing photograph was happy. Conversely, when a negative image was subliminally flashed on the screen, subjects overwhelmingly assessed the person in the dishwashing photograph as in a bad mood.[2] When asked after the experiment if they realized there were subliminal images, everyone said that they were completely unaware.

Similar effects have been found with a range of other stimuli, including graphic sexual imagery. People found ordinary photos slightly arousing when shown a sexually explicit subliminal prime right before viewing them. And again, participants reported being completely unaware of the prime itself.[3] That scene in *Fight Club* where Brad Pitt's character, Tyler Durden, is splicing single frames of pornography into family films for a kick is not as implausible as you might think.

However, testing the effectiveness of subliminal techniques in the consumer world has yielded mixed results. One study [4] found that subliminally flashing the word *LIPTON* gave people an increased preference for Lipton Iced Tea. However, this preference only increased if the participants were already thirsty. For participants who weren't thirsty, the effect disappeared. It's pretty creepy nonetheless.

The discomfort surrounding subliminal marketing is amplified by the fact that not only does it directly impact our behavior, it does so outside our awareness. And if something happens outside of our awareness, we can't consent to it.

One of the original critiques of Vicary in 1957 captures this intuition:

The subconscious mind is the most delicate part of the most delicate apparatus in the entire universe. It is not to be smudged, sullied, or twisted in order to boost the sales of popcorn or anything else. Nothing is more difficult in the modern world than to protect the privacy of the human soul.

The nonconsensual nature of subliminal marketing has thankfully been recognized by lawmakers, and it might reassure you to know that the US Federal Communications Commission explicitly bans the use of what this book calls "pure" subliminal techniques,[5] as do the UK, Australia, and many other countries. However, where is the line between subliminal priming and mainstream marketing? Consider the wording used by the UK's Committee of Advertising Practice when describing its prohibition of "subliminal priming": "No advertisement may use images of very brief duration, or any other technique that is likely to influence consumers, without their being fully aware of what has been done."[6] If you omit the first clause banning advertisements that "use images of very brief duration," what you're left with is a fairly agreeable description of . . . well, *marketing*.

Imagine this: Fast-food company KFC creates two near-identical commercials selling their one-dollar "Snacker" chicken sandwich. Both commercials show college students looking for a cheap place to grab lunch, discovering the Snacker, and ending up at KFC. The commercials then cut to a close-up of the sandwich before ending. But in version one of the commercial, just before cutting to the close-up, the words "buy now" are flashed across the screen for 3,000 milliseconds—three full seconds. And in version two, a thimble-sized image of a dollar bill appears on the lettuce throughout the concluding four-second close-up of the commercial.

Does one of these commercials feel more acceptable to you than the other?

Chances are, you feel version one, with the subliminal "buy now," is worse—but why? Let's say the commercials each result in a 20 percent increase in sales of the Snacker, as compared to a third version that uses neither tactic. Do you still feel the same way? Neither commercial has a lasting long-term effect on the consumer, other than making them more likely to buy a particular sandwich. Furthermore, neither tactic breaches viewers' conscious awareness. How different are they, really?

The good news is, because subliminal messaging is illegal, version one is a work of fiction. The bad news is that version two, with the hidden dollar bill, is a very real KFC commercial and is 100 percent legal. See for yourself.[7] ⑤

Many aspects of brand marketing operate on a comparably covert level. While not purely *sub*liminal, these *midliminal* tactics are part and parcel of being a successful brand marketer. And compared to subliminal priming, which we only see in controlled studies, these midliminal approaches are much more common, and have a much more potent effect on our psychology and behavior.

MIDLIMINAL PRIMING

Recall that a subliminal prime is any stimulus that can influence you and your behavior without your conscious awareness. But primes don't need to be subliminal to work. They can still affect our behavior in ways we are unconscious of even when we *are* (or at least *could be*) conscious of having been exposed to them. Often the most effective primes aren't flashed before us too quickly for our eyes to process. Instead, they are right in front of us, hiding in plain sight. Welcome to what we call *midliminal priming*.

For a prime to be midliminal, you must be *able* to see it, yet it must typically go unrecognized. Like the second KFC commercial, where we can see the dollar bill image once someone points it out, midliminal messages do not have to be faster than 50 ms to escape your awareness. In fact, midliminal messages sit right in front of you the entire time, speaking directly to your subconscious. Take the FedEx logo, for instance. Ever notice the arrow in between the E and the X? How about the smile in the Amazon logo, which starts at the A and ends at the Z?

The arrow in the FedEx logo primes you to associate the company with fast delivery. Amazon's logo with a visual smile nudges a mirroring positive emotional reaction from you while emphasizing the message that Amazon carries everything from A to Z.

Midliminal messaging works because of the brain's tendency to fall for priming, whether that priming is intentional or not. Priming works by impacting the mental models our brain creates (remember chapter one?). And whether or not a given prime ultimately impacts our behavior some-where down the line, it still leaves an imprint in our brains.

These midliminal primes can therefore be more potent than you might assume. Think of all the watch advertisements you've seen in your life. Across all of the different brands and models, have you noticed any particular pattern? The hands of the watch are typically always set at the same time: 10:10. This isn't a coincidence; all of those photo shoots didn't just happen to be scheduled for the same time of day. This is deliberate design. The 10:10 position makes the hands of the clock look as if the clock is "smiling." And this is not simply watch-industry superstition, either. In controlled studies,[8] positioning the hands of a clock at 10:10, compared to a neutral time like 11:30, leads to a significant positive effect on the viewer's emotions, and an increase in their willingness to buy. All of this without subjects explicitly noticing that the watch hands were smiling. ☺

In a way, *all* advertising is midliminal priming. Store displays are primes. Celebrity endorsements are primes. Product placements in film and television are primes. Priming is all about exposure. And the less you notice it, the better it works.

WHY PRODUCT PLACEMENT IS SO EXPENSIVE

Here's a story of an accidental prime via product placement.

While working on the script for the movie *Cast Away,* one of the screenwriters deliberately stranded himself on an island for a week. During this time, he came across a volleyball—and this is how Wilson was born. In case you've forgotten: in *Cast Away,* Tom Hanks plays a FedEx employee whose FedEx plane crashes on an uninhabited island. One of the items that survives the crash is a volleyball, which Hanks names Wilson (after the brand name stamped across its middle), and with which he shares many conversations throughout the movie.

The whole point of product placement is to present a brand or product to the viewer in a subtle enough way that the viewer's conscious mind does not ask why the product is there. Wilson does this handsomely by organically becoming a character in the movie, and one of the reasons he is so effective has to do with the nature of our exposure to him.

Remember the mere exposure effect from chapter eight: The more we see something, the more we like it. And this effect is magnified when we're *not* consciously thinking about each additional exposure.[9] With primes like Wilson, we're not thinking to ourselves, *There's that Wilson volleyball again,* each time he pops up. Instead, we're engrossed in the movie, and in Wilson as a character. But your subconscious still registers Wilson as a volleyball—a product—and his name as the brand.

This is why product placements are a multimillion-dollar industry: the "advertising" happens on a subconscious level, and is more effective for it. You may not have noticed that four of the Transformers vehicles in the 2007 movie were GMC vehicles (Chevrolet Camaro, Pontiac Solstice, GMC TopKick, and Hummer H2[10]), but your brain likely did. While Wilson was not a paid product placement, it functioned the same way. The over 100 million people who viewed *Cast Away* heard the brand Wilson mentioned thirty-four times. Had Wilson had been a paid product placement, he would have cost upward of $12 million.[11]

In a similarly effective instance of accidental product placement, Starbucks got a boost when one of the *Game of Thrones* crew accidentally left a disposable coffee cup, clearly visible in the final cut, on set during an eighth-season episode. Screenshots of the moment quickly went viral. Social media monitoring platform Talkwalker counted more than 193,000 mentions within forty-eight hours on Twitter and elsewhere that cited either Starbucks, *Game of Thrones*, or a variation of the series' hashtag.[12] The total estimated value of all of this free PR? Over $2 billion. And the real irony? The to-go cup wasn't even from Starbucks! (The shot was too dark to clearly see the logo, but it looked enough like Starbucks that fans just assumed.)

Primes like this, where the brand is seamlessly integrated into the story (or, in *Game of Thrones*' case, obviously unintentional), are more effective because they feel authentic. They never trigger your suspicion, because they don't look like an ad. You're still being marketed to; you just don't realize it.

If you watch a movie in which the main character chases down the bad guy wearing a pair of Nikes, the next time you're at Foot Locker, you might be slightly more likely to go for Nikes over Adidas—without having any idea that your cinematic experience influenced your preference. Watching *Cast Away*, you think you're just sitting back, enjoying a movie, but every time you see that adorable volleyball, you're also, slowly and unconsciously, gaining an appreciation for the Wilson brand.

To double down on their free product placement, Wilson (the sporting goods company, not the character) created a promotional ball, complete with the facial markings seen in the film. Judging by its five-hundred-plus reviews on Amazon (full of countless puns), the volleyball was a success. The only downside: Amazon used UPS to deliver Wilson, not FedEx.

Of course, product placement isn't always about serendipity. Usually, it's paid for—and handsomely. Consider the 2013 reboot of Superman, *Man of Steel*, starring Henry Cavill. The movie grossed $160 million in revenue before a single movie ticket was sold. How? By breaking the record for most product placements sold in a movie. In fact, companies paid nearly $9 billion for product placements in 2018 in the US alone.[13] Priming is big business.

MIDLIMINAL PRIMES FOR THE SENSES

We've talked so far about fairly complex visual primes, like the position of watch hands and product placements in movies, but priming can occur from far simpler stimuli. And primes don't need to be visual; we can be primed via any of our senses.

Let's take a deeper dive into the neuroscience of senses, and how brands use midliminal primes on each of them to affect your behavior.

VISION

Humans are primarily visual creatures. As you may recall from chapter one, vision is the sense with the largest amount of brain mass devoted to it—roughly a third of the cortex—and there are over thirty distinct pathways linking input from our eyes to the brain. The brain also dedicates very specific regions for very specific visual functions. We have an area exclusively concerned with seeing motion, for instance. Another very specialized region, the fusiform gyrus, is selectively concerned with the processing of faces; people with damage here can see everything under the sun, *except* for faces. As a result of this share of brain volume and specialization, vision has primacy over all our other senses.

Even the simplest visual stimuli can prime a specific response or feeling because of the associations they carry. Color is a prime (no pun intended!) example. Colors are key players in the midliminal marketing game, and can be used intentionally to prime your behavior.

One recent experiment shows the fascinating priming effect the color red can have on our perception of someone's attractiveness.[14] The experiment placed female hitchhikers on a road, where they propositioned passersby for a ride. Turns out, heterosexual male drivers stopped twice as often when the same female hitchhikers wore red shirts. (The red shirts had no measurable effect on heterosexual female drivers.) Similar effects have been found with waitresses: male guests tip waitresses donning a red outfit up to 24 percent more than those wearing any other color.[15]

In Western cultures, the color red is often associated with love and sexuality, and brands use that association to influence how we think of their products. Louboutin famously branded the soles of their high-heel stilettos a particular shade of red, and has attempted numerous times to actually patent the use of the color in this way.[16] Virgin Airlines has doubled down on red as the visual representation of its flirty brand image. Virgin's commercials, safety videos, flight attendant uniforms, and the logo itself are heavy on the color red. Virgin was the first airline to introduce an airplane-wide digital chatroom app, which was baked into the headrest TV screen. The app lets passengers chat each other up, both via private direct message and a public room shared by all passengers. The name of this app? Red.

What do Burger King, McDonald's, In-N-Out, Wendy's, KFC, and Carl's Jr. have in common, aside from selling fast food? They use red and yellow in their logos. Recall from chapter one that blue acts as an appetite suppressant; we also eat less from a blue bowl than we do any other color. Red seems to have the opposite effect. It's a long-held belief among marketers that red, being a physiologically stimulating color, subconsciously communicates urgency in the same way yellow subconsciously communicates friendliness and happy feelings. Urgency and friendliness are beneficial associations for fast-food chains. The scientific research here is muddy, but that hasn't stopped the top fast-food companies from the gratuitous use of ~~ketchup and mustard~~ red and yellow in their logos. Can you think of a fast-food logo that isn't red or yellow?

The color orange is believed to affect behavior by priming physical movement. The theory is that orange indicates energy and hence, action. Again, direct scientific evidence is murky. Yet, brands large and small act upon this orange theory. One company took the sentiment literally by calling itself Orange Theory Fitness. The product? A gym focusing on group workouts. OTF is famous for intense classes that push fitness junkies to their physical limits. The company takes fitness to another level by providing each participant with a heart rate monitor and broadcasting their heart rates live on a leaderboard, with extra points awarded to those who can stay in "peak burn" zone. The name of this zone? Orange Zone.

Similarly, the core sentiment behind the DIY (do-it-yourself) movement is action. So it is unsurprising that Home Depot, the one-stop retail DIY shop with a market cap of over $233 billion, has invested unapologetically in the color orange. Everything from the store's logo to its interior aisle signs, checkout lanes, and employee aprons demonstrates its commitment to orange and, symbolically, action.

One surprising area where color can make a difference? The prescription drug industry. Pfizer is one of the leading pharmaceutical companies in the world, and between 2003 and 2017, one single product of theirs was responsible for $26.5 billion of revenue—Viagra. Famously known as the "little blue pill," it opened up an entirely new product market. Competing pharma giants went into action to create profitable alternatives, and Bayer and GlaxoSmithKline succeeded in doing just that with Levitra.

In developing Levitra, their market research concluded that consumers didn't resonate with the imagery of Viagra. Specifically, they found that the pill's blue color was too cool, too calm, and they equated it with being sick. The differentiation strategy doubled down on this insight. What better color to prime action (in the sexual sense) than orange? The Levitra logo is orange. The pill itself is orange. When asked why, Nancy K. Bryan, VP of marketing for Bayer, said, "Orange is vibrant and energetic." Bryan also revealed Bayer's internal name for the campaign to beat Viagra: "Beat the Blues."

Not to be outdone, fellow pharma giant Eli Lilly jumped in on the boner bandwagon with Cialis. The logo? Orange. The box? Orange. The pill? Orange. But Eli Lilly took the visuals one step further: by strategically changing the shape of the pill to further punctuate the action conveyed by orange.

HEARING

Hearing—or as a neuroscientist would call it, auditory processing—is as fascinating as vision. Through a long series of almost purely mechanical processes, the ear takes in vibrating air waves from the outside world, interprets simple features like pitch and volume in the cochlea, and then sends this input through the auditory nerve to the brain for further processing.

Compared to visual stimuli, sounds have a more subtle but still important effect on us. The sounds of an airplane, for instance, can have a deep impact on people who reside along regular flight paths. Studies show chronic aircraft noise exposure impairs reading comprehension and long-term memory in children, and may be associated with raised blood pressure in both children and adults.[17]

At a more fundamental level, specific sounds give specific impressions. In fact, the brain has a strong tendency to personify sounds—to assign feeling to them—and brands use this tendency to create or build on the personality they want to have.

Take a look at the following objects. Imagine one of them is named Bouba and the other is named Kiki. Which one do you think is which?

These images are from a classic test of what's called the *Bouba/Kiki effect*. If you're like most people, you naturally assume that the spiky-looking object on the left is called Kiki and the bulbous-looking one on the right is called Bouba. *Kiki* "sounds" sharp and spiky; *Bouba* sounds round and bulbous.

You might be thinking that this effect is linguistic and therefore cultural, given the similarities in sound between the names and adjectives that describe them (spiky = kiki; bulbous = bouba). But the Bouba/Kiki effect shows amazing cross-linguistic consistency,[18] suggesting that these sounds carry meaning in and of themselves, even if nobody knows for sure why.

As they've done with red and visual priming, Virgin Airlines uses sound as a priming aid in perhaps its ultimate execution. Virgin has specific music it plays during boarding and deplaning, tracks that can be described as sensual, flirty, hip, and vibey. And when you combine the music with the reddish lighting, the vividly red seats, and the equally vivid flight attendant uniforms, you have a very real, very palpable brand personality. Think about it: What makes you pick one airline over another? All prices being (roughly) equal, it is a brand's subjective, differentiated personality that makes you choose it over and over again. Virgin America was bold to double down on brand personality when it launched in 2007, a time when existing airlines were struggling to stay in business. But ten years later, Alaska Airlines bought Virgin America for a whopping $2.6 billion. Hope the purchase included the playlist!

When music sounds a certain way, it can deeply affect our behavior in the consumer world. Research has found that slower-paced music in supermarkets is associated with slower-paced movement but more overall sales and more expensive purchases.[19] Music can change your buying preferences in other ways, as well. In a series of controlled studies, researchers found that the ambient music playing in a wine store had a major impact on their ultimate wine purchase. Playing German music increased sales of German wines, French music primed customers to reach for French wines,[20] and so forth. And despite these significant behavioral effects, a questionnaire at the end of the shopping experience revealed that customers were completely unaware of the background music. Similar findings have been noted with restaurant wine sales (classical and other "high class" music leads to more expensive wine selections).[21]

Good sound design isn't just about what you hear. Sometimes it's about what you don't hear. One feature that makes luxury cars, well, luxurious, is a cabin that insulates passengers from noise of the road, engine, and outside world. This is unlike, say, sports cars, where a big part of the appeal is how they sound when driven to the limit. Of course, if you make luxury sports cars like BMW does, this presents a problem. Their solution? Programming in enhanced engine sounds, which react to how hard the driver pushes the car and are delivered via the cabin's speakers. BMW is open about this sound augmentation. They're also not alone. Lexus hired

Yamaha's musical instrument division to fine-tune the engine sounds of the Lexus LFA sports car.[22]

TOUCH

There's nothing like human touch. For infants, skin-on-skin contact is paramount. It bolsters important physiological processes, and galvanizes the parent–child bond. This contact is so crucial that it's common practice across America, and in many other countries, to immediately place the child on the chest of the mother right after birth.

Touch is not just something that helps cement an emotional bond. It also affects our trajectory of development. Infants who are denied physical contact during certain crucial periods can develop a rare condition known as psychosocial dwarfism, characterized by stunted growth. The famous author J. M. Barrie suffered from this condition due to a traumatic childhood and it became a central theme in his writing; he is the author of *Peter Pan*, about children who never grow up.

The importance of touch fades into the background as we mature into adults, but it's always there. And when it comes to marketing and midliminal priming, human touch can have a significant impact on our purchasing. One study actually found that when a store employee touched a customer's arms (respectfully, of course!), the consumer was more likely to make a purchase, and rated their overall experience as being much more pleasant.[23]

And this is just one way touch can factor into our decision to buy. Think about car shopping. There are many objective ways to rate a car before buying. How quickly it goes from zero to sixty. Miles to the gallon. Number of doors. Stereo system wattage. Cost. And yet one of the most influential factors we consider when it comes to making a final purchase is the way driving the car "feels."

Car brands use touch and texture to communicate the personality of their cars to prospective drivers and make a positive impression. Jaguar garnered a lot of attention when it changed its gear shift from the most common form, a stick, to a dial. Moreover, the dial was designed to usually remain hidden, flush inside the armrest. When the driver enters the seat, the car "wakes up" and the dial rises, begging the driver to touch and twist it from park to drive. This novel touch experience is exactly the type of data the brain uses to calculate your ultimate opinion of the car you just test drove.

E-commerce companies like Amazon have driven many book and record chains, like Borders and Tower Records, out of business. But the companies that are surviving, even thriving, against Amazon are doing so by doubling down on offering customers what Amazon and its ilk don't: the ability to touch their products. People can touch and feel the new Galaxy phone at Best Buy's Samsung showcase or test the ripeness of a peach before (over)paying at Whole Foods. (No wonder Amazon bought the grocery chain in August 2017 for $13.7 billion.)

SMELL

You generally don't notice smells, but when you do, they have a very particular impact. Scents are very situation-specific in a way vision isn't. Memories encoded through vision last longer, but smell memories are much more specific and closely tied to episodic memory—in other words, memories of specific experiences, as opposed to specific pieces of information.[24] Say you find an old Yankees baseball cap. If you only looked at it, you would be reminded of the Yankees in general: how their season is going, if you like their manager or not, and so on. In contrast, if you were to pick it up and smell it, you might vividly recall the first time you went to Yankee Stadium with your father during a particular trip to NYC.

Since humans smell things less often than they see things, it is easier to attach associations to a smell than it is to, say, a color. Think of the last time you walked by a Subway sandwich shop. For better or worse, you've come to associate Subway with its very unique smell. This is a 1:1 association. You've seen lots of things that *look* a bit like a Subway shop, but the *smell* of the Subway shop is uniquely Subway. Therefore, when you smell this "Subway smell" again, your brain has no memories to pull up except for the ones associated with Subway.

Knowing all this, companies take advantage of the impact of smells on consumers' experiences. Consider the classic use of smell within real estate, for example, where scents like pine, vanilla, or fresh cookies are used during open houses to help sell homes. Dating back to 1991, researchers like Alan Hirsch were testing the impact of scent on buying behavior.[25] In one instance, scientists put an identical pair of running shoes in two rooms. One of the rooms was filled with purified air, the other with a floral smell. After exploring both rooms, 84 percent of the test subjects said they were more inclined to buy the sneakers in the scented room. Today, Nike experiments with scent at their retail locations. Steven Semoff, president of the Scent Marketing Institute, claims Nike's experiments with scent have yielded an 80 percent increase in the customer's intent to purchase.[26]

Cinnabon chooses retail locations based on their ability to trap smells, because a space that smells like cinnamon rolls helps prime passersby to purchase. M&M World Store in London smells like chocolate, which makes sense, right? They're selling chocolate. But M&Ms are sold in sealed packages. The store has to use a spray. Lastly, Singapore Airlines has one-upped Virgin America's use of sensory marketing by using a specific scent in the hot towels they offer passengers before meals. It's a combination of floral and citrus and, if you must know, has a name: Stefan Floridian Waters. The midliminal information Stefan provides the brain informs your impression of the airline.

In one study, subjects were given a crumbly biscuit to eat. Half of the subjects were exposed to the citrusy scent of a cleaning product while eating, and the other half were not. The results? The half in the scented room were much cleaner and tidier when eating the biscuit, despite reporting being completely unaware of the scent.[27] Another experiment found slot machines in Las Vegas sprayed with a pleasant scent received 45 percent more play than those left unscented.[28] Similarly, diners were found to have spent 20 percent more money and 15 percent more time in a restaurant when it was scented with lavender than they did when it was scented with lemon.[29]

A key theme running through many, if not all, of the studies we've discussed here is participants' complete lack of awareness of any of these sensory primes. Remember: A midliminal prime is one where you *can* perceive the prime via conscious awareness, but you just typically do not. When asked why they selected the French wine over the Australian, none of the subjects ever, ever said it was the music playing in the store. No one referenced the scent, or the color of the aisle, or whatever other sensory factor proved to influence their purchase, when explaining their behavior—because they weren't aware that any of these factors influenced their behavior. Most people don't notice the sensory prime itself, let alone its impact on their behavior, whether that prime is a song, someone brushing their arm, or anything else. And yet, repeatedly, and across all of our sensory domains, these subtle midliminal marketing tactics have massive effects on our behavior.

NOT-SO-FREE WILL?

What does this mean for marketing as a whole? Current marketing ethics explicitly assumes that consumers have free choice over how they react to any given advertisement or campaign,[30] and that while advertisements help influence consumers one way or another, consumers ultimately retain final, autonomous say. In fact, this assumption of consumer autonomy provides license for a large range of marketing practices. Regardless of the marketing act (offline ads, digital campaigns, product positioning, etc.), the consumer ultimately gets to *choose* how they react and respond to it—or so the reasoning goes. No matter what bells and whistles they use, brands cannot force your hand to buy; because of this, the ball is ultimately in the consumer's court. But is this assumption of consumer autonomy justified?

In short, no. There is no good evidence to suggest that we consumers always retain full control over pushing the buy button. If we aren't aware of these factors—the scent in the room, the music playing—or the ways in which they influence our decisions, then how can we say we're in control?

The conversation about marketing ethics has to restart by reconsidering the psychological impact of marketing itself—and in particular, the power of factors outside our awareness that drive our thoughts, feelings, and behavior. The starting point for marketers, consumers, and lawmakers must be the science of human autonomy. Any fair ethical framework must incorporate an appreciation for the potency of these unconscious forces.

Think of psychology, and you think of Freud. Of course, think of Freud, and a range of bizarre ideas instantly come to mind. If you chew on your pen, you are obsessed with penises. If you like drinking coffee as an adult, you have repressed childhood trauma. And of course, we all have a secret desire to have sex with our parents. If you bring up Freud in most circles, you can reliably expect to be greeted with skepticism, if not ridicule.

Yet we also owe Freud a great debt. Above all, he was the first prominent thinker to recognize that much of mental life exists below the surface of our awareness, which he called the unconscious. Freud's greatest contribution to modern psychology, and his lasting legacy, is this: *We never really know why we do the things we do.*

Over eighty years since Freud's death, the evidence in support of this general claim continues to mount. We know now that patients with brain damage that prevents them from forming new conscious memories, as we saw with Michelle Philpots in chapter three, can successfully improve skills (e.g., riding a bike) across several sessions, even though they have no conscious recollection of previous training.[31] That words flashed at us at a rate too rapid for conscious processing (i.e., subliminal priming) can create subtle emotional and behavioral changes.[32] That something about a new place, or a new person, can trigger an unconscious memory that gives an eerie feeling despite our being unaware we've made this association. And then there's blindsight. There's a lot going on beneath the surface of which we're unaware.

The closer we look, the more mysterious the situation gets. Through modern technology like functional magnetic resonance imaging (fMRI), we can now examine the brain's activity while it carries out a range of different mental functions. Eavesdropping on someone's brain as they make judgments and decisions is particularly fascinating, and it has revealed that a striking majority of our decision making takes place completely outside of our awareness.

In a now-classic study published in *Nature Neuroscience*, John-Dylan Haynes had participants make a simple decision: to push a button with their right hand or their left hand. They were free to make this decision at any time, but needed to note at what specific point they made up their mind about their choice. Astonishingly, researchers found that activity deep in the brain could predict, with absolute certainty, what a subject's decision would be before the subject did. And researchers could do so not merely a second or two before the subjects knew, but rather *a full seven seconds* before a person "made" their choice.[33]

Imaging work has found similar effects within the consumer world.[34]

Even when you aren't paying attention to a product, outside of your awareness your brain is registering important information about it. And the traces of this stimulus in the brain can later predict, with uncanny accuracy, your preference for those products later.

Haynes's study highlights the humbling degree of ignorance we have about our own brain activity, and observations like his have contributed compelling evidence to the ongoing neuro-philosophical debate over whether our sense of free will is just an illusion. For the current discussion, however, it is sufficient to note this: our conscious attention is simply unaware of the cascade of neural activity that drives our thoughts and ultimately our behaviors. What we consider and feel to be a "decision" is the unfolding of an unconscious process happening much earlier than we realize.

Not only are we unaware of these underlying processes, but random factors can easily shift our behavior without us realizing it. Imagine Jill, responding to an ad at her university, signs up for an experiment that will pay her $20 to evaluate faces. That day, she arrives a little late because someone bumped her into the hallway, but she is relieved to find the experimenter is friendly and understanding. He sits her down at an empty white table and explains the experiment.

First, Jill is asked to read a brief description of a person along with their picture. Then, she is asked to answer a series of questions on what she thinks about the person—how friendly they are, how generous they are, and the like. There are no right or wrong answers; the experimenter is just interested in personal judgments. Last, she is given a brief questionnaire to fill out with her age, gender, and other demographic information. The final question reads: *Why did you rate this person the way you did?*

"What do you mean, why?" Jill responds. "Because that's what I thought when I read their description. What else is there?"

It turns out that the clumsy person—let's call him Jack—who bumped into her in the hallway on her way in was part of the experiment. As part of an ingeniously elaborate setup devised by researchers at UC Boulder,[35] when Jack dropped his papers from bumping into Jill, he handed her a cup of coffee to hold while he recovered them. The researchers had Jack give half the participants a cold cup of coffee, and the other half a warm cup. Each participant held the cup for less than a minute—but it made a difference. Turns out, those who received the warm cup rated others as being much more generous and friendly than those who were given the cold cup. And the most consistent finding of all? Exactly zero participants made any connection between their feelings of warmth toward the faces in the experiment and the temperature of the coffee they held. And why would they?

To paraphrase Freud's insight: *We never really choose the things we choose.*

Midliminal marketing works just as well as, if not better than, subliminal marketing. And as important as it is to draw an ethical line between subliminal marketing and midliminal marketing, it is equally important to consider the ethics of *priming* generally, whether subliminal or midliminal. The brain is constantly taking in information, but it is selective about the parts of that information it shares with "you." The parts it shares are your conscious experiences. The rest, though unnoticed by you, still impacts your thoughts, emotions, and behaviors.

To prime your behavior, brands bypass you to speak directly to your unsharing brain. They can use touch to drive a purchase, sound to convey a personality, smell to differentiate themselves from their competitors, and sight for all of the above.

Communicating with our senses in ways our brains can't perceive—subliminal marketing—is outlawed, but doing so in ways we *can* perceive (even if often unconsciously) is not. But this line in the sand can feel fairly arbitrary, when the evidence shows that even the smallest factors can have massive, covert influences on our buying behavior. While we like to think that we are in complete control of our consumer lives, the science suggests otherwise.

Outlawing subliminal marketing was the first step. It was also the easiest step. The second step is addressing midliminal marketing. This is less black and white, especially since it can be argued all branding involves midliminal primes. It requires addressing marketing ethics through the lens of neuroscience. And this, coincidentally, is the topic of the next and final chapter. Read on.

Chapter 12

THE FUTURE OF MARKETING

Nature is full of interesting relationships, from the birds that pick at the food in alligators' teeth, to the barnacles that catch rides on whales, to the bees that only pollinate a single species of flower.

But the award for greatest nature BFFs would have to go to sloths and the algae that coats their backs. The tree sloth gets a constant source of nutrients from eating the green algae, as well as camouflage from potential predators. In return, the algae gets its own source of energy: moths that land, and die, on the sloth throughout the day. In fact, the notoriously economical sloth will venture down its tree once a week to attract moths from its own dung, just for the algae. What a pal!

The relationship between sloth and algae is unique in how close and interconnected it has evolved to be: they both need each other, and their lives are not just shaped but maintained through their interactions. The sloth would be a very different creature without the algae, and vice versa. They're so intertwined that the lines between them are blurred.

This is the kind of deep, interconnected relationship we, as consumers, are in with consumption. It's one that we depend on, that invariably shapes us, and that blurs boundaries. It's difficult to know where the consumer world ends and we, as consumers, begin. When you watch a great movie and then excitedly share this experience with a close friend, you are operating naturally in the consumer world. You are also unwittingly engaging in the most powerful form of marketing there is: word of mouth. And today, thanks to the rise of influencer culture, depending on the size of your online platform and how persuasive you are, talking about a great movie you watched can be a business. As Jay-Z famously said, "I'm not a businessman, I'm a *business*, man."

We aren't passive recipients in this relationship. The consumer world is built around and conforms to us, just as we conform to it. Every day, we use products and technologies that were only built on the premise that we would buy and use them. Every day, we participate in services and have experiences that were designed around our specific psychological responses. The consumer world is the way it is because we, as human consumers, are the way we are, and its history follows the ebb and flow of consumer values. When companies have shifted their approach, it is largely because consumers themselves have changed. Beverage companies have introduced healthier, less sugary options because consumer attitudes toward health have shifted. American sedans have become smaller and more fuel-efficient because environmental attitudes have shifted. Fashion retailers are now shying away from fast fashion because views on sustainability have begun affecting consumer preferences. And that's to say nothing of the ways advertising has shifted. The list of consumer-led changes goes on and on.

Whether we like it or not, we're in a deep, dynamic, complex relationship with the consumer world. And keeping that relationship healthy starts with understanding the nature of marketing, the nature of our psychology, and our role as consumers in navigating both.

WHEN THE STORK IS AN ALGORITHM

In 2011, a father demanded to speak to the manager at his local Target store, angry about the coupons being sent to his teenage daughter. They all fit a specific theme: baby bottles, diapers, and maternity clothes. "She's still in high school, and you're sending her coupons for baby clothes and cribs? Are you trying to encourage her to get pregnant?" His next conversation with the manager was apologetic. Turns out, Target knew what the father did not: his daughter was pregnant.[1]

What was interesting about the Target case is the daughter hadn't browsed any pregnancy-related items. Instead, Target's advanced algorithms had picked up on associated patterns of purchasing behavior: more unscented lotion than normal, slightly different produce items, some extra (not prenatal) vitamins. Even back in 2011, Target could assign a reliable pregnancy prediction score based on three sources—credit card data, Target coupon card use, and email data—and twenty-five data points. The data used for this prediction was largely from in-store purchases, not web browsing. And this was before Facebook went public, one year before it bought Instagram, three years before it bought WhatsApp, and three years before Apple brought smartwatches to the mainstream with the first-generation Apple Watch. Just think about what Target could figure out about you now.

THE FUTURE OF NEUROMARKETING

The future of marketing technology is inextricably linked to psychology, because as more data reveals more of your psychology, marketing departments will only get better at persuasion. For instance, take the way technology has amplified personality science.

In the world of psychology-based personality theories, one stands above the rest in its ability to model and predict future behavior: OCEAN analysis. The acronym OCEAN represents five different core personality traits: Openness, Conscientiousness, Extraversion, Agreeableness, and Neuroticism. Your OCEAN profile is your score on each trait scale.

OPENNESS
Do you enjoy new experiences?

CONSCIENTIOUSNESS
Do you prefer plans and order?

EXTRAVERSION
Do you like spending time with others?

AGREEABLENESS
Do you put other people's needs before your own?

NEUROTICISM
Do you tend to worry a lot?

In controlled studies, OCEAN analysis has proved effective at predicting a range of outcomes, from relationship success (high agreeableness) to racism (low openness). It's far from perfect, but it's the most valid measure of personality available. And anything that helps understand customers better, and can be incorporated into data-rich algorithms, is a huge plus for companies.

Thanks to the increasingly large amounts of increasingly robust data being analyzed through increasingly sophisticated algorithms, these models get more detailed, and more effective, every day. And by combining your purchase data and digital data with personality science, companies get a monumental psychological advantage.

The potency of this granular, personality-based approach was in full force in the 2016 election, when Donald Trump's election team hired UK-based Cambridge Analytica to help move the needle on his campaign. Cambridge created a simple survey, which 270,000 people took. The actual questions and results of the survey were trivial; what was important was that taking it provided access to all of each survey taker's Facebook user data—all of the likes, the comments, the pictures, everything. This was true not only for those 270,000 people, but—thanks to Facebook's leaky security—for all of their social networks as well. All told, Cambridge Analytica collected data from 87 million people[2]—and they did so legally.

Using predictive analytics, they used the data to derive a unique OCEAN personality profile for each person. Then, this profile was used to target potential voters with custom advertisements. For example, people who were highly neurotic and conscientious (and therefore maybe a bit paranoid) were shown a pro-Trump advertisement that depicted a break-in by a burglar and read: "The Second Amendment isn't just a right. It's an insurance policy. Defend the right to bear arms." In other words, each voter saw something uniquely catered to their specific OCEAN profile.

Exactly how much influence Cambridge Analytica had over the 2016 election is difficult to quantify. But their work does still provide a shocking preview of the likely future of advertising: granular and personal, with increasingly high levels of accuracy and curation. As Alexander Nix described in 2015 as the firm's CEO, "Today, communication is becoming ever increasingly targeted. It's being individualized for every single person in this room." By combining the psychology of personalities with digital data, Cambridge showed a preview of the future.

IN THE FUTURE, YOU WILL MARKET TO YOURSELF

What do Shudu Gram and Miquela Sousa have in common? Both are supermodels with massive online followings, 200,000 and 1.6 million respectively. The thing is, neither are real people. They are *deepfakes*—digitally generated supermodels who have convinced consumers of their existence and have sponsorships with the likes of Gucci, Fendi, and beyond.

If the technology to create convincing deepfakes exists today, what's to stop someone from creating a deepfake of you? This isn't a matter of if, but when, for instance, a company like Ray-Ban will show you a model in a digital ad who looks like you wearing the newest model of aviators.

The tactic is sure to work because of something neuroscientists call the *cocktail party effect*. Imagine this scenario: You're at a crowded party, catching up with a close friend. You're engrossed in the conversation, oblivious to the chatter of voices in the background. Then, all of a sudden, twenty feet behind you, you hear it: your name. Ten seconds ago, you had no idea the person who said it was even there, but now your ears are glued to their conversation. It's an effect that has been replicated by a series of psychological studies dating back to the 1950s.

Now combine that effect with today's incredibly accurate facial recognition technology and tomorrow's ability to create deepfake models. Recent research suggests that we have a special kind of attention not just for our own names, but for our own faces, as well.[3] In other words, there's a *visual* cocktail party effect.

Your brain recognizes your face even when you consciously don't. If you were asked to watch a quick-moving series of faces on a screen, you wouldn't be able to describe any individual face. But if you were hooked up to an electroencephalography (EEG) machine that detects what your brain is picking up, your brain activity would show your attention shifting when your face is flashed on the screen. And importantly, this isn't true for faces generally; it's only true when it's your own face.

In 2019, FaceApp attracted users by allowing them to see what they might look like forty to fifty years down the road. All good fun, but it re-ignited concerns about data safety and privacy. *Forbes* estimates that FaceApp now owns the faces of over 150 million Facebook users.

And while it's easy to point the finger (once again) at Facebook for failures in data security, it's far from the only party interested in harvesting face data. From Apple's Face ID feature to facial recognition in surveillance, face data—and the software to use it—is everywhere.

As Lorrie Cranor, a computer science professor at Carnegie Mellon University, recently told *Bloomberg Businessweek*, "Facial recognition technology is now cheap enough where you can put it in every Starbucks and have your coffee ready when you're in the front of the line."[4]

It's not a matter of whether our faces will be used by advertisers to persuade us, but when and how. Here are two speculative ways:

Social media marketing. Imagine scrolling mindlessly through your newsfeed on the subway, when you see an ad that catches your eye. Maybe you're not the type of person who typically clicks on ads, but how could you not when the person modeling these trendy new shoes is . . . you?

In the crowded attention economy, advertisers on social media apps are in a perpetual arms race in an effort to catch your gaze. The technique of embedding users' faces into ads that appear within the platform will be a game changer and an easy brand differentiator. And remember: You don't have to *consciously* see that it's your face. The mere presence of your face in an ad image will *unconsciously* drive your attention to it.

Personalized "FaceSwap" ad videos. The technology also exists for ads to put you into full-on videos. Deepfake videos of politicians like Nancy Pelosi already pose difficult ethical questions. But a message is never going to be as attention-grabbing and persuasive coming from someone else as it would be coming from you. And the technology of a speculative FaceSwap company will make this easy by allowing your face to be mapped onto another's not only in pictures but in videos.

Some of the uses we've seen so far for face-swapping technology are perfectly harmless, and the type of content the internet is beloved for. For example, earlier in summer 2019, the face of Nick Offerman (a.k.a. Ron Swanson from *Parks and Recreation*) was mapped onto the characters of *Full House*.[5] Also in 2019, Chinese company Momo released an app called Zao that allows you to insert "yourself" as any main character in a famous movie.[6] (An ad used to introduce the app depicted incredibly realistic scenes from *Inception*, with another person's face acting out the role of Leonardo DiCaprio.[7] ⌐⊙)

But FaceSwap video technology has plenty of potential for amplifying existing marketing tactics in ways that start to feel uncomfortably manipulative. Recall from chapter six how, because humans are naturally loss averse, fear is a powerful motivator. Imagine FaceSwap's hyper-personalized approach being used to advertise something like, say, insurance. What could provoke fear more effectively than a vividly realistic video of your corpse being pulled from a horrible car wreck?

The exact form of this new wave of personalized ads remains to be seen. But one thing is clear: the future of face-based, personalized marketing is here. Along with it comes a new horizon of opportunity for marketers, a fresh headache for regulators, and new puzzles for ethicists.

CONSUMERISM 2.0

Data and psychology will define the next generation of marketing, but what about the consumers? Consumers will need to update their own behavior to version 2.0. To stay vigilant and look out for their own best interests, consumers will need to know more about how the sausage is made, and then engage with the consumer world with heightened self-awareness.

Philip Kotler, the godfather of marketing, who literally wrote the book on the subject (*Principles of Marketing* is used globally in both undergraduate and graduate courses), defines marketing as "managing profitable relationships." Stripped of jargon, the definition is that marketing is much more human. Marketing is *trading value*. And to successfully navigate the future, consumers must understand what value is being traded and how.

Long before graphic design, before social media, before product managers, and, heck, even before brand logos, marketing was simple. There were two parties, a seller and a buyer. The seller had a product, and the buyer had money (or other goods) to offer in exchange for that product. That was business. The trading of value was simple. The closest thing to a logo was the face of the seller.

Over time, as competition grew, so did the need for differentiation.

Prices being equal, a seller needed to provide additional value beyond just the product to earn value (in the form of payment) from buyers. Details such as how the seller greeted customers, the breadth of their catalog, and the cleanliness of their shop all became additional ways for a seller to provide value outside of the product itself.

Fast-forward to today. Marketing remains a trade of value, with buyers now called *consumers* and the moniker *seller* covering businesses, nonprofits, and governmental organizations—any group that provides and receives value. All that's evolved is how buyers and sellers trade value.

Today's buyer often provides value beyond payment. They can provide word of mouth, email a referral code to a friend, post about the seller on Facebook, or applaud the seller on Yelp. Today's buyers might as well be doing free labor for sellers, considering all the value user-generated content brings to sellers. Really, it should be called *buyer*-generated content. Every time you create a playlist on Spotify, write a review on Amazon, or post a photo on Instagram, you are providing the company *tremendous* value outside of payment. And while Amazon and Spotify would live on without buyer-generated content, companies like Instagram, where money isn't exchanged by the end user, would cease to exist if users stopped providing that value. This new world of value exchange gives the buyer immense untapped power.

Today's seller also provides new kinds of value, for the same reason sellers from generations past provided safe, clean environments to shop—out of necessity, due to the evolving business environment. Today, there are more things we can buy than needs we can fill, which means sellers have to provide much more value to earn our money. Each possible touchpoint between seller and buyer is an opportunity for the seller to provide value. From telephone hold music to shopping bag design to product packages to award-winning blogs, modern sellers have to work harder to market, differentiate, and connect.

It's worth pointing out that, despite all our talk in this book of the ways in which companies use the blind spots in human psychology to their advantage, marketers *can* genuinely increase a product's value for the consumer. That marketing alters our perception of reality doesn't in itself mean what we feel in response to that marketing is fake or superficial. Regular wine sipped from a crystal glass truly does taste better for the drinker, right down to the level of the brain. Remember: As humans, we never experience the world directly; all we ever experience is our brain's model of it. The pleasure we derive from knowing a wine is rare and expensive can be just as real as the pleasure we feel from the taste of the wine hitting our tongue.

Walking into an Apple Store feels better than walking into a Fry's electronics store. Running in a pair of new Nike Joyride running shoes provides a different, elevated experience than running in a generic brand. All that time, money, and careful effort behind Nike's branding has a tangible effect on us. As we saw in chapter one, this branding itself can directly enhance our experience through a placebo-like effect. And recall from that same chapter that controlled studies found we hit golf balls better and farther with what we're told is a Nike-branded driver than we do a generically branded one—despite their physical qualities being identical.[8] These types of performance placebo effects are everywhere, and we have marketers to thank for them.

In other words, there's reason to *not* be cynical about marketing tactics, generally speaking. Marketing can and does provide a genuine boost in our happiness and fulfillment, and that's worth appreciating. For the person who genuinely loves the feeling of putting on their Nikes for their morning run—conjuring a super-athlete identity the marketing team worked hard to craft in the process—the extra $30 they spent on them over a generic brand is well worth it.

In the value exchange between buyer/consumer and seller/business, the goal of a business is to optimize the value they extract from the consumer. The goal of a consumer should be the same: to optimize the value they receive from the business. In a fair exchange of value, both parties are happy. However, most consumers are unaware of the extent of the value exchange taking place. Some may be nebulously aware of how the roles of buyers and sellers have evolved, as just outlined. However, there are newer, less transparent exchanges of value taking place that, while visible to sellers, are invisible to buyers. This makes the value exchange unfairly one-sided, to the benefit of the business. And it is here, when the value exchange is unfair, that we run into ethical problems.

MARKETING IS ABOUT PERSUASION

Within the consumer–corporation relationship, persuasion is key. The success of a marketing tactic (branding, advertisements, etc.) is defined by its ability to persuade. Persuasion is key to making the value exchange work.

And the persuasive effect of any given marketing tactic isn't binary. Instead, it rests on a spectrum. Imagine a simple scale from 0 to 10, where 0 means having no effect on future behavior, and 10 means having a guaranteed effect on future behavior. At the far right of the spectrum, a person is guaranteed to undertake a desired behavior as a direct result of an ad; at the far left, the marketing tactic has no impact on whether or not the desired behavior occurs.

No   Guaranteed
Effect   Effect

---

0   10

This spectrum helps contextualize the ethical conversation surrounding unfair value exchanges. At what point along this spectrum of persuasiveness are you, as a consumer, not comfortable? Most of us feel immediately uncomfortable with the idea that a marketing tactic could have deterministic impact on their behavior, effectively extinguishing our personal autonomy. But where on the spectrum should the line be drawn, then? At tactics with no more than 80 percent effectiveness? 70 percent? The job of marketers is to inch ever closer to the right. Those whose work is too far to the left—those whose work has little or no impact on the consumer—are, by definition, bad marketers. So where should the line of acceptability be drawn?

The marketing landscape is changing faster than ever because the relationship between buyers and sellers is growing faster than ever. At its core, that relationship is still one based on value exchange, but the type of value that is being exchanged has shifted, as have the ways in which companies extract it.

These changes are resulting in a massive shift along the persuasiveness continuum, thanks to the biggest change to marketing in millennia: personal data.

For now, personal technologies, digital habits, and the connected lives of consumers provide more data than there are people or AI to crunch effectively. But personal data collection is just at its beginning; 90 percent of all data ever collected was harvested in 2016 and 2017.[9] Brands will only get better at processing, understanding, and using this data to persuade with each passing day.

Imagine the most persuasive person you know. Now imagine them having your digital data, list of past purchases, and personality type. Imagine them knowing, too, all of your private text conversations, and your medical history. How persuasive would they be then? It might be impossible for them *not* to persuade you. And while advertising that has a *guaranteed* effect might never be possible, the trajectory of companies' ability to persuade is an asymptote, inching ever closer to near certainty.

Where is the "right" place along the persuasiveness continuum? Does it make a difference if marketers are trying to persuade us to do something that is ultimately in our own best interest, like exercise more or adopt a healthier diet? Marketing ethics is a complex issue, and your authors' ongoing research is probing these issues.[10] We've barely scratched the surface of variables and factors in this brief chapter that should inform an updated model of marketing ethics. But one thing should be clear: marketers are not going to get any worse at their jobs. Marketers are only going to become more effective at persuasion.

Given that, what is the path forward for us as consumers? What can and should we do—as the other piece in this complex, intertwined relationship—to look out for our own interests?

THE PATH FORWARD: REGULATION AND THE CONSUMER (MOSTLY THE CONSUMER)

Unfair value exchanges in the business world are not new, and neither are laws that protect consumers and markets from them. Antitrust laws, for example, safeguard consumers (and the economy at large) from monopolies, which stifle competition and enable the extortion of customers. While the dangers of monopolies have been well recognized for centuries, this new era of big data has ushered in a new set of concerns and calls for regulation. Examples like the Cambridge Analytica scandal have put data privacy squarely on the map. Still, it is unclear what regulation will come of it, if any. Our elected officials' understanding of new technology like AI seems to go only as far as spelling it.

While regulation will no doubt have an important role to play in shaping the future collection and utilization of user data, the lion's share of the responsibility for balancing the value exchange between businesses and consumers will lie with consumers. By changing what we value—and what, and where, we derive that value from—we have incredible power to shape the buyer/seller relationship . . . and in doing so, balance the scale.

There's an important role for regulation, to be sure, but the lion's share of the responsibility rests with the consumer. While it is easy to point a finger at Facebook and say, "You are creating addictive products and abusing data," we must also consider the three fingers pointing back at us. Data companies like Facebook are not nonprofits; they need to make money to survive. Running a digital country of almost 2.3 billion digital citizens is not free. If consumers aren't willing to pay to use platforms like Facebook, Instagram, and WhatsApp, these companies must find another way to survive financially—like mining your attention for data, and then selling that data to marketers.

As the old saying goes, "There is no free lunch." In the digital world, there is no free app. It is time for consumers to shake off the hangover of "free." If you're not paying with cash, you're paying with something else you and marketers both value: your attention, your data, or both. And the sooner we realize this, the sooner we can start navigating our relationship with the consumer world more effectively.

We're not passive recipients here; we have the power to change the nature of our relationship with the consumer world—to force the consumer world to adjust to us. If we all immediately swore off technology and threw our smartphones into the sea, it would cause massive waves in the consumer world. Apple may be a global leader in market capitalization, but even they would need to make drastic changes just to survive, much less remain profitable. Companies need customers even more than customers need them.

We could take a cue from the food and beverage industry, and demand transparency about what companies get out of the business/consumer value exchange and what consumers do. Alcohol and cigarettes come with health warnings. Movies and video games come with age restrictions. Yet preteens can download social media apps and stream, swipe, and like away without any oversight. And instead of being hidden in terms and conditions, how value is being extracted from you should be presented transparently, as part of the value companies themselves offer.

Especially with tech products, it often isn't clear what exactly the consumer is providing to a company, value-wise, and a relationship in which one party doesn't know what's actually being exchanged is clearly immoral. You would never sign a prenup written in a language you don't speak—yet you do it every time you click *agree* on a set of terms and conditions.

Whether we like it or not, we're in a deep relationship with the consumer world. But this realization can actually be empowering. You're a partner in this exchange. What you value shapes the relationship. By changing *what* you consider valuable, and how you delegate your own value, you can alter it. As a buyer, you can push sellers to adapt and provide a more balanced, mutually beneficial relationship. Heck, maybe the consumer world can even become the algae to your sloth.

Over the past few hundred pages, you have gained the ability to see the unseen—you've gained blindsight. You are aware of the invisible quirks of your psychology and know what to expect when your brain meets brand. You've confronted some of the major paradoxes of human psychology: pain and pleasure, logic and emotion, perception and reality, and attraction to both danger and safety. You now understand the neuroscience of memory, decision making, empathy, connection, storytelling, subliminal messaging, attention, and experience, all in the context of consumerism.

The authors ask just one favor: that you empower others with this knowledge by passing the book on to a fellow consumer—or even (especially!) a marketer, so they better understand the psychological consequences of their campaigns.

You have graduated from being a passenger to a pilot, able to navigate the consumer world on your own terms. CONGRATULATIONS! Where you fly to now is up to you.

ACKNOWLEDGMENTS

I f you're lucky, a couple times in life you may experience a moment that feels like the universe made it happen. For us, meeting Lisa Gallagher, our agent, was one of those moments. Somewhere in the middle of your vacation in Mexico, you decided to check your email, and we are here because of it. From the bottom of our lucky hearts, Lisa, thank you. Thank you for believing in us. Thank you for preparing us. And thank you for sharpening our vision. Book publishing is a team sport, and you drafted us.

While Lisa drafted us, Leah Wilson, our editor, was our coach. Cultivating raw material into a final piece of genuine value is one hell of a challenge. You are the master of it. We eagerly waited for (and celebrated) every one of your revisions because we knew our writing would instantly level up. On our first phone call, we requested you to be fiercely direct with your feedback, and you did precisely that, revision after revision, month after month. Thank you for helping us see the forest when we were too close even to see the trees. Thank you for being the voice of reason. Lastly, thank you for being the objective tie-breaker that you are. We love you for it, Coach Leah! We always referred to this book as "our baby," and we could imagine no better hands to have brought it into the world.

Glenn Yeffeth and the rest of the BenBella team—we owe you the utmost gratitude for taking in two first-time authors and making us feel like A-listers. Glenn, we are grateful for your instant recognition of our vision from day one. Thank you to you and the rest of the hard-working BenBella team for enabling that vision to become reality. Any authors who are reading this: you would be hard-pressed to find a publisher who cares as much as BenBella.

We also want to thank Lyn Melwani. Lyn, if there were such a thing as a Best Mentee Award, we would rename it the Lyn Award. Your desire to grow is insatiable, and we are lucky to have had your support throughout this project!

Thank you to Alan Johnson and Camila Silva for your creative energy and inspiration. You were there for us when we needed rescuing; your aesthetic influence is what you are currently holding. We hope you are proud of it; we know we are.

And last but not least, a shout-out to our first class of interns: Valeria Esparza, Per Stubing, Josephine Gatus, and Carol Alencar. It was a pleasure having you along for the journey, and we hope you enjoyed the ride!

Matt would like to thank his wife, Marlene. Without your love, support, patience, and good humor, this book would not have been possible. To his son, Santiago—thank you for your cheer and your curiosity, and for always putting a smile on everyone's faces. Thank you to his parents-in-law, Magnolia and Chencho, for all of their support and their warmth, and for being especially patient caregivers for Santiago. Matt would also like to (again) thank his parents, Stan and Sandy, for always encouraging his writing, and his brother, Alan Johnson, for his creative input on the book cover, and for the always-interesting conversations about the interaction of psychology and art.

Prince would like to thank Heather Hutchinson for her divine patience during the intense writing periods. He would also like to thank his parents, Satnam and Ruby Ghuman, for their unwavering support. A special thank you goes out to the most okayest sister in the world, Sweety Ghuman, for reminding him to balance work and play. The book would not have crossed the finish line without constant encouragement from Prince's "MySpace Top 8"; you know who you are. He would also like to single out Faraz

Ellahie for providing invaluable feedback on tone and humor. He would also like to thank his dog child, Schmeckle, for being the muse who never left his lap and provided all the emotional support a writer could ever need. Lastly, Prince would like to thank LeBron James for joining the Lakers and bringing shine to the purple and gold.

NOTES

THE POWER OF BLINDSIGHT

1 B. De Gelder, M. Tamietto, G. van Boxtel, R. Goebel, A. Sahraie, J. van den Stock, B.M.C. Steinen, L. Weiskrantz, A. Pegna, "Intact navigation skills after bilateral loss of striate cortex," Current Biology 18(2009):R1128–R1129.

CHAPTER 1: EATING THE MENU

1 J. Bohannon, R. Goldstein, and A. Herschkowitsch, "Can People Distinguish Pâté From Dog Food?" (American Association of Wine Economists Working Paper No. 36, April 2009), https://www.wine-economics.org/dt_catalog/working-paper-no-36/.

2 G. Morrot, F. Brochet, & D. Dubourdieu, "The Color of Odors." Brain & Language 79 (2001): 309–20.

3 H. McGurk and J. MacDonald J., "Hearing Lips and Seeing Voices," Nature 264, no. 5588 (1976): 746–48, doi:10.1038/264746a0.

4 Sixesfullofnines, "McGurk effect – Auditory Illusion – BBC Horizon Clip," video, 0:54, November 6, 2011, https://www.youtube.com/watch?v=2k8fHR9jKVM.

5 M. Nishizawa, W. Jiang, and K. Okajima, "Projective-AR System for Customizing the Appearance and Taste of Food," in Proceedings of the 2016 Workshop on Multimodal Virtual and Augmented Reality (MVAR '16) (New York: ACM, 2016), 6, doi:10.1145/3001959.3001966.

6 G. Huisman, M. Bruijnes, and D. K. J. Heylen, "A Moving Feast: Effects of Color, Shape and Animation on Taste Associations and Taste Perceptions," in Proceedings of the 13th International Conference on Advances in Computer Entertainment Technology (ACE 2016) (New York: ACM, 2016), 12, doi:10.1145/3001773.3001776.

7 M. Suzuki, R. Kimura, Y. Kido, et al., "Color of Hot Soup Modulates Postprandial Sati-

ety, Thermal Sensation, and Body Temperature in Young Women," Appetite 114 (2017): 209–16.

8 Angel Eduardo, "George Carlin - Where's the Blue Food?," video, 1:09, May 25, 2008. https://www.youtube.com/watch?v=l04dn8Msm-Y

9 Author Matt had this precise scenario play out when he was living abroad in China. On a trip to Hangzhou, he was enjoying a very well-prepared meal and was thoroughly impressed by the flavorful dishes, especially his main entrée. Not wanting to be rude, he dug into it the meat in front of him without asking what it was. Then, a colleague revealed what the dish was—horse face. Suddenly, the entree tasted much different.

10 Wan-chen Lee, Jenny Mitsuru Shimizu, Kevin M. Kniffin, et al., "You Taste What You See: Do Organic Labels Bias Taste Perceptions?" Food Quality and Preference 29, no. 1 (2013): 33–39, doi:10.1016/j.foodqual.2013.01.010.

11 James C. Makens, "Effect of Brand Preference upon Consumers' Perceived Taste of Turkey Meat," Journal of Applied Psychology 49, no. 4 (1964): 261–63.

12 H. Plassmann, J. O'Doherty, B. Shiv, et al., "Marketing Actions Can Modulate Neural Representations of Experienced Pleasantness," Proceedings of the National Academy of Sciences of the USA 105 (2008): 1050.

13 Jeffrey R. Binder and Rutvik H. Desai, "The Neurobiology of Semantic Memory," Trends in Cognitive Sciences 15, no. 11 (2011): 527–36,

14 Karalyn Patterson, Peter J. Nestor, and Timothy T. Rogers, "Where Do You Know What You Know? The Representation of Semantic Knowledge in the Human Brain," Nature Reviews Neuroscience 8 (2007): 976–87.

15 R. Lambon and A. Matthew, "Neural Basis of Category-Specific Semantic Deficits for Living Things: Evidence from Semantic Dementia, HSVE and a Neural Network Model," Brain 130, no. 4 (2007): 1127–37.

16 J. R, Saffran, R. N. Aslin, and E. L. Newport, "Statistical Learning in 8-Month Olds," Science 274, no. 5294 (1996): 1926–28.

17 Interbrand, "Best Global Brands 2019 Ranking," accessed October 28, 2019, https://www.interbrand.com/best-brands/best-global-brands/2019/ranking/.

18 S.I. Lee, interview with the authors in San Francisco, November 2018.

19 S. M. McClure, J. Li, D. Tomlin, et al., "Neural Correlates of Behavioral Preference for Culturally Familiar Drinks," Neuron 44 (2004): 379–87.

20 Yann Cornil, Pierre Chandon, and Aradhna Krishna, "Does Red Bull Give Wings to Vodka? Placebo Effects of Marketing Labels on Perceived Intoxication and Risky Attitudes and Behaviors," Journal of Consumer Psychology 27, no. 4 (2017): 456–65.

21 Pascal Tétreault, Ali Mansour, Etienne Vachon-Presseau, et al., "Brain Connectivity Predicts Placebo Response across Chronic Pain Clinical Trials, PLoS Biology, October 27, 2016, https://doi.org/10.1371/journal.pbio.1002570.

22 T. D. Wager and L. Y. Atlas, "The Neuroscience of Placebo Effects: Connecting Context, Learning and Health," Nature Reviews: Neuroscience 16, no. 7 (2015): 403–18.

23 Gary Greenberg, "What If the Placebo Effect Isn't a Trick?" New York Times, November 7, 2018, https://www.nytimes.com/2018/11/07/magazine/placebo-effect-medicine.html.

24 A. M. Garvey, F. Germann, and L. E. Bolton, "Performance Brand Placebos: How Brands Improve Performance and Consumers Take the Credit," Journal of Consumer Research 42, no. 6 (2016): 931–51.

CHAPTER 2: DROPPING ANCHORS

1 C. Escera, K. Alho, I. Winkler, et al., "Neural Mechanisms of Involuntary Attention to Acoustic Novelty and Change," Journal of Cognitive Neuroscience 10 (1998): 590–604.

2 M. Banks and A. P. Ginsburg, "Early Visual Preferences: A Review and New Theoretical Treatment," in Advances in Child Development and Behavior, ed. H. W. Reese (New York: Academic Press, 1985), 19: 207–46.

3 L. B. Cohen, "Attention-Getting and Attention-Holding Processes of Infant Visual Preferences," Child Development 43 (1972): 869–79.

4 M. Milosavljevic, V. Navalpakkam, C. Koch, et al., "Relative Visual Saliency Differences Induce Sizable Bias in Consumer Choice," Journal of Consumer Psychology 22, no. 1 (2012): 67–74, https://doi.org/10.1016/j.jcps.2011.10.002.

5 Milosavljevic et al., "Relative Visual Saliency Differences."

6 Felicity Murray, "Special Report: Vodka Packaging Design," thedrinksreport, September 13, 2013, https://www.thedrinksreport.com/news/2013/15045-special-report-vodka-packaging-design.html.

7 Katie Calautti, phone interview with the authors, February 28, 2019.

8 Macegrove, "Cadbury's Gorilla Advert," video, 1:30, Aug 31, 2017, https://www.youtube.com/watch?v=TnzFRV1LwIo.

9 Nikki Sandison, "Cadbury's Drumming Gorilla Spawns Facebook Group," Campaign, September 11, 2007, https://www.campaignlive.co.uk/article/cadburys-drumming-gorilla-spawns-facebook-group/737270.

10 "Cadbury's Ape Drummer Hits the Spot," Campaign Media Week, September 25, 2007, https://www.campaignlive.co.uk/article/brand-barometer-cadburys-ape-drummer-hits-spot/740054.

11 A. Gallagher, R. Beland, P. Vannasing, et al., "Dissociation of the N400 Component between Linguistic and Non-linguistic Processing: A Source Analysis Study," World Journal of Neuroscience 4 (2014): 25–39.

12 M. Kutas and K. D. Federmeier, "Thirty Years and Counting: Finding Meaning in the N400 Component of the Event-Related Brain Potential (ERP)," Annual Review of Psychology 62 (2011): 621–47.

13 Dan Hughes, "6 of the Most Memorable Digital Marketing Campaigns of 2018…So Far," Digital Marketing Institute, accessed November 28, 2019, https://digitalmarketinginstitute.com/en-us/the-insider/6-of-the-most-memorable-digital-marketing-campaigns-of-2018.

14 Daniel J. Simons and Daniel T. Levin, "Failure to Detect Changes to People during a Real-World Interaction," Psychonomic Bulletin and Review 5, no. 4 (1998): 644–49, https://msu.edu/course/psy/802/snapshot.afs/altmann/802/Ch2-4a-SimonsLevin98.pdf.

15 Daniel Simons, "The 'Door' Study," video, 1:36, March 13, 2010, https://www.youtube.com/watch?v=FWSxSQsspiQ.

16 Daniel J. Simons and Christopher F. Chabris, "Gorillas in our midst: sustained inattentional blindness for dynamic events," Perception 28 (1999): 1059–74, http://www.chabris.com/Simons1999.pdf.

17 Daniel Simons, "Selective Attention Test," video, 1:21, March 10, 2010, https://www.youtube.com/watch?v=vJG698U2Mvo.

18 William Poundstone, Priceless: The Myth of Fair Value (and How to Take Advantage of It) (New York: Hill and Wang, 2011), 15; Brian Wansink, Robert J. Kent, and Stephen J. Hoch, "An Anchoring and Adjustment Model of Purchase Quantity Decisions," Journal of Marketing Research 35 (February 1998): 71–81.

19 Wansink, Kent, and Hoch, "Anchoring and Adjustment Model."

CHAPTER 3: MAKING THE MOMENT

1 D. I. Tamir, E. M. Templeton, A. F. Ward, et al., "Media usage diminishes Memory for Experiences," Journal of Experimental Social Psychology 76 (2018): 161–68.

2 L. A. Henkel, "Point-and-Shoot Memories: The Influence of Taking Photos on Memory for a Museum Tour," Psychological Science 25, no. 2 (2014): 396–402.

3 A. Barasch, G. Zauberman, and K. Diehl, "Capturing or Changing the Way We (Never) Were? How Taking Pictures Affects Experiences and Memories of Experiences," European Advances in Consumer Research 10 (2013): 294.

4 C. Diemand-Yauman, D. M. Oppenheimer, and E. B. Vaughan, "Fortune Favors the Bold (and the Italicized): Effects of Disfluency on Educational Outcomes," Cognition 118 (2011): 114–18.

5 RMIT University, "Sans Forgetica" (typeface download page), 2018, http://sansforgetica.rmit/.

6 "Sans Forgetica: New Typeface Designed to Help Students Study," press release, RMIT University, October 26, 2018, https://www.rmit.edu.au/news/all-news/2018/oct/sans-forgetica-news-story.

7 E. Fox, R. Russo, R. Bowles, et al., "Do Threatening Stimuli Draw or Hold Visual Attention in Subclinical Anxiety?" Journal of Experimental Psychology: General 130, no. 4 (2001): 681–700, doi:10.1037/0096-3445.130.4.681.

8 E. A. Kensinger and S. Corkin, "Memory Enhancement for Emotional Words: Are Emotional Words More Vividly Remembered Than Neutral Words?" Memory and Cognition 31 (2003):1169–80.

9 Paulo Ferreira, Paulo Rita, Diogo Morais, et al., "Grabbing Attention While Reading Website Pages: The Influence of Verbal Emotional Cues in Advertising," Journal of Eye Tracking, Visual Cognition and Emotion (June 2, 2011), https://revistas.ulusofona.pt/index.php/JETVCE/article/view/2057.

10 Jonathan R. Zadra and Gerald L. Clore, "Emotion and Perception: The Role of Affective Information," Wiley Interdisciplinary Reviews: Cognitive Science 2, no. 6 (2011): 676–85, https://www.ncbi.nlm.nih.gov/pmc/articles/PMC3203022/.

11 A. D. Vanstone and L. L. Cuddy, "Musical Memory in Alzheimer Disease," Aging, Neuropsychology, and Cognition 17(1): 2010; 108–28.

12 A. Baird and S. Samson, "Memory for Music in Alzheimer's Disease: Unforgettable?" Neuropsychology Review 19, no. 1 (2009): 85–101.

13 D. J. Levitin, This Is Your Brain on Music: The Science of a Human Obsession (New York: Dutton/Penguin, 2006).

14 T. L. Hubbard, "Auditory Imagery: Empirical Findings," Psychological Bulletin 136 (2010): 302–29.

15 Andrea R. Halpern and James C. Bartlett, "The Persistence of Musical Memories: A Descriptive Study of Earworms," Music Perception: An Interdisciplinary Journal 28, no. 4 (2011): 425–32.

16 Ronald McDonald House Charities, "Our Relationship with McDonald's," accessed October 28, 2019, https://www.rmhc.org/our-relationship-with-mcdonalds.

17 "Ronald McDonald School Show Request," n.d., accessed October 28, 2019, https://www.mcdonaldssocal.com/pdf/School_Show_Request_Form.pdf.

18 D. Kahneman, D. L. Fredrickson, C. A. Schreiber, et al., "When More Pain Is Preferred to Less: Adding a Better End," Psychological Science 4 (1993): 401–5.

19 Event Marketing Institute, EventTrack 2015: Event & Experiential Marketing Industry Forecast & Best Practices Study (Norwalk, CT: Event Marketing Institute, 2015), http://cdn.eventmarketer.com/wp-content/uploads/2016/01/EventTrack2015_Consumer.pdf.

20 Google.org, "Impact Challenge Bay Area 2015," accessed October 28, 2019, https://impactchallenge.withgoogle.com/bayarea2015.

21 Tony Chen, Ken Fenyo, Sylvia Yang, et al., "Thinking inside the Subscription Box: New Research on E-commerce Consumers," McKinsey, February 2018, https://www.mckinsey.com/industries/high-tech/our-insights/thinking-inside-the-subscription-box-new-research-on-ecommerce-consumers

22 Gerken, Tom (Sep 2018), "Kevin Hart: Fans kicked out for using mobile phones at gigs," BBC News, accessed October 28, https://www.bbc.com/news/world-us-canada-45395186.

23 Katie Calautti, phone interview with the authors, February 28,2019.

24 Music Industry Research Association and Princeton University Survey Research Center, "Inaugural Music Industry Research Association (MIRA) Survey of Musicians," June 22, 2018, https://img1.wsimg.com/blobby/go/53aaa2d4-793a-4400-b6c9-95d6618809f9/downloads/1cgjrbs3b_761615.pdf

25 RIAA, "U.S. Sales Database," accessed October 28, 2019, https://www.riaa.com/u-s-sales-database/.

26 Statista, "Music Events Worldwide," accessed October 28, 2019, https://www.statista.com/outlook/273/100/music-events/worldwide.

CHAPTER 4: MEMORY REMIXED

1 Linda Rodriguez McRobbie, "Total Recall: The People Who Never Forget," The Guardian, February 8, 2017, https://www.theguardian.com/science/2017/feb/08/total-recall-

the-people-who-never-forget.

2 Valerio Santangelo, Clarissa Cavallina, Paola Colucci, et al., "Enhanced Brain Activity Associated with Memory Access in Highly Superior Autobiographical Memory," Proceedings of the National Academy of Sciences 115, no. 30 (July 9, 2018), doi:10.1073/pnas.1802730115.

3 Bart Vandever, "I Can Remember Every Day of My Life," BBC Reel, February 28, 2019, https://www.bbc.com/reel/video/p0722s3y/-i-can-remember-every-day-of-my-life-.

4 "Coca Cola Commercial - I'd Like to Teach the World to Sing (In Perfect Harmony) - 1971," YouTube video, 0:59, posted by "Shelly Kiss," December 29, 2008, https://www.youtube.com/watch?v=ib-Qiyklq-Q.

5 Shelly Kiss, "Coca Cola Commercial - I'd Like to Teach the World to Sing (In Perfect Harmony) – 1971," video, 0:59, December 29, 2008, https://www.youtube.com/watch?v=ib-Qiyklq-Q.

6 Accenture. "Who Are the Millenial Shoppers? And What Do They Really Want?", accessed December 2, 2019, https://www.accenture.com/us-en/insight-outlook-who-are-millennial-shoppers-what-do-they-really-want-retail.

7 Andrew Webster, "Nintendo NX: Everything We Know So Far," The Verge, September 23, 2016, https://www.theverge.com/2016/4/27/11516888/nintendo-nx-new-console-news-date-games.

8 InternetExplorer, "Microsoft's Child of the 90s Ad for Internet Explorer 2013," video, 1:40, Jan 23, 2013, https://www.youtube.com/watch?v=qkM6RJf15cg.

9 "Elizabeth Loftus: How Can Our Memories Be Manipulated?" NPR, TED Radio Hour, October 13, 2017, https://www.npr.org/2017/10/13/557424726/elizabeth-loftus-how-can-our-memories-be-manipulated.

10 E. F. Loftus and J. E. Pickrell, "The Formation of False Memories," Psychiatric Annals 25, no. 12 (1995): 720–25.

11 Lawrence Patihis, Steven J. Frenda, Aurora K. R. LePort, et al., "False Memories in Superior Autobiographical Memory," Proceedings of the National Academy of Sciences of the USA, 110, no. 52 (December 24, 2013): 20947–952, doi:10.1073/pnas.1314373110.

12 Daniel M. Bernstein, Nicole L.M. Pernat, and Elizabeth F. Loftus, "The False Memory Diet: False Memories Alter Food Preferences," Handbook of Behavior, Food and Nutrition (January 31, 2011): 1645–63.

13 John Glassie, "The False Memory Diet," New York Times, December 11, 2005, https://www.nytimes.com/2005/12/11/magazine/falsememory-diet-the.html.

14 Kathryn Y. Segovia and Jeremy N. Bailenson, "Virtually True: Children's Acquisition of False Memories in Virtual Reality," Media Psychology 12 (2009): 371–93, https://vhil.stanford.edu/mm/2009/segovia-virtually-true.pdf.

15 D. R. Godden and A. D. Baddeley, "Context-Dependent Memory in Two Natural Environments: On Land and Underwater," British Journal of Psychology, 66 (1975): 325–331. doi:10.1111/j.2044-8295.1975.tb01468.x.

16 Hajo Adam and Adam D. Galinsky, "Enclothed Cognition," Journal of Experimental Social Psychology 48, no. 4 (July 2012): 918–25.

17 Jason Notte, "5 Champagne Beers for New Year's Toasting," The Street, December 21,

2011, https://www.thestreet.com/story/11350740/1/5-champagne-beers-for-new-years-toasting.html.

18 Alix Spiegel, "What Vietnam Taught Us about Breaking Bad Habits," NPR Shots, January 2, 2012), https://www.npr.org/sections/health-shots/2012/01/02/144431794/what-vietnam-taught-us-about-breaking-bad-habits.

19 "Drug Facts: Heroin," National Institute on Drug Abuse, June 2019, http://www.drugabuse.gov/publications/drugfacts/heroin.

20 B. P. Smyth, J. Barry, E. Keenan, et al., "Lapse and Relapse Following Inpatient Treatment of Opiate Dependence," Irish Medical Journal 103, no. 6 (2010): 176–79.

21 Wendy Wood and David T. Neal, "The Habitual Consumer," Journal of Consumer Psychology 19 (2009): 579–92, https://dornsife.usc.edu/assets/sites/545/docs/Wendy_Wood_Research_Articles/Habits/wood.neal.2009._the_habitual_consumer.pdf.

22 P. B. Seetheraman, "Modeling Multiple Sources of State Dependence in Random Utility Models: A Distributed Lag Approach," Journal of Marketing Science 23, no. 2 (2004): 263–71.

23 Verena Vogel, Heiner Evanschitzky, and B. Ramaseshan, "Customer Equity Drivers and Future Sales," Journal of Marketing 72, no. 6 (2008): 98–108.

24 L. Festinger and J. M. Carlsmith, "Cognitive Consequences of Forced Compliance," Journal of Abnormal and Social Psychology 58 (1959): 203–10.

25 "Nissan Xterra Commercial (2002)," YouTube video, 0:29, posted by "Vhs Vcr," November 23, 2016, https://www.youtube.com/watch?v=SVmn_tlxpYU.

26 M. Moscovitch, "Confabulation," in Memory Distortion, ed. D. L. Schacter, J. T. Coyle, G. D. Fischbach et al. (Cambridge, MA: Harvard University Press, 1995), 226–51.

27 Sandra Blakeslee, "Discovering That Denial of Paralysis Is Not Just a Problem of the Mind," New York Times, August 2, 2019, https://www.nytimes.com/2005/08/02/science/discovering-that-denial-of-paralysis-is-not-just-a-problem-of-the.html.

28 T. Feinberg, A. Venneri, and A. M. Simone A.M. et al., "The Neuroanatomy of Asomatognosia and Somatoparaphrenia," Journal of Neurology, Neurosurgery & Psychiatry 81 (2010): 276–81.

29 Petter Johansson, Lars Hall, Sverker Sikström, et al., "Failure to Detect Mismatches between Intention and Outcome in a Simple Decision Task," Science, October 2005, 116–19.

30 L. Hall, P. Johansson, B. Tärning, et al., "Magic at the Marketplace: Choice Blindness for the Taste of Jam and the Smell of Tea," Cognition 117 (2010): 54–61, doi: 10.1016/j.cognition.2010.06.010

31 Anat Keinan, Ran Kivetz, and Oded Netzer, "The Functional Alibi," Journal of the Association for Consumer Research 1, no. 4 (2016), 479–96.

32 Rory Sutherland, Alchemy: The Dark Art and Curious Science of Creating Magic in Brands, Business, and Life (New York: William Morrow), loc. 3645, Kindle.

33 Ruth Westheimer, "You've Decided to Break Up with Your Partner. Now What?," Time, January 4, 2018, http://time.com/5086205/dr-ruth-breakup-advice/.

CHAPTER 5: OF TWO MINDS

1 Daniel Kahneman and Shane Frederick, "Representativeness Revisited: Attribute Substitution in Intuitive Judgment," in Heuristics and Biases: The Psychology of Intuitive Judgment, ed. Thomas Gilovich, Dale Griffin, and Daniel Kahneman (New York: Cambridge University Press), 49–81.

2 Kara Pernice, "F-Shaped Pattern of Reading on the Web: Misunderstood, But Still Relevant (Even on Mobile)," Nielsen Norman Group, November 12, 2017, https://www.nngroup.com/articles/f-shaped-pattern-reading-web-content/.

3 SimilarWeb, "Youtube.com Analytics – Market Share Stats & Traffic Ranking," accessed October 2019, SimilarWeb.com/website/youtube.com.

4 P. Covington, J. Adams, and E. Sargin, "Deep Neural Networks for YouTube Recommendations," in Proceedings of the 10th ACM Conference on Recommender Systems (New York: ACM, 2016), 191–98.

5 A. Alter, Irresistible: The Rise of Addictive Technology and the Business of Keeping Us Hooked (New York: Penguin, 2016).

6 J. Koblin, "Netflix Studied Your Binge-Watching Habit. That Didn't Take Long," New York Times, June 9, 2016, https://www.nytimes.com/2016/06/09/business/media/netflix-studied-your-binge-watching-habit-it-didnt-take-long.html.

7 E. J. Johnson, J. Hershey, J. Meszaros, et al., "Framing, Probability Distortions, and Insurance Decisions," Journal of Risk and Uncertainty 7 (1993): 35–51, doi:10.1007/BF01065313.

8 James C. Cox, Daniel Kreisman, and Susan Dynarski, "Designed to Fail: Effects of the Default Option and Information Complexity on Student Loan Repayment," National Bureau of Economic Research Working Paper No. 25258, November 2018, https://www.nber.org/papers/w25258.

9 S. Davidai, T. Gilovich, and L. Ross, "The Meaning of Default Options for Potential Organ Donors," Proceedings of the National Academy of Sciences of the USA 109, no. 38 (2012): 15201–205.

10 Jennifer Levitz, "You Want 20% for Handing Me a Muffin? The Awkward Etiquette of iPad Tipping," Wall Street Journal, October 17, 2018, https://www.wsj.com/articles/you-want-20-for-handing-me-a-muffin-the-awkward-etiquette-of-ipad-tipping-1539790018?mod=e2fb.

11 Phil Barden, Decoded: The Science Behind Why We Buy (Hoboken, NJ: John Wiley & Sons), 150, Kindle.

12 Daniel Burstein, "Customer-First Marketing Chart: Why Customers Are Satisfied (and Unsatisfied) with Companies," Marketing Sherpa, February 21, 2017, https://www.marketingsherpa.com/article/chart/why-customers-are-satisfied.

13 NPR/Marist Poll results, April 25–May 2, 2018, accessed October 28, 2019, http://maristpoll.marist.edu/wp-content/misc/usapolls/us180423_NPR/NPR_Marist%20Poll_Tables%20of%20Questions_May%202018.pdf#page=2.

14 J. Clement, "Online shopping behavior in the United States - Statistics & Facts." Statista Report, August 30, 2019, https://www.statista.com/topics/2477/online-shopping-behavior/.

15 Sapna Maheshwari, "Marketing through Smart Speakers? Brands Don't Need to Be Asked Twice," New York Times, December 2, 2018, https://www.nytimes.com/2018/12/02/business/media/marketing-voice-speakers.html.

16 "Cavs Player Timofey Mozgov Accidentally Speaks Russian," YouTube video, 0:34, posted by FOX Sports, March 19, 2015, https://www.youtube.com/watch?v=mL-2wnGbDQSs.

17 T. W. Watts and G. J. Duncan, "Controlling, Confounding, and Construct Clarity: A Response to Criticisms of 'Revisiting the Marshmallow Test'" (2019), https://doi.org/10.31234/osf.io/hj26z.

18 Aimee Picchi, "The American Habit of Impulse Buying," CBS News, January 25, 2016, https://www.cbsnews.com/news/the-american-habit-of-impulse-buying/.

19 Sienna Kossman, "Survey: 5 in 6 Americans admit to impulse buys," CreditCards.com, January 25, 2016, https://www.creditcards.com/credit-card-news/impulse-buy-survey.php.

20 Phillip Hunter, "Your Decisions Are What You Eat: Metabolic State Can Have a Serious Impact on Risk-Taking and Decision-Making in Humans and Animals," European Molecular Biology Organization 14, no. 6 (2013): 505–8.

21 S. Danziger, J. Levav, J., and L. Avnaim-Pesso, "Extraneous Factors in Judicial Decisions," Proceedings of the National Academy of Sciences of the USA 108, no. 17 (2011): 6889–94.

22 Though see for a critique Keren Weinshall-Margel and John Shapard, "Overlooked Factors in the Analysis of Parole Decisions," Proceedings of the National Academy of Sciences of the USA 108 no. 42 (2011): E833, https://www.pnas.org/content/108/42/E833.long.

23 Malcolm Gladwell, "The Terrazzo Jungle," The New Yorker, March 15, 2004, https://www.newyorker.com/magazine/2004/03/15/the-terrazzo-jungle.

24 "The Gruen Effect," May 15, 2015, in 99% Invisible, produced by Avery Trufelman, MP3 audio, 20:10, https://99percentinvisible.org/episode/the-gruen-effect/.

25 David Derbyshire, "They Have Ways of Making You Spend," Telegraph, December 31, 2004, https://www.telegraph.co.uk/culture/3634141/They-have-ways-of-making-you-spend.html.

26 A. Selin Atalay, H. Onur Bodur, and Dina Rasolofoarison, "Shining in the Center: Central Gaze Cascade Effect on Product Choice," Journal of Consumer Research 39, no. 4 (December 2012): 848–66.

27 LivePerson, The Connecting with Customers Report: A Global Study of the Drivers of a Successful Online Experience," November 2013, https://docplayer.net/8484776-The-connecting-with-customers-report-a-global-study-of-the-drivers-of-a-successful-online-experience.html.

28 "Ebates Survey: More Than Half (51.8%) of Americans Engage in Retail Therapy—63.9% of Women and 39.8% of Men Shop to Improve Their Mood," Business Wire, April 2, 2013, http://www.businesswire.com/news/home/20130402005600/en/Ebates-Survey-51.8-Americans-Engage-Retail-Therapy%E2%80%94.

29 Selin Atalay and Margaret G. Meloy, "Retail Therapy: A Strategic Effort to Improve Mood," Psychology & Marketing 28, no. 6 (2011): 638–59.

30 Emma Hall, "IPA: Effective Ads Work on the Heart, Not on the Head," Ad Age, July 16, 2017, https://adage.com/article/print-edition/ipa-effective-ads-work-heart-head/119202/.

31 Francisco J. Gil-White, "Ultimatum Game with an Ethnicity Manipulation," in Foundations of Human Sociality: Economic Experiments and Ethnographic Evidence from Fifteen Small-Scale Societies, ed. Joseph Henrich, Robert Boyd, Samuel Bowles, et al. (New York: Oxford University Press, 2004), https://www.oxfordscholarship.com/view/1 0.1093/0199262055.001.0001/acprof-9780199262052-chapter-9.

32 Carey K. Morewedge, Tamar Krishnamurti, and Dan Ariely, "Focused on Fairness: Alcohol Intoxication Increases the Costly Rejection of Inequitable Rewards," Journal of Experimental Social Psychology 50 (2014): 15–20.

33 J. A. Neves. "Factors influencing impulse buying behaviour amongst Generation Y students," accessed December 2, 2019, https://pdfs.semanticscholar.org/4e37/7f-c1680020a106de47f9996e8fea07a6f9e8.pdf/.

34 Brian Boyd, "Free Shipping & Free Returns," Clique (website), April 15, 2016, http://cliqueaffiliate.com/free-shipping-free-returns/.

35 Sarah Getz, "Cognitive Control and Intertemporal Choice: The Role of Cognitive Control in Impulsive Decision Making" (PhD diss., Princeton University, September 2013), http://arks.princeton.edu/ark:/88435/dsp019s161630w.

36 S. J. Katz and T. P. Hofer, "Socioeconomic Disparities in Preventive Care Persist Despite Universal Coverage: Breast and Cervical Cancer Screening in Ontario and the United States," JAMA 1994;272(7):530–534.

37 Manju Ahuja, Babita Gupta, and Pushkala Raman, "An Empirical Investigation of Online Consumer Purchasing Behavior," Communications of the ACM 46, no. 12 (December 2003): 145–51. doi:https://doi.org/10.1145/953460.953494.

38 Anandi Mani, Sendhil Mullainathan, Eldar Shafir, et al., "Poverty Impedes Cognitive Function," Science 341, no. 6149 (2013): 976–80.

39 Jiaying Zhao, Skype interview with the authors, December 7, 2018.

40 New York Stock Exchange, PGR stock pricing, January 1996–January 1997.

41 Emily Peck, Felix Salmon, and Anna Szymanski, "The Dissent Channel Edition," September 29, 2018, in The Slate Money Podcast, MP3 audio, 59:44, http://www.slate.com/articles/podcasts/slate_money/2018/09/slate_money_on_thinking_in_bets_why_elon_musk_should_get_some_sleep_and.html.

42 N. Mazar, D. Mochon, and D. Ariely, "If You Are Going to Pay within the Next 24 Hours, Press 1: Automatic Planning Prompt Reduces Credit Card Delinquency," Journal of Consumer Psychology 28, no. 3 (2018): https://doi.org/10.1002/jcpy.1031.

CHAPTER 6: PLEASURE – PAIN = PURCHASE

1 Artangel, "Michael Landy: Break Down," February 10–24, 2001, https://www.artangel.org.uk/project/break-down/.

2 Alastair Sooke, "The Man Who Destroyed All His Belongings," BBC Culture, July 14, 2016, http://www.bbc.com/culture/story/20160713-michael-landy-the-man-who-destroyed-all-his-belongings.

3 A. Pertusa, R. O. Frost, M. A. Fullana, et al., "Refining the Boundaries of Compulsive Hoarding: A Review," Clinical Psychology Review 30, no. 4 (2010): 371–86, doi:10.1016/j.cpr.2010.01.007.

4 B. Knutson, S. Rick, G. E. Wimmer, et al., "Neural Predictors of Purchases," Neuron 53, no. 1 (2007): 147–56, http://doi.org/10.1016/j.neuron.2006.11.010.

5 Silvia Bellezza, Joshua M. Ackerman, and Francesca Gino, "Be Careless with That! Availability of Product Upgrades Increases Cavalier Behavior Toward Possessions," Journal of Marketing Research 54, no. 5 (2017): 768–84.

6 "EA SPORTS FIFA Is the World's Game," BusinessWire, press release, September 5, 2018, https://www.businesswire.com/news/home/20180905005646/en/.

7 Gregory S. Burns, Samuel M. McLure, Giuseppe Pagnoni, et al., "Predictability Modulates Human Brain Response to Reward," Journal of Neuroscience 21, no. 8 (2001): 2793–98.

8 Jerry M. Burger and David F. Caldwell, "When Opportunity Knocks: The Effect of a Perceived Unique Opportunity on Compliance," Group Processes & Intergroup Relations 14, no. 5 (2011): 671–80, http://gpi.sagepub.com/content/14/5/671.full.pdf+html.

9 Clive Schlee, "Random Acts of Kindness," Pret a Manger website, April 27, 2015, https://www.pret.com/en-us/random-acts-of-kindness.

10 Ryan Spoon, "Zappos Marketing: Surprises & Delights," Business Insider, March 11, 2011, https://www.businessinsider.com/zappos-marketing-surprises-and-delights-2011-3.

11 Stan Phelps, "Zappos Goes Door to Door Surprising and Delighting an Entire Town for the Holidays," Forbes, December 9, 2015, https://www.forbes.com/sites/stanphelps/2015/12/09/zappos-goes-door-to-door-surprising-and-delighting-an-entire-town-for-the-holidays/#3058e0f4f6ca.

12 Mauro F. Guillén and Adrian E. Tschoegl, "Banking on Gambling: Banks and Lottery-Linked Deposit Accounts," Journal of Financial Services Research 21, no. 3 (2002): 219–231, http://www-management.wharton.upenn.edu/guillen/PDF-Documents/Gambling_JFSR-2002.pdf.

13 Shankar Vedantam, "'Save To Win' Makes Saving as Much Fun as Gambling," NPR Hidden Brain, January 6, 2014, https://www.npr.org/2014/01/06/260119038/save-to-win-makes-saving-as-much-fun-as-gambling.

14 Barry Schwartz, "More Isn't Always Better," Harvard Business Review, June 2006, https://hbr.org/2006/06/more-isnt-always-better.

15 S. S. Iyengar and M. R. Lepper, "When Choice Is Demotivating: Can One Desire Too Much of a Good Thing?" Journal of Personality and Social Psychology 79, no. 6 (2000): 995–1006.

16 Alexander Chernev, U. Böckenholt, and J. K. Goodman, "Choice Overload: A Conceptual Review and Meta-analysis," Journal of Consumer Psychology 25 (2015): 333–58.

17 Sarah C. Whitley, Remi Trudel, and Didem Jurt, "The Influence of Purchase Motivation on Perceived Preference Uniqueness and Assortment Size Choice," Journal of Consumer Research 45, no. 4 (2018): 710–24, doi: 10.1093/jcr/ucy031.

18 Thomas T. Hills, Takao Noguchi, and Michael Gibbert, "Information Overload or Search-Amplified Risk? Set Size and Order Effects on Decisions from Experience,"

Psychonomic Bulletin & Review 20, no. 5 (October 2013): 1023–1031, doi:10.3758/s13423-013-0422-3.

19 Accenture, "Accenture Study Shows U.S. Consumers Want a Seamless Shopping Experience Across Store, Online and Mobile That Many Retailers Are Struggling to Deliver," press release, April 15, 2013, http://newsroom.accenture.com/news/accenture-study-shows-us-consumers-want-a-seamless-shopping-experience-across-store-online-and-mobile-that-many-retailers-are-struggling-to-deliver.htm.

20 Corporate Executive Board, "Consumers Crave Simplicity Not Engagement," press release, May 8, 2012, https://www.prnewswire.com/news-releases/consumers-crave-simplicity-not-engagement-150569095.html.

21 Flixable, "Netflix Museum," n.d., accessed October 29, 2019, https://flixable.com/netflix-museum/.

22 Yangjie Gu, Simona Botti, and David Faro, "Turning the Page: The Impact of Choice Closure on Satisfaction," Journal of Consumer Research 40, no. 2 (August 2013): 268–83.

23 Statistic Brain Research Institute, "Arranged/Forced Marriage Statistics," n.d., accessed October 29, 2019, https://www.statisticbrain.com/arranged-marriage-statistics/.

24 Divorcescience, "World Divorce Statistics—Comparisons Among Countries," n.d. accessed October 29, 2019, https://divorcescience.org/for-students/world-divorce-statistics-comparisons-among-countries/.

25 P. C. Regan, S. Lakhanpal, and C. Anguiano, "Relationship Outcomes in Indian-American Love-Based and Arranged Marriages," Psychological Reports 110, no. 3 (2012): 915–24, doi:10.2466/21.02.07.PR0.110.3.915-924.

26 Tor Wager, "Functional Neuroanatomy of Emotion: A Meta-Analysis of Emotion Activation Studies in PET and fMRI," NeuroImage 16, no. 2 (June 2002): 331–48, doi:10.1006/nimg.2002.1087.

27 D. Prelec and G. F. Loewenstein, "The Red and the Black: Mental Accounting of Savings and Debt," Marketing Science 17 (1998): :4–28 (reference list).

28 Visa, "Visa Inc. at a Glance," n.d., accessed October 29, 2019, https://usa.visa.com/dam/VCOM/download/corporate/media/visa-fact-sheet-Jun2015.pdf.

29 BNP Paribas, "Diversification of Payment Methods—A Focus on Dematerialization," June 29, 2018, https://group.bnpparibas/en/news/diversification-payment-methods-a-focus-dematerialization.

30 George Loewenstein, "Emotions in Economic Theory and Economic Behavior," American Economic Review 90, no. 2 (2000): 426–32, doi:10.1257/aer.90.2.426.

31 Alberto Alesina and Francesco Passarelli, "Loss Aversion in Politics," National Bureau of Economic Research Working Paper No. 21077, April 2015, https://www.nber.org/papers/w21077.

32 F. Harinck, E. Van Dijk, I. Van Beest, et al., "When Gains Loom Larger Than Losses: Reversed Loss Aversion for Small Amounts Of Money," Psychological Science 18, no. 12 (2007): 1099–1105, doi:10.1111/j.1467-9280.2007.02031.x.

33 Lü Dongbin, The Secret of the Golden Flower, http://thesecretofthegoldenflower.com/index.html.

34 Daugirdas Jankus. Effects of cognitive biases and their visual execution on consumer behavior in e-commerce platforms. Master's Thesis (2016): ISM Vadybos ir ekonomikos universitetas.

CHAPTER 7: ADDICTION 2.0

1 HFR. "25 Shocking Caffeine Addiction Statistics," accessed October 28, 2019, https://healthresearchfunding.org/shocking-caffeine-addiction-statistics/.

2 HealthReseachFunding.org, "7 Unbelievable Nicotine Addiction Statistics," n.d., accessed October 29, 2019, https://healthresearchfunding.org/7-unbelievable-nicotine-addiction-statistics/.

3 Statista, "Tobacco Products Report 2019—Cigarettes," n.d., accessed October 29, 2019, https://www.statista.com/study/48839/tobacco-products-report-cigarettes/.

4 Alexa, "Top Sites in the United States," https://www.alexa.com/topsites/countries/US.

5 Alex Hern, "Facebook should be 'regulated like the cigarette industry', says tech CEO," accessed December 2, 2019, https://www.theguardian.com/technology/2018/jan/24/facebook-regulated-cigarette-industry-salesforce-marc-benioff-social-media.

6 G. S. Berns and S. E. Moore, "A Neural Predictor of Cultural Popularity," Journal of Consumer Psychology 22 (2012): 154–60.

7 Daniel J. Lieberman and Michael E. Long, The Molecule of More: How a Single Chemical in Your Brain Drives Love, Sex, and Creativity—and Will Determine the Fate of the Human Race (Dallas: BenBella, 2018), 6.

8 Áine Doris, "Attention Passengers: your Next Flight Will Likely Arrive Early. Here's Why," KelloggInsight, November 6, 2018, https://insight.kellogg.northwestern.edu/article/attention-passengers-your-next-flight-will-likely-arrive-early-heres-why.

9 Debi Lilly, phone interview with the authors, March 6, 2019.

10 "#4: Oprah Relives the Famous Car Giveaway | TV Guide's Top 25 | Oprah Winfrey Network," YouTube video, 5:01, posted by OWN, September 25, 2012, https://www.youtube.com/watch?v=WmCQ-V7c7Bc.

11 OWN, "#4: Oprah Relives the Famous Car Giveaway | TV Guide's Top 25 | Oprah Winfrey Network," video, 5:05, September, 25, 2012, https://www.youtube.com/watch?v=WmCQ-V7c7Bc.

12 Michael D. Zeiler, "Fixed and Variable Schedules of Response Independent Reinforcement," Journal of the Experimental Analysis of Behavior 11, no. 40 (1968): 405–14.

13 R. Schull, "The Sensitivity of Response Rate to the Rate of Variable-Interval Reinforcement for Pigeons and Rats: A Review," Journal of the Experimental Analysis of Behavior 84, no. 1 (2005): 99–110.

14 Olivia Solon, "Ex-Facebook President Sean Parker: Site Made to Exploit Human 'Vulnerability,'" The Guardian, November 9, 2017, https://www.theguardian.com/technology/2017/nov/09/facebook-sean-parker-vulnerability-brain-psychology.

15 Ruchi Sanghvi, "Yesterday Mark reminded it was the 10 year anniversary of News Feed," Facebook, September 6, 2016, https://www.facebook.com/ruchi/posts/10101160244871819.

16 Shea Bennett, "Users Spend More Time on Pinterest Than Twitter, LinkedIn and

Google+ Combined," Adweek, February 18, 2012, http://www.adweek.com/digital/usa-social-network-use/#/.

17 B. Zeigarnik, "On Finished and Unfinished Tasks," in A Sourcebook of Gestalt Psychology, ed. W. D. Ellis (New York: Humanities Press, 1967), 300–14.

18 The Numbers, "Box Office History for Marvel Cinematic Universe Movies," accessed December 2, 2019, https://www.the-numbers.com/movies/franchise/Marvel-Cinematic-Universe.

19 Michael Sebastian, "Time Inc. Locks in Outbrain's Headline Recommendations in $100 Million Deal," Ad Age, November 18, 2014, http://adage.com/article/media/time-deal-outbrain-worth-100-million/295889/.

20 Craig Smith, "38 Amazing BuzzFeed Statistics and Facts (2019)," DMR by the Numbers, September 6, 2019, https://expandedramblings.com/index.php/business-directory/25012/buzzfeed-stats-facts/.

21 Sam Kirkland, "Time.com's Bounce Rate Down by 15 Percentage Points Since Adopting Continuous Scroll," Poynter, July 20, 2014, https://www.poynter.org/news/time-coms-bounce-rate-down-15-percentage-points-adopting-continuous-scroll.

22 Bianca Bosker, "The Binge Breaker: Tristan Harris Believes Silicon Valley Is Addicting Us to Our Phones. He's Determined to Make It Stop," The Atlantic, November 2016, https://www.theatlantic.com/magazine/archive/2016/11/the-binge-breaker/501122/.

23 Tristan Harris, "A Call to Minimize Users' Distraction & Respect Users' Attention, by a Concerned PM & Entrepreneur" (slide deck), February 2013, LinkedIn SlideShare, uploaded by Paul Mardsen, August 13, 2018, https://www.slideshare.net/paulsmarsden/google-deck-on-digital-wellbeing-a-call-to-minimize-distraction-and-respect-users-attention.

24 Brian Resnick, "What Smartphone Photography Is Doing to Our Memories," Vox, March 28, 2018, https://www.vox.com/science-and-health/2018/3/28/17054848/smartphones-photos-memory-research-psychology-attention.

25 Devin Coldewey, "Limiting Social Media Use Reduced Loneliness and Depression in New Experiment," TechCrunch, November 9, 2018, https://techcrunch.com/2018/11/09/limiting-social-media-use-reduced-loneliness-and-depression-in-new-experiment/.

26 Haley Sweetland Edwards, "You're Addicted to Your Smartphone. This Company Thinks It Can Change That," Time, April 12, 2018, updated April 13, 2018, http://amp.timeinc.net/time/5237434/youre-addicted-to-your-smartphone-this-company-thinks-it-can-change-that.

27 Digital Detox Retreats (website), accessed October 29, 2019, http://digitaldetox.org/retreats/.

28 Molly Young, "What an Internet Rehabilitation Program Is Really Like," Allure, January 21, 2018, https://www.allure.com/story/internet-addiction-rehab-program.

29 Adi Robertson, "Google's CEO Had to Remind Congress That Google Doesn't Make iPhones," The Verge, December 11, 2018, https://www.theverge.com/2018/12/11/18136377/google-sundar-pichai-steve-king-hearing-granddaughter-iphone-android-notification.

30 Nicolas Thompson, "Our Minds Have Been Hijacked by Our Phones. Tristan Harris

Wants to Rescue Them," Wired (July 26, 2017), https://www.wired.com/story/our-minds-have-been-hijacked-by-our-phones-tristan-harris-wants-to-rescue-them/.

31 "Venture Investment in VR/AR Startups," PitchBook, n.d., accessed October 29, 2019, https://files.pitchbook.com/png/Venture_investment_in_VR_AR.png.

32 Bernard Yack, The Problems of a Political Animal: Community, Justice, and Conflict in Aristotelian Political Thought (Berkeley: University of California Press, 1993).

CHAPTER 8: WHY WE LIKE WHAT WE LIKE

1 Jennifer Thorpe, "Champions of Psychology: Robert Zajonc," Association for Psychological Science, January 2005, https://www.psychologicalscience.org/observer/champions-of-psychology-robert-zajonc.

2 Margalit Fox, "Robert Zajonc, Who Looked at Mind's Ties to Actions, Is Dead at 85," New York Times, December 6, 2008, https://www.nytimes.com/2008/12/07/education/07zajonc.html.

3 R. B. Zajonc, "Mere Exposure: A Gateway to the Subliminal," Current Directions in Psychological Science 10, no. 6 (2001): 224.

4 R. F. Bornstein, "Exposure and Affect: Overview and Meta-analysis of Research, 1968–1987," Psychological Bulletin, 106 (1989): 265–89.

5 Robert B. Zajonc "Attitudinal Effects Of Mere Exposure," Journal of Personality and Social Psychology 9, no. 2, Pt. 2 (1968): 1–27. doi:10.1037/h0025848.

6 Zajonc, "Mere Exposure."

7 Jan Conway, "Coca-Cola Co.: Ad Spend 2014–2018," Statista, August 9, 2019, https://www.statista.com/statistics/286526/coca-cola-advertising-spending-worldwide/.

8 Aleksandra, "63 Fascinating Google Search Statistics," SEO Tribunal, September 26, 2018, https://seotribunal.com/blog/google-stats-and-facts/.

9 Robert F. Bornstein and Paul R. D'Agostino, "Stimulus Recognition and the Mere Exposure Effect," Journal of Personality and Social Psychology 63, no. 4 (1992): 545–52, https://faculty.washington.edu/jdb/345/345%20Articles/Chapter%2006%20Bornstein%20&%20D%27Agostino%20(1992).pdf.

10 Joseph E. Grush, "Attitude Formation and Mere Exposure Phenomena: A Nonartifactual Explanation of Empirical Findings," Journal of Personality and Social Psychology 33, no. 3 (1976): 281–90, http://psycnet.apa.org/record/1976-22288-001.

11 Sylvain Delplanque, Géraldine Coppin, Laurène Bloesch, et al., "The Mere Exposure Effect Depends on an Odor's Initial Pleasantness," Frontiers in Psychology, July 3, 2015, https://doi.org/10.3389/fpsyg.2015.00920.

12 A. L. Alter and D. M. Oppenheimer, "Predicting Short-Term Stock Fluctuations by Using Processing Fluency," Proceedings of the National Academy of Sciences of the USA 103, no. 24 (2006): 9369–72, doi:10.1073/pnas.0601071103.

13 Michael Bernard, Bonnie Lida, Shannon Riley, et al., "A Comparison of Popular Online Fonts: Which Size and Type Is Best?" Usability News 4, no. 1 (2018), https://pdfs.semanticscholar.org/21a3/2bc134881ef07726c0e45e3d01923418f14a.pdf?_ga=2.217085078.1679975153.1572354996-1611920395.1572354996.

14 Christian Unkelbach, "Reversing the Truth Effect: Learning the Interpretation of Processing Fluency in Judgments of Truth," Journal of Experimental Psychology: Learning, Memory, and Cognition 33, no. 1 (2007): 219–30, doi:10.1037/0278-7393.33.1.219.

15 Karen Riddle, "Always on My Mind: Exploring How Frequent, Recent, and Vivid Television Portrayals Are Used in the Formation of Social Reality Judgments," Media Psychology 13 , no. 2 (2010): 155–79, doi:10.1080/15213261003800140.

16 Stephanie Clifford, "Video Prank at Domino's Taints Brand," New York Times, April 15, 2019, https://www.nytimes.com/2009/04/16/business/media/16dominos.html.

17 "Domino's President Responds to Prank Video," YouTube video, 2:01, posted by "swift-tallon," April 18, 2009, https://www.youtube.com/watch?v=dem6eA7-A2I.

18 Cornelia Pechmann and David W. Stewart, "Advertising Repetition: A Critical Review of Wearin and Wearout," Current Issues and Research in Advertising 11, nos. 1–2 (1988): 285–329.

19 R. F. Bornstein, "Exposure and Affect: Overview and Meta-analysis of Research, 1968–1987," Psychological Bulletin 106 (1989): 265–89, doi:10.1037/0033-2909.106.2.265.

20 R. Bornstein and P. D'Agostino, "Stimulus Recognition and Mere Exposure," Journal of Personality and Social Psychology 63 (1992):4;545-552.

21 Stewart A. Shapiro and Jesper H. Nielsen, "What the Blind Eye Sees: Incidental Change Detection as a Source of Perceptual Fluency," Journal of Consumer Research 39, no. 6 (April 2013): 1202–1218.

22 Bornstein and D'Agostino, "Stimulus Recognition and Mere Exposure."

23 Derek Thompson, "The four-letter code to selling just about anything," The Atlantic, January 2017,

24 https://nypost.com/2015/02/14/fifty-shades-of-grey-whips-sex-toy-sales-into-a-frenzy/.

CHAPTER 9: EMPATHY AND THE HUMAN CONNECTION

1 This refers to the broad, "language-sensitive" network of the brain, spanning the left temporal cortex, auditory cortex, and Broca's area, as described in Hasson's work, and consistent with E. Fedorenko and N. Kanwisher, "Functionally Localizing Language-Sensitive Regions in Individual Subjects with fMRI," Language and Linguistics Compass 5, no. 2 (2011): 78–94.

2 G. Stephens, L. Silbert, and U. Hasson, "Speaker–Listener Neural Coupling Underlies Successful Communication," Proceedings of the National Association of Sciences of the USA 107, no. 32 (2010): 14425–30.

3 M. Pickering and S. Garrod, "Toward a Mechanistic Psychology of Dialogue," Behavioral and Brain Sciences 27, no. 2 (2004): 169–90. http://www.psy.gla.ac.uk/~simon/CD8063. Pickering_1-58.pdf

4 Scott Neuman, "Company's Line of Rainbow Themed Swastika T-Shirts Back-fires," NPR The Two-Way, August 7, 2017, http://www.npr.org/sections/thet-wo-way/2017/08/07/542068985/companys-line-of-rainbow-themed-swastika-t-shirts-backfires.

5 Libby Hill, "Pepsi Apologizes, Pulls Controversial Kendall Jenner Ad," Los Angeles Times,

April 5, 2019, https://www.latimes.com/entertainment/la-et-entertainment-news-up-dates-april-2017-htmlstory.html#pepsi-apologizes-pulls-controversial-kendall-jenner-ad.

6 L. Steinberg and K. C. Monahan, "Age Differences in Resistance to Peer Influence," Developmental Psychology 43 (2007): 1531–43.

7 David Bambridge, Teenagers: A Natural History (London: Portobello Books, 2009).

8 Nielsen, "Nielsen Unveils First Comprehensive Study on the Purchasing Power and Influence of the Multicultural Millennial," press release, January 18, 2017, http://www.nielsen.com/us/en/press-room/2017/nielsen-unveils-first-comprehensive-study-on-the-purchasing-power-of-multicultural-millennial.html.

9 Claire Suddath, "Harley-Davidson Needs a New Generation of Riders," Bloomberg Businessweek, August 23, 2018, https://www.bloomberg.com/news/features/2018-08-23/harley-davidson-needs-a-new-generation-of-riders.

10 Robert Ferris, "Harley-Davidson's electric motorcycle signals a big change for the legendary, but troubled, company," CNBC, November 11, 2018, https://www.cnbc.com/2018/11/09/harley-davidsons-electric-motorcycle-is-a-big-change-for-the-company.html.

11 L. Fogassi, P. F, Ferrari, B. Gesierich, et al., "Parietal Lobe: From Action Organization to Intention Understanding," Science 308, no. 5722 (2005): 662–67.

12 Pier Francesco Ferrari and Giacomo Rizolatti, "Mirror Neurons: Past and Present," Philosophical Transactions of the Royal Society of London B: Biological Sciences 369, no. 1644 (2014): 20130169, https://doi.org/10.1098/rstb.2013.0169.

13 M. Iacoboni, "Imitation, Empathy, and Mirror Neurons," Annual Review of Psychology 60 (2009): 653–70.

14 S. Bekkali, G. J. Youssef, P. H. Donaldson, et al., "Is the Putative Mirror Neuron System Associated with Empathy? A Systematic Review and Meta-Analysis," PsyArXiv Preprints (March 20, 2019), https://doi.org/10.31234/osf.io/6bu4p.

15 "Taste the Feeling - Sam Tsui, Alyson Stoner, Josh Levi, Alex G. Diamond, & KHS," YouTube video, 3:11, posted by Kurt Hugo Schneider, August 13, 2016, https://www.youtube.com/watch?v=5-uXzOW6SLo.

16 Adobe Marketing Cloud, "8 Marketers Doing Big Data Right," Mashable, May 6, 2013, https://mashable.com/2013/05/06/cmo-data/#2rNcAJeGpPq5.

17 Binkley, Christina, "More Brands Want You to Model Their Clothes," The Wall Street Journal, May 15, 2013, https://www.wsj.com/articles/SB10001424127887324216004578483094260521704.

18 L. Budell L., et al "Mirroring Pain in the Brain: Emotional Expression Versus Motor Imitation," PLoS One 10, no. 2 (2015): e0107526.

19 P. Slovic, "'If I Look at the Mass I Will Never Act'": Psychic Numbing and Genocide," Judgment and Decision Making 2 (2007): 79–95.

20 P. Slovic and D. Västfjäll, "The More Who Die, the Less We Care: Psychic Numbing and Genocide," in Imagining Human Rights, ed. S. Kaul & D. Kim (Berlin: De Gruyter, 2015), 55–68.

21 Wendy Koch, "Lives of Indelible Impact," USA Today, May 29, 2007.

22 M. Johnson, L. Detter, and P. Ghuman. "Individually Driven Narratives Facilitate Emotion and Consumer Demand," The European Conference on Media, Communications & Film: Official Conference Proceedings, 2018.

23 M. Fidelman, "5 of the Best Sports Marketing Campaigns That Went Viral in 2015," Forbes, June 9, 2015, https://www.forbes.com/sites/markfidelman/2015/06/09/here-are-5-of-the-best-sports-marketing-campaigns-that-went-viral-in-2015/#7d-c3a18a401d.

24 C. Nass, Y. Moon, B. Fogg, et al., "Can Computer Personalities Be Human Personalities?" International Journal of Human–Computer Studies 43 (1995): 223–39; C. Nass, Y. Moon, and P. Carney, "Are People Polite to Computers? Responses to Computer-Based Interviewing Systems," Journal of Applied Social Psychology 29, no. 5 (1999): 1093–1110; C. Nass and Y. Moon, "Machines and Mindlessness: Social Responses to Computers," Journal of Social Issues 56, no. 1 (2000): 81–103.

25 P. Karr-Wisniewski and M. Prietula, "CASA, WASA, and the Dimensions of Us," Computers in Human Behavior 26 (2010): 1761–71.

26 R. Sager, "Do Celebrity Endorsements Actually Work?" MarketWatch, March 11, 2011, http://www.marketwatch.com/story/do-celebrity-endorsements-work-1300481444531.

27 Kit Yarrow, Decoding the New Consumer Mind: How and Why We Shop and Buy (Hoboken, NJ: John Wiley & Sons), 145, Kindle.

28 Johnny Green, "Under Armour - Misty Copeland - I Will What I Want," video, 1:40, March 15, 2016, https://www.youtube.com/watch?v=zWJ5_HiKhNg.

CHAPTER 10: THE ESSENCE OF EVERYTHING

1 Mattha Busby, "Woman Who Bought Shredded Banksy Artwork Will Go Through with Purchase," The Guardian, October 11, 2018, https://www.theguardian.com/artanddesign/2018/oct/11/woman-who-bought-shredded-banksy-artwork-will-go-through-with-sale.

2 Elizabeth Chuck, "Purchaser of Banksy Painting That Shredded Itself Plans to Keep It," NBC News, October 12, 2018, https://www.nbcnews.com/news/world/purchaser-banksy-painting-shredded-itself-plans-keep-it-n91941.1.

3 B. M. Hood and P. Bloom, "Children Prefer Certain Individuals over Perfect Duplicates," Cognition 106, no. 1 (2008): 455–62, doi10.1016/j.cognition.2007.01.012.

4 Chris Dwyer, "How a 'Chef' Can Sway Fine Diners into Preferring Inferior Food," August 20, 2015, http://www.cnn.com/travel/article/chef-fools-diners-taste-test/index.html.

5 Brian Wansink, Collin R. Payne, and Jill North, "Fine as North Dakota Wine: Sensory Expectations and the Intake of Companion Foods," Physiology & Behavior 90, no. 5 (2007): 712–16.

6 Eustacia Huen, "How Stories Can Impact Your Taste in Food," Forbes, September 29, 2018, https://www.forbes.com/sites/eustaciahuen/2018/09/29/story-food/#7c34f5393597.

7 Anna Bernasek and D. T. Morgan, All You Can Pay: How Companies Use Our Data to Empty Our Wallets (New York: Hachette Book Group, 2015).

8 "Perrier Orson Welles," YouTube video, 0:29, posted by Retronario, March 9, 2014, https://www.youtube.com/watch?v=2qHv4yh4R9c.

9 Bruce G. Posner, "Once Is Not Enough: Why the Marketing Genius Who Made Perrier a Household Word Has Fizzled as a Small-Business Consultant," Inc., October 1, 1996, https://www.inc.com/magazine/19861001/7075.html.

10 Retrontario, "Perrier Orson Welles 1979," video, 0:29, March 9, 2014. https://www.youtube.com/watch?v=2qHv4yh4R9c.

11 Nestlé, "Perrier: Perrier Brand Focus," n.d., accessed November 1, 2019, https://www.nestle.com/investors/brand-focus/perrier-focus.

12 Dan Shapley, "Almost Half of All Bottled Water Comes from the Tap, but Costs You Much More," Good Housekeeping, August 12, 2010, https://www.goodhousekeeping.com/home/a17834/bottled-water-47091001/.

13 Posner, "Once Is Not Enough."

14 "Significant Objects," website, accessed November 1, 2019, http://significantobjects.com/.

15 "5 minutes with . . . a 1926 Bottle of The Macallan Whisky," Christie's, December 12, 2018, https://www.christies.com/features/5-minutes-with-a-1926-bottle-of-The-Macallan-whisky-9384-1.aspx.

16 "Lot 312: The Macallan 1926, 60 Year-Old, Michael Dillon" (auction listing), Christie's, accessed November 1, 2019, https://www.christies.com/lotfinder/wine/the-macallan-1926-60-year-old-michael-dillon-6180404-details.aspx?from=salesummary&intObjectID=6180404&lid=1.

17 Dean Small, phone interview with the authors, February 13, 2019.

18 "Bertha Benz: The Journey That Changed Everything," YouTube video, 4:02, posted by Mercedes-Benz, March 6, 2019, https://www.youtube.com/watch?v=vsGrFYD5Nfs.

19 "Mercedes Benz - Company History Commercial," YouTube video, 0:33, posted by "TheRealBigBlack," November 30, 2019, https://www.youtube.com/watch?v=ynzZxHy-9jrs.

20 "Macy's 150 Years Commercial," YouTube video, 1:00, posted by "Frenite," https://www.youtube.com/watch?v=4oORxFJJc88.

21 Emily Glazer, "Wells Fargo to Pay $185 Million Fine over Account Openings," Wall Street Journal, September 8, 2016, https://www.wsj.com/articles/wells-fargo-to-pay-185-million-fine-over-account-openings-1473352548?mod=article_inline.

22 "Wells Fargo Re-established 2018," Vimeo video, 1:01, posted by "craigknelson," https://vimeo.com/270298076.

23 "The Fédération Internationale de l'Automobile (FIA)," FIA Heritage Museums website, , accessed November 1, 2019, fiaheritagemuseums.com.

24 Evangeline Holland, "The Spirit of Ecstasy," Edwardian Prominence (blog), May 3, 2008, http://www.edwardianpromenade.com/love/the-spirit-of-ecstasy/.

25 Daniel Kahneman, Alan B. Krueger, David Schkade, et al., "A Survey Method for Characterizing Daily Life Experience: The Day Reconstruction Method," Science 306, no.

5702 (December 3, 2004): 1776–1780.

26 Amir Mandel, "Why Nobel Prize Winner Daniel Kahneman Gave Up on Happiness," Haaretz, October 7, 2018, https://www.haaretz.com/israel-news/.premium.MAGA-ZINE-why-nobel-prize-winner-daniel-kahneman-gave-up-on-happiness-1.6528513.

CHAPTER 11: MIDLIMINAL

1 William M. O'Barr, "'Subliminal' Advertising," Advertising & Society Review 6, no. 4 (2005), doi:10.1353/asr.2006.0014.

2 J. A. Krosnick, A. L. Betz, L. J. Jussim, et al., "Subliminal Conditioning of Attitudes," Personality and Social Psychology Bulletin 18, no. 2 (1992): 152–62, doi:10.1177/0146167292182006.

3 Omri Gillath, Mario Mikulincer, Gurit E. Birnbaum, et al., "Does Subliminal Exposure to Sexual Stimuli Have the Same Effects on Men and Women?" The Journal of Sex Research 44, no. 2 (2007): 111–21, doi:10.1080/00224490701263579.

4 J. Karremans, W. Stroebe, and J. Claus, "Beyond Vicary's Fantasies: The Impact of Subliminal Priming and Brand Choice," Journal of Experimental Social Psychology 42, no. 6 (2006): 792–98. doi:10.1016/j.jesp.2005.12.002.

5 Federal Communications Commission, "Press Statement of Commissioner Gloria Tristani, Re: Enforcement Bureau Letter Dismissing a Request by Senators Ron Wyden and John Breaux for an Investigation Regarding Allegations of the Broadcast of Subliminal Advertising Provided by the Republican National Committee," press release, March 9, 2001, https://transition.fcc.gov/Speeches/Tristani/Statements/2001/stgt123.html.

6 Committee on Advertising Practice, BCAP Code: The UK Code of Broadcast Advertising, "03 Misleading Advertising," section 3.8, n.d., accessed November 1, 2019, https://www.asa.org.uk/type/broadcast/code_section/03.html.

7 "Subliminal Message in KFC Snacker," YouTube Video, 0:12, posted by "defying11," May 18, 2008, https://www.youtube.com/watch?v=zrRDEjPoeGw.

8 A. A. Karim, B. Lützenkirchen, E. Khedr, et al., "Why Is 10 Past 10 the Default Setting for Clocks and Watches in Advertisements? A Psychological Experiment," Frontiers in Psychology 8 (2017): 1410, https://doi.org/10.3389/fpsyg.2017.01410.

9 R. B. Zajonc. "Mere Exposure: A Gateway to the Subliminal." Current Directions in Psychological Science, 10(6) (2001): 224-228.

10 Associated Press, "'Transformers' a GM Ad in Disguise," NBC News, July 3, 2007, http://www.nbcnews.com/id/19562215/ns/business-autos/t/transformers-gm-ad-disguise/.

11 Michael L. Maynard and Megan Scale, "Unpaid Advertising: A Case of Wilson the Volleyball in Cast Away," Journal of Popular Culture 39, no. 4 (2006), https://onlinelibrary.wiley.com/doi/abs/10.1111/j.1540-5931.2006.00282.x.

12 Sarah Whitten, "Starbucks Got an Estimated $2.3 Billion in Free Advertising from 'Game of Thrones' Gaffe, and It Wasn't Even Its Coffee Cup," CNBC, May 7, 2019, https://www.cnbc.com/2019/05/07/starbucks-got-2point3-billion-in-free-advertising-

from-game-of-thrones-gaffe.html.

13 "U.S. Product Placement Market Grew 13.7% in 2017, Pacing for Faster Growth in 2018, Powered by Double-Digit Growth in Television, Digital Video and Music Integrations," PRWeb, press release, June 13, 2018, https://www.pqmedia.com/wp-content/uploads/2018/06/US-Product-Placement-18.pdf.

14 Nicolas Guéguen, "Color and Women Hitchhikers' Attractiveness: Gentlemen Drivers Prefer Red," Color Research & Application 37 (2012): 76–78, doi:10.1002/col.20651.

15 Nicolas Guéguen and Céline Jacob, "Clothing Color and Tipping: Gentlemen Patrons Give More Tips to Waitresses with Red Clothes," Journal of Hospitality & Tourism Research, April 18, 2012, http://jht.sagepub.com/content/early/2012/04/16/1096348012442546.

16 Elizabeth Paten, "Can Christian Louboutin Trademark Red Soles? An E.U. Court Says No," New York Times, February 6, 2018, https://www.nytimes.com/2018/02/06/business/christian-louboutin-shoes-red-trademark.html.

17 Stephen A. Stansfeld and Mark P. Matheson, "Noise Pollution: Non-auditory Effects on Health," British Medical Bulletin 68, no. 1 (2003): 243–57, https://doi.org/10.1093/bmb/ldg033.

18 Torø Graven and Clea Desebrock, "Bouba or Kiki with and Without Vision: Shape-Audio Regularities and Mental Images," Acta Psychologica 188 (2018): 200–12.

19 Ronald E. Milliman, "Using Background Music to Affect the Behavior of Supermarket Shoppers," Journal of Marketing 46, no. 3 (1982): 86–91.

20 Adrian C. North, David J. Hargreaves, and Jennifer McKendrick, "The Influence of In-Store Music on Wine Selections Article," Journal of Applied Psychology 84, no. 2 (1999): 271–76.

21 Adrian C. North, Amber Shilcock, and David J. Hargreaves, "The Effect of Musical Style on Restaurant Customers' Spending," Environment and Behavior 35, no. 5 (2003): 712–18.

22 K. C. Colwell, "Faking It: Engine-Sound Enhancement Explained," Car and Driver, April 2012, https://www.caranddriver.com/features/faking-it-engine-sound-enhancement-explained-tech-dept.

23 M. Lynn, J. Le, and D. Sherwyn, "Reach Out and Touch Your Customers," Cornell Hotel and Restaurant Administration Quarterly, 39(3) (1998): 60–65.

24 Christopher Bergland, "The Neuroscience of Smell Memories Linked to Place and Time," Psychology Today, July 31, 2018, https://www.psychologytoday.com/us/blog/the-athletes-way/201807/the-neuroscience-smell-memories-linked-place-and-time.

25 N. R. Keinfield, "The Smell of Money," New York Times, October 25, 1992, https://www.nytimes.com/1992/10/25/style/the-smell-of-money.html.

26 "The Smell of Commerce: How Companies Use Scents to Sell Their Products," The Independent, August 16, 2011 https://www.independent.co.uk/news/media/advertising/the-smell-of-commerce-how-companies-use-scents-to-sell-their-products-2338142.html.

27 Geke D. S. Ludden and Hendrik N. J. Schifferstein, "Should Mary smell like biscuit? In-

vestigating scents in product design," International Journal of Design 3(3) (2009): 1–12.

28 Hancock, G.D. (2009). The Efficacy of fragrance use for enhancing the slot machine gaming experience of casino patrons.

29 N. Gueguen and C. Petr, "Odors and consumer behavior in a restaurant," International Journal of Hospitality Management 25 (2) (2006): 335–339.

30 P. E. Murphy, "Research in Marketing Ethics: Continuing and Emerging Themes," Recherche et Applications En Marketing (English edition) 32, no. 3 (2017): 84–89.

31 B. Milner, "The Medial Temporal-Lobe Amnesic Syndrome," Psychiatric Clinics of North America 28 (2005): 599–611.

32 A. J. Marcel, "Conscious and Unconscious Perception: Experiments on Visual Masking and Word Recognition," Cognitive Psychology 15 (1983): 197–237.

33 C. S. Soon, M. Brass, H.-J. Heinze, et al., "Unconscious Determinants of Free Decisions in the Human Brain," Nature Neuroscience 11, no. 5 (2008): 543–45, doi:10.1038/nn.2112.

34 A. Tusche, S. Bode, and J. Haynes, "Neural Responses to Unattended Products Predict Later Consumer Choices," The Journal of Neuroscience 30, no. 23 (2000): 8024–31.

35 L. E. Williams and J. A. Bargh, "Experiencing Physical Warmth Promotes Interpersonal Warmth," Science 322 (2008): 606–7.

CHAPTER 12: THE FUTURE OF MARKETING

1 Charles Duhigg, "How Companies Learn Your Secrets," New York Times, February 16, 2012, https://www.nytimes.com/2012/02/19/magazine/shopping-habits.html.

2 Associated Press and NBC News, "Facebook to send Cambridge Analytica Data-Use Notices to 87 Million Users Monday," NBC News, April 9, 2018, https://www.nbcnews.com/tech/social-media/facebook-send-cambridge-analytica-data-use-notices-monday-n863811.

3 M. Wojcik, M. Nowicka, M. Bola, and A. Nowicka, "Unconcious Detection of One's Own Image," Psychological Science 30:4 (2019): 471-480

4 Joel Stein, "I Tried Hiding From Silicon Valley in a Pile of Privacy Gadgets," Bloomberg Businessweek, August 8, 2019, https://www.bloomberg.com/news/features/2019-08-08/i-tried-hiding-from-silicon-valley-in-a-pile-of-privacy-gadgets.

5 DrFakenstein, "Full House of Mustaches - Nick Offerman [deepfake]," video, 1:01, August 11, 2019, https://www.youtube.com/watch?v=aUphMqs1vFw.

6 Grace Shao and Evelyn Cheng, "The Chinese face-swapping app that went viral is taking the danger of 'deepfake' to the masses," CNBC, September 4, 2019, https://www.cnbc.com/2019/09/04/chinese-face-swapping-app-zao-takes-dangers-of-deepfake-to-the-masses.html.

7 NBC News Now "The Future Is Zao: How A Chinese Deepfake App Went Viral," video, 3:12, September 4, 2019, https://www.youtube.com/watch?v=dJYTMhKXCAc.

8 A. M. Garvey, F. Germann, and L. E. Bolton, "Performance Brand Placebos: How Brands

Improve Performance and Consumers Take the Credit," Journal of Consumer Research 42, no. 6 (2016): 931–51.

9 Domo, "Data Never Sleeps 5.0," infographic, n.d., accessed November 1, 2019, https://www.domo.com/learn/data-never-sleeps-5.

10 M. Johnson, P. Ghuman, and R. Barlow, "Psychological Coordinates of Marketing Ethics for the Modern World" (forthcoming); see http://www.popneuro.com.

INDEX

Dr. Matt A. Johnson

Prince Ghuman

A MARKETER AND
A SCIENTIST WALKED
INTO A BAR . . .
(About the Authors)

A Marketer and a Scientist walked into a bar. Or more specifically, they walked into a bar in San Francisco, a decade after their college days together at UC San Diego.

After college, their lives had taken very different turns. The Scientist had completed a PhD in cognitive neuroscience at Princeton University, and had spent the past eighteen months working as a consultant in Shanghai. The Marketer had just been featured in the Movers & Shakers column in the *San Francisco Chronicle* and was the Head of Global Marketing at OFX, a publicly traded Fin-Tech firm.

But, as they discovered during that fateful bar conversation, they were driven towards the same fundamental goal: to understand and predict human behavior. The Neuroscientist looked around San Francisco and thought, *What is it about the human brain that enables someone to willingly pay $20 for a salad merely because it's labeled* artisanal? The Marketer thought, *This is how they could charge $30 for it.*

This is the story of the two authors of *Blindsight*: Prince Ghuman, the marketer, and Dr. Matt Johnson, the neuroscientist. The partnership has resulted in undergraduate and postgraduate courses in neuromarketing, the development of an ethical framework for modern marketing, and primary research into consumer behavior. Today, they are full-time professors at Hult International Business School in San Francisco, and hold workshops for practitioners to ethically apply neuroscience to business.

The pair's most important undertaking has been this book, which combines their over twenty-five years of experience. But the journey does not stop at *Blindsight*. The consumer world is ever-evolving and the neuroscientific community continues to learn more about the mysteries of the brain. If you'd like to continue learning, enjoy bite-size consumer psychology content on the Pop Neuro blog, at https://www.popneuro.com/neuromarketing-blog. If you'd like to go one step further toward understanding how to apply neuroscience to business in an ethical way, take a look at https://www.popneuro.com/neuromarketing-bootcamp.

Thank you for your purchase of *Blindsight*; we hope it continues to add value to your consumer life. Questions and comments are welcomed at hello@popneuro.com.